The Rebel of the School

by

L. T. Meade

Double 9
BOOKS

The Rebel of the School
by L. T. Meade

ISBN: 978-93-58595-93-2

Published by

DOUBLE 9 BOOKS

2/13-B, Ansari Road
Daryaganj, New Delhi – 110002
info@double9books.com
www.double9books.com
Tel. 011-40042856

This book is under public domain

ABOUT THE AUTHOR

Elizabeth Thomasina Meade Smith (1844-1914), a prolific author of novels for girls, used the pen name L. T. Meade. She was the daughter of Rev. R. T. Meade of Nohoval, County Cork, and was born in Bandon, Ireland. In September 1879, she wed Alfred Toulmin Smith after relocating to London. In her lifetime, she wrote over 280 volumes, starting when she was just 17 years old. She was so productive that eleven new books with her name on them appeared in the first few years after her passing. She was most recognized for her young adult novels, the most well-known of which was A World of Girls, which was released in 1886. 37,000 copies of A World of Girls were sold, and it had a significant impact on novels about girls' schools written in the 20th century. She did, however, also write "sentimental" and "sensational" tales, religious tales, historical novels, journeys, romances, and mysteries, some of which had male co-authors. Meade was a pioneer club member and a feminist. Meade wrote The Cleverest Woman in England, a novel based on the life of women's rights activist and Pioneer Club founder Emily Langton Massingberd (1847-1897), after her passing in 1898.

CONTENTS

CHAPTER I.
SENT TO COVENTRY!

The school was situated in the suburbs of the popular town of Merrifield, and was known as the Great Shirley School. It had been endowed some hundred years ago by a rich and eccentric individual who bore the name of Charles Shirley, but was now managed by a Board of Governors. By the express order of the founder, the governors were women; and very admirably did they fulfil their trust. There was no recent improvement in education, no better methods, no sanitary requirements which were not introduced into the Great Shirley School. The number of pupils was limited to four hundred, one hundred of which were foundationers and were not required to pay any fees; the remaining three hundred paid small fees in order to be allowed to secure an admirable and up-to-date education under the auspices of the great school.

There came a day in early autumn, shortly after the girls had reassembled after their summer vacation, when they streamed out of the building in groups of twenties and thirties and forties. They stood about and talked as girls will.

The Great Shirley School, well as it was managed, had perhaps a larger share than many schools of those temptations which make school a world—a world for the training either for good or evil of those who go to it. There were the girls who attended the school in the ordinary way, and there were the girls who were drafted on to the foundation from lower schools. These latter were looked down upon by the least noble and the meanest of their fellow-scholars.

There was a slight rain falling, and two or three girls standing in a group raised their umbrellas, but they still stood beside the gates.

"She's quite the very prettiest girl I ever saw," cried Alice Tennant; "but of course we can have nothing to do with her. She entered a week ago. She doesn't pay any of the fees; she has no pretence to being a lady. Oh, here she comes! Did you ever see such a face?"

A slight, shabbily dressed little girl, with her satchel of books slung on her arm, now appeared. She looked to right and left of her as though she were slightly alarmed. Her face was beautiful in the truest sense of the world; it did not at all match with the shabby, faded clothes which she wore. She had large deep-violet eyes, jet-black hair, and a sweet, fresh complexion. Her expression was bewitching, and when she smiled a dimple came in her cheek.

"Look—look!" cried Mary Denny. "Isn't she all that I have said?"

"Yes, and more. What a pity we can't know her!" said Alice Tennant.

"But can't we? I really don't see why we should make the poor child miserable," said Mary Denny.

"It is not to be thought of. We must worship the beautiful new star from afar. Perhaps she will do something to raise herself into our set; but as it is, she must go with Kate Rourke and Hannah Johnson and Clara Sawyer, and all the rest of the foundationers."

"Well, we have seen her now," said Mary, "so I suppose we needn't stand talking about her any longer. Will you come home and have tea with me, Alice? Mother said I might ask you."

"I wish I could come," said Alice; "but we are expecting Kathleen."

"Oh, the Irish girl! Is it really arranged that she is to come?"

"Yes, of course it is. She comes to-night. I have never seen her. We are all pleased, and expect that she will be a very great acquisition."

"Irish girls always are," said Mary. "They're so gay and full of life, and are so ridiculously witty. Don't you remember that time when we had Norah Mahoney at the school? What fun that was!"

"But she got into terrible scrapes, and was practically dismissed," said Alice. "I only hope Kathleen won't be in that style."

"But do you know anything about her? The Irish are always so terribly poor."

"She is not poor at all. She has got an uncle and aunt in Chicago, and they are as rich as can be; and her uncle is coming to see her at Christmas. And besides that, her father has an awfully old castle in the south-west of Ireland. He is never troubled on account of the Land League or anything else, and Kathleen will have lots and lots of money. I know she is paying mother well for giving her a home while she is being educated at the Shirley School."

"I can't imagine why she comes to our school if she is so rich," said Mary. "It seems almost unfair. The Great Shirley School is not meant for rich girls: a girl of the kind you have just described ought not to become a member of the school."

"Oh, that is all very fine; but it seems her mother was educated here, and swore a sort of vow that when Kathleen was old enough she should come to this school and to no other. Her mother's name is Mrs. O'Hara, and she wrote to Miss Ravenscroft and asked if there was a vacancy for Kathleen, and if she knew of any one who would be nice to her and with whom she could live. Miss Ravenscroft thought of mother; she knew that mother would like to have a boarder who would pay her well. So the whole thing was settled; mother has been corresponding with Mrs. O'Hara, and Kathleen comes to-day. I really can't stay another moment, Mary. I must rush home; there are no end of things to be attended to."

"All right," said Mary. "I will watch for you and the beautiful Irish heiress—"

"I don't know that she is an heiress."

"Well, whatever she is—the bewitching Irish girl—to-morrow morning. Ta-ta for the present."

Mary turned to the left, and Alice continued her walk. She walked quickly. She was a well-made, rather pretty girl of fifteen. Her hair, very light in colour, hung down her back. She had a determined walk and a good carriage. As she hurried her steps she saw Ruth Craven, the pretty foundation girl, walking in front of her. Ruth walked slowly and as if she were tired. Once she pressed her hand to her side, and Alice, passing her, hesitated and looked back. The face that met hers was so appealing and loving that she could not resist saying a word.

"Are you awfully tired, Ruth Craven?" she said.

"I shall get used to it," replied Ruth. "I have had a cold for the last few days. Thank you so much, Miss Tennant!"

"Don't thank me," said Alice, frowning; "and don't say 'Miss Tennant,' It isn't good form in our school. I hope you will be better to-morrow. I am sure, at least, that you will like the school very much."

"Thank you," said the girl again.

The girls parted at the next corner. When Ruth found herself alone she paused and looked behind her. Tears rose to her eyes; she took out her handkerchief to wipe them away. She paused as if troubled by some thought; then her face grew bright, and she stepped along more briskly.

"I am a coward, and I ought to be ashamed of myself," she thought. "Now, when I go in and grandfather sees me, he will think he has done quite wrong to let me go to the Shirley School. I must not let him think that. And granny will be still more vexed. I have had my heart's desire, and because things are not quite so pleasant as I hoped they would have been, it is no reason why I should be discontented."

The next moment she had lifted the latch at a small cottage and entered. It was a little better than a workman's house, but not much; there were two rooms downstairs and two rooms upstairs, and that was all. To the front of the little house was the tiny parlour, at the back an equally tiny kitchen. Upstairs was a bedroom for Ruth and a bedroom for her grandparents. Mr. and Mrs. Craven did not keep any servants. The moment Ruth entered now her grandmother put her head out of the kitchen door.

"Ruthie," she said, "the butcher has disappointed us to-day. Here is a shilling; go to the shop and bring in some sausages. Be as quick as you can, child, or your grandfather won't have his supper in time."

Ruth took the money without a word. She went down a small lane, turned to her right, and found herself in a mean little street full of small shops. She entered one that she knew, and asked for a pound and a half of pork sausages. As the woman was wrapping them up in a piece of torn newspaper, she looked at Ruth and said:

"Is it true, Miss Craven, that you are a scholar at the Great Shirley School?"

"I am," replied Ruth. "I went there for the first time to-day."

"So your grandparents are going to educate you, miss, as if you were a lady."

"I am a lady, Mrs. Plowden. My grandparents cannot make me anything but what I am."

Mrs. Plowden smiled. She handed Ruth her sausages without a word, and the young girl left the shop. Her grandmother was waiting for her in the porch.

"What a time you have been, child!" she said. "I do hope this new school and the scholars and all this fuss and excitement of your new life won't turn your head. Whatever happens, you have got to be a little servant to me and a little messenger to your grandfather. You have got to make yourself useful, and not to have ideas beyond your station."

"Here are the sausages, granny," answered Ruth in a gentle tone.

The old lady took them from her and disappeared into the kitchen.

"Ruth—Ruth!" said a somewhat querulous but very deep voice which evidently issued from the parlor.

"Yes, granddad; coming in a moment or two," Ruth replied. She ran up the tiny stairs, and entered her own little bedroom, which was so wee that she could scarcely turn round in it, but was extremely neat.

Ruth removed her hat, brushed out her black hair, saw that her dress, shabby as it was, was in apple-pie order, put on a neat white apron, and ran downstairs. She first of all entered the parlor. A handsome old man, with a decided look of Ruth herself, was seated by the fire. He was holding out his thin, knuckly hands to the blaze. As Ruth came in he turned and smiled at her.

"Ah, deary!" he said, "I have been missing you all day. And how did you like your school? And how is everything?"

"I will tell you after supper, grandfather. I must go and help granny now."

"That's right; that's a good girl. Oh! far be it from me to be impatient; I wouldn't be for all the world. Your granny has missed you too to-day."

Ruth smiled at him and went into the kitchen. There were eager voices and sounds of people hurrying about, and then a fragrant smell of fried sausages. A moment later Ruth appeared, holding a brightly trimmed lamp in her hand; she laid it on a little centre-table, drew down the blinds, pulled the red curtains across the windows, poked up the fire, and then proceeded to lay the cloth for supper. Her pile of books, which she had brought in her satchel, lay on a chair.

"I can have a look at your books while I am waiting, can't I, little woman?" said the old man.

Ruth brought him over the pack of books somewhat unwillingly. He gave a sigh of contentment, drew the lamp a little nearer, and was lost for the time being.

"Now, child," said old Mrs. Craven, "you heat that plate by the fire. Have you got the pepper and salt handy? Sausages ain't worth touching unless you eat them piping hot. Your grandfather wants his beer. Dear, dear! What a worry that is! I never knew that the cask was empty. What is to be done?"

"I can go round to the shop and bring in a quart," said Ruth.

"But you—a member of the Shirley School! No, you mustn't. I'll do it."

"Nonsense, granny! I'll leave school to-morrow if you don't let me work for you just the same as ever."

Mrs. Craven sank into her chair.

"You are a good child," she said. "All day I have been so fretting that we were taking you out of your station; and that is a sad mistake—sad and terrible. But you are a good child. Yes, go for it, dear; it won't do you any harm."

Ruth wrapped an old shawl round her head, picked up a jug, and went off to the nearest public-house. They were accustomed to see her there, for old Mr. Craven more often than not had his little cask of beer empty. She went to a side entrance, where a woman she knew served her with what she required.

"There, Ruth Craven," she said—"there it is. But, all the same, I'm surprised to see you here to-night."

"But why so?" asked Ruth.

"Isn't it true that you are one of the Shirley scholars now?"

"I am; I joined the school to-day."

"And yet you come to fetch beer for your old grandfather!"

"I do," said Ruth, with spirit. "And I shall fetch it for him as long as he wants it. Thank you very much."

She took the jug and walked carefully back to the cottage.

"She's the handsomest, most spirited, best little thing I ever met," thought the landlady of the "Lion," and she began to consider in her own mind if one of her men could not call round in the morning and leave the necessary beer at the Cravens'.

Supper was served, and was eaten with considerable relish by all three.

"Now," said old granny when the meal had come to an end, "you stay and talk to your grandfather—he is all agog to hear what you have got to say—and I will wash up. Now then, child, don't you worry. It isn't everybody who has got loving grandparents like us."

"And it isn't many old bodies who have got such a dear little granddaughter," said the old man, smiling at Ruth.

Mrs. Craven carried the supper things into the kitchen, and Ruth sat close to her grandfather.

"Now, tell me, child, tell me," he said. "What did they do? What class did they put you into?"

"I am in the third remove; a very good class indeed—at least they all said so, grandfather."

"I don't understand your modern names; but tell me what you have got to learn, dear. What sort of lessons are they going to put into that smart little head of yours?"

"Oh, all the best things, grandfather—French, German, English in all its branches, music, and Latin if I like. I am determined to take up Latin; I want to get to the heart of things."

"Quite right—quite right, too. And you are ever so pleased at having got in?"

"It does seem a grand thing for me, doesn't it, grandfather?"

"Most of the girls are ladies, aren't they?"

"It is a big school—between three and four hundred girls. I don't suppose they are all ladies."

"Well, you are, anyhow, my little Ruth."

"Am I, granddad? That is the question."

"What do you think yourself?"

"I think so; but what does the world say?"

"Ruth, I never told you, but your mother was a lady. You know what your father was. I saved and stinted and toiled and got him a commission in the army. He died, poor fellow, shortly after you were born. But he was a commissioned officer in the Punjab Infantry. Your mother was a governess, but she was a lady by birth; her father was a clergyman. Your parents met in India; they fell in love, and married. Your mother died at your birth, and you came home to us. Yes, child, by birth you are a lady, as good as any of them—as good as the best."

"They are dead," said Ruth. "I don't remember them. I have a picture of my father upstairs; it is taken with his uniform on. He looks very handsome. And I have a little water-color sketch of my mother, and she looks fair and sweet and interesting. But I never knew them. Those I knew and know and love are you, grandfather, and granny."

"Well, dear, when I had the power and the brains and the strength, I kept a shop—a grocer's shop, dear; and my wife, she was the daughter of a harness-maker. Your grandparents were both in trade; there's no way out of it."

"But a gentleman and lady for all that," said the girl.

She pressed close to the old man, took one of his weather-beaten hands between both of her own, and stroked it.

"That is as people think, Ruthie; but we weren't in the position, and never expect to be, of those who are high up in the world."

"I am glad you told me about my father and mother," said the girl. "I love both their memories. I am glad to think that my father served the Queen, and that my mother was the daughter of a clergyman. But I am more glad to think that there never was such an honorable man as you, granddad, and that you made the grocery trade one of the best in the world."

"It was a bad trade, my darling. I had several severe losses. It was very unfortunate my lending that money."

"What money?"

"Oh, I will tell you another time; it doesn't really matter. There was a little bit of ingratitude there, but it doesn't matter. Only I made no fortune by grocery—barely enough to put my boy into the army and to educate him for it, and enough to keep us with a pittance now that we are old. But I have nothing to leave you, sweetest. You just have your pension from the Government, which don't count for nothing at all."

Ruth rose to her feet.

"I am glad I got into the school," she said. "I hope to do wonders there. I mean to take every scrap of good the place opens out to me. I mean to work as hard as ever I can. You shall be desperately proud of me; and so shall granny, although she doesn't hold with much learning."

"But I do, little girl; I love it more than anything. I have got such a lovely scheme in my head. I will work alongside of you, Ruth—you and I at the same things. You can lend me the books when you don't want them."

"What a splendid idea!" said Ruth, clapping her hands.

"You look quite happy, my dear."

"And so I am. I am about the happiest girl on earth. And now, may I begin to look through my lessons for to-morrow?"

The old man arranged the lamp where its light would be most comfortable for the keen young eyes, and Ruth sat down to the table, got out her books, and worked for an hour or two. Mrs. Craven came in, looked at her proudly, wagged her head, and returned to the kitchen. After a time she came to the door and beckoned to the old man to follow her. But the old man had taken up one of Ruth's books and was absorbed in its contents; he was muttering words over under his breath.

"Coming, wife—coming presently," he said.

Ruth's head was bent over her books. Mr. Craven rose and went on tiptoe into the kitchen.

"We mustn't disturb her, Susan," he said. "We must let her have her own way. She must work just as long as she likes. She is going to be a great power in the land, is that child, with her beauty and her talent; there's nothing she can't aspire to."

"Now don't you be a silly old man," said Mrs. Craven. "And what on earth were you whispering about to yourself when I came in?"

"I am going to work with her. It will be a wonderful stimulation, and a great interest to me. I always was keen for book-learning."

Mrs. Craven suppressed a sigh.

"If I even had fifty pounds," she said, "I wouldn't let that child spend every hour at school. I'd dress up smart, and take her out, and get her the very best husband I could. Why, old man, what does a woman want with all that learning?"

"If a woman has brains she's bound to use them," replied the old man, as he sat down by the kitchen fire.

Meanwhile Ruth went on with her lessons. After a time, however, she uttered a sigh. She flung down her books and looked across the room.

"If he only knew," she said under her breath—"if he only knew that I was practically sent to Coventry—that none of the nice girls will speak to me. But never mind; I won't tell him. Nothing would induce me to trouble him on the subject."

CHAPTER II.
HIGH LIFE AND LOW LIFE.

Amongst the many girls who attended the Great Shirley School was one who was known by the name of Cassandra Weldon. She was rapidly approaching the proud position of head girl in the school. She had entered the Shirley School when quite a little child, had gone steadily up through the different classes and the various removes, until she found herself nearly at the head of the sixth form. She was about to try for a sixty-pound scholarship, renewable for three years; if she got it she would go to Holloway College, and eventually support herself and her mother. Mrs. Weldon was the widow of a man who in his time had a very successful school for boys, and she herself had been a teacher long ago in the Great Shirley School. Cassandra and her mother, therefore, were from the very first surrounded by scholarship; they belonged, so to speak, to the scholastic world.

Mrs. Weldon could scarcely talk of anything else. Evening after evening she would question her daughter eagerly with regard to this accomplishment and the other, to this change or that, to this chance which Cassandra might have and to the other. The girl was extremely clever, with a sort of all-round talent which was most remarkable; for in addition to many excellent accomplishments, she was distinctly musical. Her musical talent very nearly amounted to genius. If in the future she could not play in public, she resolved at least to earn her living as a music teacher. Mrs. Weldon hoped that Cassandra would do more than this; and, to tell the truth, the girl shared her mother's dreams. Besides music, she had worked very hard at botany, at French and German, and at English literature. She would be seventeen on her next birthday, and it was against the rules for any girl to remain at the Great Shirley School after that time. Cassandra had, however, two more terms of school-life before her, and these terms she regarded as the most valuable of her whole education.

In appearance Cassandra was a tall, well-made girl, graceful in her movements, and very self-possessed in manner. Her face was full of intelligence, but was rather plain than otherwise, for her mouth was too wide and her nose the reverse of classical. She had bright intelligent brown eyes, however, a nice voice, and a pleasant way. Cassandra was looked up to by all her fellow-students, and this not because she was rich, nor because she was beautiful, but simply because she was good and honorable and trustworthy; she possessed a large amount of sympathy for nearly every one, her tact was unfailing, and she was never self-assertive.

Now Cassandra, who had many friends in the school, had amongst them, of course, her greatest friend. This girl was called Florence Archer. Florence was pretty and clever, but she had neither Cassandra's depth nor power of intellect. She was naturally vain and frivolous, except in the presence of her dearest friend. She was easily influenced by others, and it was her habit to follow the one who gave her the last advice. Her passionate love for Cassandra was perhaps her best and strongest quality; but of late she had exhibited a sense of almost unwarrantable jealousy when any other girl showed a preference for her special friend. Florence was a very nice girl, but jealousy was her bane. She thought a good deal of herself, for her father was a rich man, and only took advantage of the Great Shirley education because it was incomparably the best in the place. There was no rule against any one attending the school, and he had long ago secured a niche in it for his favorite daughter. Florence loved it and hated it at the same time. She was fond of her own companions, but she could not bear the foundation girls. These girls made a large percentage in the school. In all respects they were supposed to be Florence's equals, but as a matter of fact they were kept in a very subordinate position by the paying girls. On every possible occasion they were avoided, and there must be something very special about any one of them if she was taken up by the aristocrats—as they termed themselves—of the school.

But Cassandra as a rule was perfectly sweet and pleasant to the foundation girls, and this trait in her friend's character annoyed Florence more than anything else.

On the morning after Ruth Craven had been admitted to the school Cassandra was one of the first arrivals. She was standing in the wide courtyard waiting for the school doors to be opened. She looked, as usual, bright and capable. A stream of girls were surrounding her, each smiling and trying to draw her attention. Cassandra was a girl of few words, and after nodding to her companions, she gave them to understand that she did not intend to enter into any special conversation. Her neat satchel of school-books was slung on her arm. She wore a very dark-blue serge dress, and her white sailor-hat looked correct and pretty on her shining brown hair. Cassandra, with her face beaming as the sun, made a sort of figure-head for the smaller girls. Presently three foundation girls entered the gates side by side and glanced up at her. This trio formed perhaps the most objectionable set in the school. One was called Kate Rourke; she was a girl of fifteen years of age, showily dressed, with flashing eyes, long earrings in her ears, false jewellery round her neck, and a smart, rather shabby hat, trimmed with a lot of flowers, placed at the back of her head. Hanging on Kate's arm might have been seen Hannah Johnson, in all respects that young lady's double. Clara Sawyer, a fair-haired little girl about fourteen, with a heavy fringe right down to her eyebrows, completed the trio.

They glanced at Cassandra, and then nodded to one another and joked and laughed.

"I have no doubt," said Kate, "that Cassie will take her up."

She said the word "Cassie" in a loud voice. Cassandra heard her, but she took not the slightest notice.

"She is safe to," continued Kate. "Now, such a girl oughtn't to be on the foundation at all. If you only knew the snubbing she gave me yesterday. I quite hate her, with all her pretty face and her mincing ways."

"Never mind, Kitty," said Hannah Johnson. "She may snub you as much as she likes, but you have got me to cling on to."

"And you've got me, too, Kitty," said Clara Sawyer. She snuggled close up to Kate and slipped her hand through her arm.

"Nasty thing!" said Hannah. "I feel every word you say, Kate. Do you know, I offered to walk home with her yesterday, and she said, 'No, I thank you; I prefer to walk home alone,'"

As Hannah made this speech she adopted the mincing tones which she supposed Ruth Craven had used. The two other girls burst out laughing.

"Oh, do say what you are laughing about!" said another girl, running up to the group at this moment. Her name was Rosy Myers. "You always have a joke among you three, and I want to share it. Do say—do say! I've got a lot of toffee in my pocket."

"Hand it out, Rosy, and perhaps we'll tell you," said Kate.

Rose produced a packet of sticky sweetmeat, and a moment later the four were sucking peppermint toffee and making themselves thoroughly objectionable to their neighbors.

"But what about the girl—the person you are laughing about?" asked Rose.

"Oh, it's that stupid, tiresome Ruth Craven," answered Hannah. "Why, she's nobody. The governors and the mistress ought not to allow such a girl in the school. It's all very well to be on the foundation, but there are limits. Why, her old grandfather kept nothing better than a huckster's shop.

It doesn't seem right that a girl of that sort should belong to this school, and then take airs."

"But the question is," said Cassandra suddenly, "does she take airs?"

The girls all stopped talking, and gazed up at Cassandra with astonishment in their faces.

"I have overheard you," said Miss Weldon calmly. "I presume you are alluding to Miss Craven?"

"We are talking about Ruth Craven," said Kate Rourke; "and you will excuse me, Cassie, but I never saw a girl more chock-full of pride. She is so conceited that she is intolerable."

"I heard of her yesterday, but have not had an opportunity to form any estimate of her character," continued Cassandra. "I should prefer that you did not call me Cassie, if you please, Kate. I will watch her and find out if I agree with you. I only noticed yesterday that she is remarkably pretty. I will ask her to walk home with me to-day and have tea. I should like to introduce her to mother."

"Well, I never!" said Hannah. "And you really mean that you would introduce that girl to Mrs. Weldon?"

"I think so. Yes, I am almost certain. Here she comes. I like her face. Don't let her hear you giggling, please, Kate; it is very unkind to make a new girl feel uncomfortable."

Kate smothered a laugh and turned away. The doors of the school were now thrown open, and the girls disappeared by their special entrances.

It was just at that moment that Ruth in her shabby dress, but with her sweet and most beautiful face, joined the group of girls who were going into the school. She was without a companion. The other girls went in by twos, each clinging to her special crony. Cassandra now changed her position, and found herself within a yard or two of Ruth Craven. She was examining Ruth with great care, but not at all from the unkind point of view; hers was a sympathetic aspect. That little old serge dress made something come up in Cassandra's throat, and she longed beyond words to give her a better dress. Ruth's hat, too, left much to be desired. It was an old black sailor-hat, which had been burnt to a dull brown. But, notwithstanding the hat and the dress, there was the face. The face was most lovely, and the back of the shabby frock was covered by hair as black as jet, and curling and rippling in the sunshine.

"What wouldn't every other girl in the school give to have such a face as that, and such hair as that?" thought Cassandra. "I must speak to her."

She was just bending forward, meaning to touch Ruth on her shoulder, when there came a commotion near the entrance, and the excited face of Alice Tennant came into view. Alice was accompanied by a tall, showily dressed girl. The girl had a very vivid color in her cheeks, intensely bright and roguish dark-blue eyes, light chestnut hair touched with gold—hair which was a mass of waves and tendrils and fluffiness, and on which a little dark-blue velvet cap was placed.

"I am not going to be shy," cried the new-comer in a hearty, clear, loud voice with a considerable amount of brogue in it. "Leave off clutching me by the arm, Alice, my honey, for see my new companions I will. Ah, what a crowd of girls!—colleens we call them in Ireland. Oh, glory! how am I ever to get the names of half of them round my tongue? Ah, and isn't that one a beauty?"

"Hush, Kathleen—do hush!" said Alice. "They will hear you."

"And what do I care if they do, darling? It doesn't matter to me. I mean to talk to that girl; she's won my heart entirely."

Before Alice could prevent her, the Irish girl had sprung forward, pushed a couple of Great Shirley girls out of their places, and had taken Ruth Craven by the arm.

"It's a kiss I'm going to give you, my beauty," she said. "Oh, it's right glad I am to see you! My name is Kathleen O'Hara, and I hail from the ould country. Ah, though! it's lonely I'm likely to be, isn't it, deary? You don't deny me the pleasure of your society when I tell you that in all this vast crowd I stand solitary—solitary but for her; and, bedad! I'm not certain that I take to her at all. Let me tuck my hand inside your arm, sweetest."

A titter was heard from the surrounding girls. Ruth turned very red, then she looked into Kathleen's eyes.

"You mean kindly," she said, "but perhaps you had better not. You, too, are a stranger."

"Are you a stranger?" asked Kathleen. "Then that clinches the matter. Ah, yes; it's lonely I am. I have come from my dear mountain home to be civilised; but civilisation will never suit Kathleen O'Hara. She isn't meant to have it. She's meant to dance on the tops of the mountains, and to gather flowers in the bogs. She's made to dance and joke and laugh, and to have a gay time. Ah! my people at home made a fine mistake when they sent me to be civilised. But I like you, honey. I like the shape of your face, and the way you are made, and the wonderful look in your eyes when you glance round at me. It is you and me will be the finest of friends, sha'n't we?"

Before Ruth could reply the girls had entered the great hall, which presently became quite full.

"Don't let go of me, darling, for the life of you. It's lost I'd be in a place of this sort. Let me clutch on to you until they put me into the lowest place in the school."

"But why so?" asked Ruth, glancing at her tall companion in some astonishment. "Don't you know anything?"

"I? Never a bit, darling. I don't suppose they'll keep me here. I have no learning, and I never want to have any, and what's more—"

"Hush, girls! No talking," called the indignant voice of a form-room mistress.

Kathleen's dark-blue eyes grew round with laughter. She suddenly dropped a curtsy.

"Mum's the word, ma'am," she said, and then she glanced round at her numerous companions.

The girls had all been watching her. Their faces broke into smiles, the smiles became titters, and the titters roars. The mistress had again to come forward and ask what was wrong.

"It's only me, miss," said Kathleen, "so don't blame any of the other innocent lambs. I'm fresh from old Ireland. Oh, miss, it's a beautiful country! Were you never there? If you could only behold her purple mountains, and let yourself go on the bosom of her rushing streams! Were you ever in the old country, miss, if I might venture to ask a civil question?"

"No," said Miss Atherton in a very suppressing tone. "I don't understand impertinent questions, and I expect the schoolgirls to be orderly.—Ah, Ruth Craven! Will you take this young lady under your wing?"

"Didn't I say we were to be mates, dear?" said Kathleen O'Hara; and as they passed from the great hall, Kathleen's hand was still fondly linked on Ruth's arm.

CHAPTER III.
THE WILD IRISH GIRL.

Lessons went on in their usual orderly fashion. At eleven o'clock there was a break for a quarter of an hour. The girls streamed into the playground. The playground was very large, and was asphalted, and in consequence quite dry and pleasant to walk on. There was a field just beyond, and into this field the girls now strolled by twos and twos. Kathleen O'Hara clung to Ruth Craven's arm; she kept talking to her and asking her questions.

"You needn't reply unless you like, pet," she said. "All I want is just to look into your face. I adore beauty; I worship it more than anything else on earth. I was brought up in the midst of it. I never saw anything uglier than poor old Towser when he broke his leg and cut his upper jaw; but although he was ugly, he was the darling of my heart. He died, and I cried a lot. I can't quite get over it. Yes, I suppose I am uncivilised, and I never want to be anything else. Do you think I want to copy those nimby-pimby girls over there, or that lot, or that?"

"You had better not point, please, Miss O'Hara," said Ruth. "They won't like it."

"What do I care whether they like it or not?" said Kathleen. "I wasn't brought here to curry favor with them. What would my darling father say if I told him that I was going to curry favor with the girls of the Great Shirley School? And what would mother say? No, no; I may pick up a few smatterings, or I may not, but there is one thing certain: I mean to make a friend of you, Ruth—yes, a great big bosom friend. You will be fond of me, won't you?"

"I like you now," said Ruth. "I know you are kind, and you are very pretty."

"Why, then, darling," said Kathleen, "is it the Blarney Stone you have kissed? You have a sweet little voice of your own, although it hasn't the dear touch of the brogue that I miss so in all the other girls."

"But you like Miss Tennant don't you?" said Ruth.

"Oh, yes. Poor little Alice! She's very reserved and very, very formal, but she's a good soul, and I won't worry her. But you are the one my heart has gone out to. Ah! that is the way of Irish hearts. They go straight out to their kindred spirits. You are a kindred spirit of mine, Ruth Craven, and you can't get away from me, not even if you will."

The fifteen minutes for recreation came to an end, and the girls returned to the schoolroom. Ruth was in a high class for her age, and was already absorbed in her work. Kathleen drummed with her fingers on her desk and looked round her. Kathleen was in a low class; she was with girls a great deal smaller and younger than herself.

"How old are you, Miss O'Hara?" the English teacher, Miss Dove, had said.

"I am fifteen, bless your heart, darling!" replied Kathleen.

"Don't talk exactly like that," said Miss Dove, who, in spite of herself, was attracted by the sweet voice and sweeter eyes. "Say, 'I am fifteen, Miss Dove.'"

Kathleen made a grimace. Her grimace was so comical that all the small girls in the class burst out laughing. She was silent.

"Speak, dear," said Miss Dove in a persuasive tone.

"Yes, darling, I'm trying to."

"You mustn't use affectionate words in school."

"Oh, my heart! How am I to bear it?" said Kathleen, and she clasped a white hand over that organ.

Miss Dove paused for a moment, and then decided that she would let the question in dispute go by for the present. She began to question Kathleen as to her acquirements, and found that she must leave her with the younger children for the time being. She then went on to attend to other duties.

Kathleen sat bolt-upright in the centre of the class. It seemed absurd to see this tall, well-grown girl surrounded by tiny tots. One of the tiny tots looked towards her. Presently she thrust out a moist little hand, and out of the moisture produced a half-melted peppermint drop. Just for a second Kathleen's bright eyes fell upon the sweetmeat with disgust; then she took it up gingerly and popped it into her mouth.

"It's golloptious," she said, turning to the child, and then she drummed her fingers once more on the edge of the desk. Presently she stooped down and whispered to this small girl:

"I hate school; don't you?"

"Y—es," was the timid reply.

"Let's go out."

"But I—I can't."

"I must, then. I have nothing to do; the lessons are deadly stupid. Forgive me, girls; you are all blameless;" and the next moment she had left the room.

Half a moment later she was in the fresh air outside. Her cheeks were hot, her hair in disorder, and her hand, where she had touched the peppermint, was sticky."

"What would father say if he could see me now?" she thought. "If Aunty O'Flynn was to look at her Kathleen! Oh, why did they send me across the cold sea to a place of this sort—a detestable place? Oh, the fresh air is reviving. I was born free, and Britons never, never will be slaves. I can't stay in that horrid room. Oh, how long the morning is!"

Just then a teacher came out and beckoned to Kathleen.

"What are you doing outside, Miss O'Hara? Come in immediately and return to your class."

"I can't dear," replied Kathleen in a gentle tone. "You are young, aren't you? You don't look more than twenty. Do you ever feel your heart beat wild, dear, and your spirits all in a sort of throb? And did you, when you were like that, submit to being tied up in steel chains all round every bit of you? Answer me: did you?"

"I can't answer you, Miss O'Hara. You are a very naughty, rebellious girl. You have come to school to be disciplined. Go back immediately."

For a minute Kathleen thought of rebelling, but then she said to herself, "It isn't worth the fuss," and returned to her place once again in the centre of the class.

"I have been called back," she said in a whisper to her little peppermint companion. "I was naughty to go out, and I am called back. I am in disgrace. Isn't it a lark?"

The little girl felt quite excited. Never was there such and big and fascinating inmate of the lower fifth before. It was worth coming to school now to be in the vicinity of one so handsome and so gay.

The weary morning came to an end at last. The girls seldom returned for afternoon school, generally doing their preparations at home. Alice Tennant, however, sometimes preferred the quiet school to the noisy life she lived with her brothers at home. She looked now eagerly for Kathleen, who had shunned her from the instant they had entered the school; she stood just by the gate waiting for her. Kathleen, on her part, was looking for Ruth Craven. Ruth had been monopolised by Cassandra Weldon.

"You must come home with me," she said.

"But my grandparents will be expecting me," said Ruth.

"Never mind; we will go round by your cottage and ask them. I know all about you, and I want to know you better. You will, won't you?"

"Thank you very much," said Ruth.

"We will go on at once without waiting for the others," said Cassandra, and they walked on quickly, while Kathleen searched in vain for her chosen friend.

"Come, Kathleen; I am waiting," said Alice in a slightly cross voice. "Mother said we were to be home early to-day."

"All right," said Kathleen; "but I can't find Miss Craven anywhere."

"You can't wait for her now. Indeed, she has gone. I saw her walking down the road with Cassandra Weldon."

"And who is she?"

"The head girl of the school; and such a splendid creature! I am glad she is taking up Ruth. It isn't possible for every one to notice her; although, for my part, I have no patience with that sort of false pride. Of course, a lot of the foundation girls are very common; but when one sees a perfect lady like Ruth one ought to recognize her."

"Of course," said Kathleen, fidgeting a little as she walked.

"And how did you get on?" asked Alice, noticing the dejected tone of her voice.

"I got on abominably," said Kathleen.

"What class are you in?"

"I don't know. I am with a lot of babies; I suppose I am to be a sort of caretaker to them. There wasn't anything to learn. I am going to write to father. I can't stay in that horrid school."

"Oh, yes, you can. You will get to like it very much after a time. You have never been at school before, and of course you find it irksome."

"Is it irksome?" cried Kathleen. "Is it that she calls it? Oh, glory! It's purgatory, my dear, that's what it is—purgatory—and I haven't done anything to deserve it."

"But you want to learn; you don't want to be always ignorant."

"Bedad, then, darling, I don't want to learn at all. What do I want to know your sort of things for? I could beat you, every one of you, and the teachers, too, in some accomplishments. Put me on a horse, darling, and see what I can do; and put me in a boat, pet, and find out where I can take you. And set me swimming in the cold sea; I can turn somersaults and dive and dance on the waves, and do every mortal thing as though I were a fish, not a girl. And give me a gun and see me bring down a bird on the wing. Ah! those things ought to be counted in the education of a woman. I can do all those things, and I can mix whisky punch, and I can sing songs to the dear old dad, and I can comfort my mother when her rheumatics are bad. And I can love, love, love! Oh, no, Alice, I am not ignorant in the true sense; but I hate French, and I hate arithmetic, and I hate all your horrid school work. And I never could spell properly; and what does it matter?"

"Everything," replied Alice. "You can't go about the world if you are stupid and ignorant."

"Can't I?" exclaimed Kathleen, and she flashed her eyes at Alice and made her feel, as she said afterwards, quite uncanny.

The Tennants were, after all, not a large family. They consisted of Mrs. Tennant, Alice, and two young brothers. These brothers were schoolboys of the unruly type. Alice considered them very badly trained. Kathleen, however, was much taken by their schoolboyish ways.

As the two girls now entered the house they heard a whistle proceeding from the attic; a cat-call at the same time came from the basement.

"Oh, dear!" cried Alice, "there are those dreadful boys again. Whatever you do, Kathleen, you must not encourage them in their larks."

"But why shouldn't I? I like them both. I call David a broth of a boy. I am glad you have got brothers, Alice. I haven't any; but then I have lots of boy cousins, which comes to much the same thing."

The girls by this time had reached the large bedroom which they shared on the first floor.

"You are welcome to my brothers if you don't toss all your things about in my room," cried Alice. "If we are to sleep together we must be orderly."

"Orderly, is it?" cried Kathleen. "I don't know the meaning of the word. Well, all right, I'm ready."

She pushed her fingers through her tangled golden hair, and, without glancing at herself in the glass, marched out of the room.

"I wish mother hadn't asked her to come," said Alice to herself. "The house was bad enough before, but now she will make things past bearing."

Alice went downstairs to the sound of a cracked gong. The Tennants had their meals in a sitting-room on the second floor. It was barely furnished, and had kamptulicon instead of a carpet on the floor. Mrs. Tennant, looking careworn and anxious, was seated at the head of the table; her dress was somewhat faded. Alice entered and took her seat at the foot. Kathleen was nowhere to be seen.

"I have only soup and fish for dinner to-day," said Mrs. Tennant. "I do trust Kathleen will be satisfied."

Alice frowned at her mother in some displeasure.

"We ought to have meat—" she was beginning, when there came a bang and a scuffle, a girlish laugh, and Kathleen, leaning fondly on both the boys, appeared. Mrs. Tennant pointed to a seat, and she sat down. The Irish girl had a healthy appetite, and was indifferent to what she ate. She demanded two plates of soup, and when she had finished the second she looked at Mrs. Tennant and said emphatically:

"I have fallen in love."

"My dear Kathleen!"

"I have—with a girl, so it doesn't matter. She's the prettiest, sweetest, bonniest thing I ever saw in my life. I am going to hunt round for her immediately after dinner. I thought I'd say so, for I mean to do it."

"Oh, Kathleen!" said Alice in a distressed voice, "you really mustn't. You must come back to the school with me. I promised Miss Dove that I'd see you through your tasks.—You know, mother," continued Alice, "Kathleen is not very advanced for her age, and Miss Dove wants to get her into a proper class as quickly as possible; therefore she is to be coached a little, and I have undertaken to do it.—You will come with me, Kathleen? I must get back to the school again by half-past two. You will be sure to come, dear?"

"I think not, dear," replied Kathleen in her most aggravating tone.

"But you must.—Mustn't she, mother?"

"You ought to, Kathleen," said Mrs. Tennant. "You have been sent here to learn. Alice can teach you; she can help you very much. She means to be very kind to you. You certainly ought to do what she suggests."

"But I am afraid," said Kathleen, "that I am not going to do what I ought. I don't wish to be good at all to-day. I couldn't live if I wasn't really naughty sometimes. I mean to be terribly naughty all the afternoon. If you will let me have my fling, I do assure you, Mrs. Tennant, that I will work off the steam, and will be all right to-morrow. I must do something desperate, and if Alice opposes me I'll have to do something worse."

"You are a clipper!" said David Tennant, smiling into her face.

"All right, my boy; I expect I am," said Kathleen; and then she added, springing to her feet, "I have eaten enough, and for what we have received— Good-bye, Mrs. Tennant; I'm off."

CHAPTER IV.
THE HOME-SICK AND THE REBELLIOUS.

Kathleen O'Hara ran up to an untidy room. She banged-to the door, and standing by it for a moment, drew the bolt. Thus she had secured herself against intrusion. She then flung herself on the bed, put her two arms under her head, and gazed out of the window. Her heart was beating wildly; she had a strange medley of feelings within. She was desperately, madly lonely. She was homesick in the most intense sense of the word.

Kathleen had never left Carrigrohane Castle before. This romantic abode was situated in the extreme south-west of Ireland. It was a mile away from the sea, and stood on a rocky eminence which overlooked a very wide expanse of moor and wood, rushing streams and purple mountains, and deep dark-blue sea. In the whole world there could scarcely be found a more lovely view than that which since her birth had presented itself before Kathleen's young eyes. Her father, Squire O'Hara, was, as landlords in Ireland go, very well off. His tenantry adored him. He got in his rents with tolerable regularity. He was a good landlord, firm but also kind and indulgent. A real case of distress was never turned away from his doors, but where rent could be paid he insisted on the cottars giving him his due. He kept a rather wild establishment, however. His wife was an Irishwoman from a neighboring county, and had some of the most careless attributes of her race. The house got along anyhow. There were always shoals of visitors, mostly relatives. There were heavy feasts in the old hall, and sittings up very late at night, and no end of hunting and fishing and shooting in their seasons. In the summer a pretty white yacht made a great "divartisement," as the Squire was fond of saying; and in all things Kathleen O'Hara was free as the air she breathed. She was educated in a sort of fashion by an Irish governess, but in reality she was allowed to pursue her lessons exactly as she liked best herself.

It was just before she was fifteen that Kathleen's aunt, a maiden lady from Dublin, who rejoiced in the truly Irish name of O'Flynn, came to see them, remarked on Kathleen's wild, unkempt appearance, declared that the girl would be a downright beauty when she was eighteen, said that no one would tolerate such a want of knowledge in the present day, and advised that she should go to school. Mrs. O'Hara took Miss O'Flynn's hint very much to heart. Kathleen was consulted, and of course tabooed the entire scheme; in the end, however, the elder ladies carried the day. Miss O'Flynn took her niece to Dublin with her, and gave her an expensive and very unnecessary wardrobe; and Mrs. O'Hara, having heard a great deal of Mrs. Tennant, who had Irish relatives, decided that Kathleen should go to the Great Shirley School, where she herself had been educated long ago. Everything was arranged in a great hurry. It seemed to Kathleen now, as she lay on her bed, kicking her feet impatiently, and ruffled her beautiful hair, that the thing had come to pass in a flash. It seemed only yesterday that she was at home in the old house, petted by the servants, adored by her father, worshipped by all her relatives—the young queen of the castle, free as the air, followed by her dogs, riding on her pony—and now she was here in this hideous, poor, fifth-class house, going to that ugly school.

"I can't stand it," she thought. "There's only one way out. I must have a real desperate burst of naughtiness. What shall I do that will most aggravate them? For do that thing I will, and as quickly as possible."

Kathleen thought rapidly. She had no brothers of her own, but their loss was made up for by the adoration of about twenty young cousins who were always loafing about the place and following Kathleen wherever she turned.

"What would most aggravate Pat if he were here," thought the girl, "or dear old Michael? Ah, well! Michael—" The girl's face slightly changed. "I was never *very* naughty with Michael," she said to herself. «He is different from the others. I wouldn›t like to see that sort of sorry look in his dear dark-blue eyes. Oh, I mustn›t think of Michael now. When I was going away he said, ‹Bedad, you›ll come back a princess, and I'll be proud to see you.' No, I mustn't think of Michael. Pat, the imp, would help me, and so would Rory, and so would Ted. But what shall it be?"

She thought excitedly. There came a rattle at the handle of the door.

"Let me in, please, Kathleen; let me in," called Alice's voice.

"Presently, darling," replied Kathleen in her most nonchalant tone.

"But I am in a hurry. I must be back at school by half-past two. Let me in immediately."

"What a nuisance it all is!" thought Kathleen. "But, after all, my naughtiness needn't make that stupid old Alice late for her darling lessons."

She scrambled off the bed, drew back the bolt, and returned to her old position. Alice came quickly in. She glanced at Kathleen with disgust.

"I wish you wouldn't lie on the bed in your muddy boots."

No answer.

"I must ask you not to lock the door. It is my room as well as yours."

No answer. Kathleen's eyes were fixed on the window; they were brimful of mischief. After a time she said:

"Darling."

"I wish you wouldn't talk to me in that silly way."

"Faith! honey, then."

"I do wish—"

Kathleen suddenly sprang upright on her bed.

"Don't you like the sky when it looks as it does now? I wish you could see it from Carrigrohane. You don't know the sort of expression it has when it seems to be kissing the sea. We have a ghost at Carrigrohane. Oh, wisha, then, if you only could see it! I can tell the boys about it. Sha'n't I make them creep?"

"It is very silly to talk about ghosts. Nobody believes in them," said Alice.

"I'll ask father if I may have you at Carrigrohane in the summer, and then see if you don't believe. She wears white."

"I am going out now, Kathleen; aren't you coming with me?"

"No, thank you, my love."

"You ought to, Kathleen. I am busy preparing for my scholarship examination or I would stay and argue with you. It is an awful pity to have gone to the expense of coming here if you don't mean to do your utmost."

"Thank you, darling, but it is rather a waste of breath for you to talk so long to me. I mean to be naughty this afternoon."

"I can't help you," said Alice. "I am very sorry you ever came."

"Thank you so much, dear."

Alice ran downstairs.

"Mother," she said, rushing into her mother's presence, "we shall have no end of trouble with that terrible girl. She is lying now on the bed with her outdoor boots on, and she won't come to school, or do a single thing I want her to."

"The money her father pays will be very welcome, Alice. We must bear with some discomforts on account of that."

"I suppose so," said Alice, shrugging her shoulders. "How horrid it is to be poor, and to have such a girl as that in the house! Well, I can't stay another minute. You had better keep a sort of general eye on her, mother, for there's no saying what she will do. She has declared her intention of being naughty. She knows no fear, is not guided by any sort of principle, and would, in short, do anything."

"Well, go to school, Alice, and be quick home, for I have a great deal I want you to help me with."

Alice made no reply, and Mrs. Tennant, after thinking for a minute, went upstairs. She knocked at the door of the room which she had given up to the two girls. There was no answer. She opened it and went in. The bird had flown. There were evident signs of a stampede through the window, for it stood wide open, and there were marks of not too clean boots on the drugget, and a torn piece of ivy just without. The window was twenty feet from the ground, and Kathleen must have let herself down by the sturdy arm of the old ivy. Mrs. Tennant looked out, half expecting to see a mangled body on the ground; but there was no one in view. She returned to her darning and her anxious thoughts.

She was a widow with two sons and a daughter, and something under two hundred and fifty pounds a year on which to live. To educate the boys, to do something for Alice, and to put bread-and-butter into all their mouths was a difficult problem to solve in these expensive days. She had on purpose moved close to the Great Shirley School in order to avail herself of its cheap education for Alice. The boys went to another foundation school near by; and altogether the family managed to scrape along. But the advent of Kathleen on the scene was a great relief, for her father paid three guineas a week for Mrs. Tennant's motherly care and for Kathleen's board and lodging.

"Poor child!" thought the good woman. "What a wild, undisciplined, handsome creature she is! I must do what I can for her."

She sat on for some time darning and thinking. Her heart was full; she felt depressed. She had been working in various ways ever since six o'clock that morning, and the darning of the boys' rough socks hurt her eyes and made her fingers ache.

Meanwhile Kathleen was running along the road. She ran until she was completely out of breath. She then came to a stile, against which she leant. By-and-by she saw a girl walking leisurely up the road; she was a shabbily dressed and rather vulgar girl. Kathleen saw at once that she was one of the Great Shirley girls, so she went forward and spoke to her.

"You go to our school, don't you?" she said.

"Yes, miss," answered the girl, dropping a little curtsy when she saw Kathleen. She was a very fresh foundation girl, and recognized something in Kathleen which caused her to be more subservient than was necessary.

"Then, if you please," continued Kathleen, "can you tell me where that sweetly pretty girl, Ruth Craven, lives?"

"She isn't a lady," said the girl, whose name was Susan Hopkins. "She is no more a lady than I am."

"Indeed she is," said Kathleen. "She is a great deal more of a lady than you are."

The girl flushed.

"You are a Great Shirley girl yourself," she said. "I saw you there to-day. You are in an awfully low class. Do you like sitting with the little kids? I saw you towering up in the middle of them like a mountain."

Kathleen's eyes flashed.

"What is your name?" she asked.

"Susan Hopkins. I used to be a Board School girl, but now I am on the foundation at Great Shirley. It is a big rise for me. Are you a poor girl? Are you on the foundation?"

"I don't know what it means by being on the foundation, but I don't think I am poor. I think, on the contrary, that I am very rich. Did you ever hear of a girl who lived in a castle—a great beautiful castle—on the top of a high hill? If you ever did, I am that girl."

"Oh, my!" said Susy Hopkins. "That does sound romantic."

Her momentary dislike to Kathleen had vanished. The desire to go to the town on a message for her mother had completely left her. She stood still, as though fascinated.

"I live there," said Kathleen—"that is, I do when I am at home. I come from the land of the mountain and the stream; of the shamrock; of the deep, deep blue sea."

"Ireland? Are you Irish?" said the girl.

"I am proud to say that I am."

"We don't think anything of the Irish here."

"Oh, don't you?"

"But don't be angry, please," continued Susy, "for I am sure you are very nice."

"I am nice when I like. To-day I am nasty. I am wicked to-day—quite wicked; I could hate any one who opposes me. I want some one to help me; if some one will help me, I will be nice to that person. Will you?"

"Oh, my word, yes! How handsome you look when you flash your eyes!" said Susy Hopkins.

"Then I want to find that dear little girl, who is so beautiful that I love her and can't get her out of my head. I want to find Ruth Craven. She went away with a horrid, stiff, pokery girl called Cassandra Weldon. You have such strange names in your country. That horrid, prim Cassandra chose to correct me when I came into school, and she has taken my darling away— the only one I love in the whole of England. I want to find her. I will give you—- I will give you an Irish diamond set in a brooch if you will help me."

This sounded a very grand offer indeed to Susy Hopkins, who lived in the most modest way, and had not a jewel of any sort in her possession.

"I will help you. I will, and I can. I know where Miss Weldon lives. I can take you to her house."

"But I want Ruth."

"If she has taken Ruth home, she will be at Cassandra's house," said Susy.

"And you can take me there?" "This blessed minute."

"All right; come along."

"When will you give me the diamond set in the brooch?"

"It isn't a real diamond, you know. It is an Irish diamond set in silver— real silver. My old nurse had it made for me, and I wear it sometimes. I will bring it to you to school to-morrow."

"Oh, thank you—thank you, Miss—I forgot your name."

"O'Hara—Kathleen O'Hara."

"O'Hara is rather a difficult name to say. May I call you Kathleen?"

"Just as you please, Susan. It is more handy for me to say Susan than Hopkins. As long as I am in England I must consort, I see, with all kinds of people; and if you will make yourself useful to me, I will be good to you."

Susy turned and led the way in the direction of Cassandra Weldon's home. They had to walk across a very wide field, then down a narrow lane, then up a steep hill, and then into a valley. At the bottom of the valley was a straight road, and at each side of the road were neat little houses—small and very proper-looking. Each house consisted of two stories, with a hall door in the middle and a sitting room on each side. There were three windows overhead, and one or two attics in the roof. The houses were very compact; they were new, and were called by ambitious names. For instance, the house where the Weldons lived went by the ambitious name of Sans Souci. All through the walk Susy chatted for the benefit of her companion. She told Kathleen so much about her life that she was interested in spite of herself! and by the time they arrived outside Sans Souci, Kathleen's hand was lying affectionately on her companion's arm.

"I had best not go in, miss," she said. "Cassandra Weldon would never take the very least notice of me; and none of us foundation girls like her at all."

"Well, it is extremely unfair," said Kathleen. "From all you have been telling me, the foundation girls must be particularly clever. I tell you what it is: I think I shall take to you."

"Oh, would you, indeed, miss?" said Susy, her eyes sparkling. "There are a hundred of us, you know, in the school."

"That is a great number. And Ruth Craven is really one?"

"She is, miss. She isn't a bit better than the rest of us."

"And I love her already."

"She is no better than the rest of us," repeated Susan Hopkins.

"I have a great mind to take to you all, to make a fuss about you, and to show the others how badly they behave."

"You'd be a queen amongst us; there's no doubt about that."

"It would be lovely, and it would be a tremendous bit of naughtiness," thought Kathleen.

"Do you think you will, miss? Because, if you do, I will tell the others. We could meet you and talk over things."

"Well, I will decide to-morrow. I will enclose a letter with your brooch. Good-bye now; I must go in and kiss my darling Ruth."

Susy Hopkins stood for a minute to watch Kathleen as she went up the little narrow path of Sans Souci. When Kathleen reached the porch she waved her hand, and Susy, putting wings to her feet, ran as fast as she could in the opposite direction. She felt very much elated and really pleased. In the whole course of her life she had never met a girl of the Kathleen O'Hara type before. Her beauty, her daring and wild manner, the flash in her bright dark eyes, the glints of gold in her lovely hair, all fascinated Susy.

"What a queen she'd make!" she thought. "We must make her our queen. We'd have quite a party of our own in the school if she took us up. And she will; I'm sure she will. This is a lark. This is worth a great deal."

Meanwhile Kathleen rang the bell at Sans Souci in a very smart, imperative manner. A little maid, neatly dressed, came to the door.

"Please," said Kathleen, "will you say that Miss O'Hara has called and would be glad to see Miss Ruth Craven for a few minutes?"

The girl withdrew. Presently she returned.

"Mrs. Weldon will be pleased if you will go in, miss. She is sitting in the drawing-room. The two young ladies are out in the garden."

"Thank you," said Kathleen.

After a brief hesitation she entered the house, and was conducted across the narrow hall into a very sweet and charmingly furnished room. The room had a bay-window with French doors; these opened on to a little flower-lawn. At one side of the house was a tiny conservatory full of bright flowers. Compared to the house where the Tennants lived, this tiny place looked like a paradise to Kathleen. She gave a quick glance round her, then came up to Mrs. Weldon.

"I am one of the new girls at the Great Shirley School," she said. "My name is Kathleen O'Hara. I am Irish. I have only just crossed the cold sea. I am lonely, too. I want Ruth Craven. May I sit down a minute while your servant fetches her? I like Ruth Craven. She is very pretty, isn't she? She is the sort of girl that you'd take a fancy to when you're lonely and far from home. May I sit here until she comes?"

"Of course, my dear," said Mrs. Weldon, speaking with kindness, and looking with eyes full of interest at the handsome, striking-looking girl. "I quite understand your being lonely. I was very lonely indeed when I came home from India and left my dear father and mother behind me."

"How old were you when you came home?"

"A great deal younger than you are: only seven years old. But that is a long time ago. I should like to be kind to you, Miss O'Hara. Cassandra has been telling me about you. You are living at the Tennants', are you not? Alice Tennant and Cassandra are great friends."

"But I don't like either of them," said Kathleen in her blunt way.

Mrs. Weldon looked a little startled.

"Do you know my daughter?" she asked.

"She is much too interfering, and she is frightfully stuck-up. Please forgive me, but I am always very plain-spoken; I always tell the truth. I don't want her. I like you, and wish that I lived with you, and that you'd have Ruth Craven instead of your own daughter in the house. Then I'd be perfectly happy. I always did say what I thought. Will you forgive me?"

"I will, dear, because at the present moment you don't know my girl at all. There never was a more splendid girl in all the world, but she requires to be known. Ah! here she comes, and your little friend, Miss Craven, with her."

Ruth, looking very pretty, with a delicate flush on each cheek, now entered the room in the company of Cassandra. Kathleen sprang up the minute she saw Ruth, rushed across the room, and flung one arm with considerable violence round her neck.

"You have come," she said. "I have been hunting the place for you. How dared you go away and hide yourself? Don't you know that you belong to me? The moment I saw you I knew that you were my affinity. Don't you know what an affinity means? Well, you are mine. We were twin souls before birth; now we have met again and we cannot part. I am ever so happy when I am with you. Don't mind those others; let them stare all they like. I am going to take you foundation girls up. I have made up my mind. We will have a rollicking good time—a splendid time. We will be as naughty as we like, and we will let the others see what we are made of. It will be war to the knife between the foundation girls and the good, proper, paying girls. Let the ladies look after themselves. We of the foundation will lead our own life, and be as happy as the day is long. Aren't you glad to see me, dear, sweet, pretty Ruth? Don't you know for yourself that you are my affinity—my chosen friend, my beloved? Through the ages we have been one, and now we have met in the flesh."

"I think," said Cassandra, at last managing to get herself heard, "that you have said enough for the present, Miss O'Hara. Ruth Craven has come to spend the day with me. I know that you are an Irish girl, and you must be lonely. I shall be very pleased if you will join Ruth and me in our walk. We are going for a walk across the common.—We shall be in to tea, dear mother. Will you have it ready for us not later than five o'clock? And I am sure you will join me, mother darling, in asking Miss O'Hara to stay, too."

"But Miss O'Hara doesn't want to join either you or your 'mother darling,'" said Kathleen in her rudest tone. "It is Ruth I want. I have come here for her. She must return with me at once."

"But I can't. I am ever so sorry, Miss O'Hara."

"You mean that you won't come when I have called for you?"

"I am with Miss Weldon at present."

"Be sensible, dear," said Mrs. Weldon at that moment. "You don't quite understand our manners in this country. However attached we may be to a person, we don't enter a strange house and snatch that person out of it. It isn't our way; and I don't think—you will forgive me for saying it—that your way is as nice as ours. Be persuaded, dear, and join Cassandra and Ruth, and have a happy time."

Kathleen's face had turned crimson. She looked from Mrs. Weldon to Cassandra, and then she looked at Ruth. Suddenly her eyes brimmed up with tears.

"I don't think I can ever change my way," she said. "I am sorry if I am rude and not understood. Perhaps, after all, I am mistaken, about Ruth; perhaps she is not my real proper affinity. I am a very unhappy girl. I wish I could go back to mother and to my dad. I shouldn't be lonely if I were in the midst of the mountains, and if I could see the streams and the blue sea. I don't know why Aunt Katie O'Flynn sent me to this horrid place. I wish I was back in the old country. They don't talk as you talk in the old country and they don't look as you look. If you put your heart at the feet of a body in old Ireland, that body doesn't kick it away. I will go. I don't want your tea. I don't want anything that you have to offer me. I don't like any of you. I am sorry if you think me rude, but I can't help myself. Good-bye."

"No, no; stay. Stay and visit with me, and tell me about the old country and the sea and the mountains," said Mrs. Weldon.

But Kathleen shook her head fiercely, and the next moment left the room.

"Poor, strange little girl," thought the good woman. "I see she is about to heap unhappiness on herself and others. What is to be done for her?"

"I like her," said Ruth. "She is very impulsive, but she is———"

"Oh, yes," said Cassandra, "she has a good heart, of course; but I foresee that she is up to all sorts of mischief. She doesn't understand our ways. Why did she leave her own country?"

Ruth was silent. She looked wistful.

"Come along, Ruthie; we will be late. I have no end of schemes in my head. I mean to help you. You will win that scholarship."

Ruth smiled. Presently she and Cassandra were crossing the common arm-in-arm. In the interest of their own conversation they forgot Kathleen.

When that young lady left the house she ran back to the Tennants'.

"I will write to dad to-night and tell him that I can't stay," she thought. "Oh, dear, my heart is in my mouth! I shall have a broken heart if this sort of thing goes on."

She entered the house. There sat Mrs. Tennant with a great basket of stockings before her. The remains of a rough-looking tea were on the table. The boys had disappeared.

"Come in, Kathleen," called Mrs. Tennant, "and have your tea. I want Maria to clear the tea-things away, as I have some cutting out to do; so be quick, dear."

Kathleen entered. The untidy table did not trouble her in the least; she was accustomed to things of that sort at home. She sat down, helped herself to a thick slice of bread-and-butter, and ate it, while burning thoughts filled her mind.

"Have some tea. You haven't touched any," said Mrs. Tennant.

"I'd rather have cold water, please," Kathleen replied.

She went to the sideboard, filled a glass, and drank it off.

"Mrs. Tennant," she said when she had finished, "what possessed you to live in England? You had all the world to choose from. Why did you come to a horrible place like this?"

"But I like it," said Mrs. Tennant.

"You don't look as if you did. I never saw such a worn-out poor body. Are you awfully old?"

"You would think me so," replied Mrs. Tennant, with a smile; "but as a matter of fact I am not forty yet."

"Not forty!" said Kathleen. "But forty's an awful age, isn't it? I mean, you want crutches when you are forty, don't you?"

"Not as a rule, my dear. I trust when I am forty I shall not want a crutch. I shall be forty in two years, and that by some people is considered young."

"Then I suppose it is mending those horrid stockings that makes you so old."

"Mending stockings doesn't help to keep you young, certainly."

"Shall I help you? I used to cobble for old nurse when I was at home."

"But I shouldn't like you to cobble these."

"Oh, I can darn, you know."

"Then do, Kathleen. I should take it very kindly if you would. Here is worsted, and here is a needle. Will you sit by me and tell me about your home?"

Kathleen certainly would not have believed her own ears had she been told an hour ago that she would end her first fit of desperate naughtiness by darning stockings for the Tennant boys. She did not darn well; but then, Mrs. Tennant was not particular. She certainly—although she said she would not—did cobble these stockings to an extraordinary extent; but her work and the chat with Mrs. Tennant did her good, and she went upstairs to dress for supper in a happier frame of mind.

"I will stay here for a little," she said finally to Mrs. Tennant, "because I think it will help you. You look so terribly tired; and I don't think you ought to have this horrible work to do. I'd like to do it for you, but I don't suppose I shall have time. I will stay for a bit and see what I can make of the foundation girls."

"The foundation girls?"

"Oh, yes; don't ask me to explain. There are a hundred of them at the Great Shirley School, and I am going—No, I can't explain. I will stop here instead of running away. I meant to run away when my affinity would have nothing to do with me."

"Really, Kathleen, you are a most extraordinary girl."

"Of course I am," said Kathleen. "Did you ever suppose that I was anything else? I am very remarkable, and I am very naughty. I always was, and I always will be. I am up to no end of mischief. I wish you could have seen me and Rory together at home. Oh, what didn't we do? Do you know that once we walked across a little bridge of metal which is put between two of the stables? It is just a narrow iron rod, six feet in length. If we had either of us fallen we'd have been dashed to pieces on the cobble-stones forty feet below. Mother saw me when I was half-way across, and she gave a shriek. It nearly finished me, but I steadied myself and got across. Oh, it was jolly! I am going to set some of the foundation girls at that sort of thing. I expect I shall have great fun with them. It is principally because my affinity won't have anything to do with me; she is attaching herself to another, and that other is little better than a monster. Your Alice won't like me; and, to be frank with you, I don't like her. I like you, because you are poor and worried and seem old for your age—although your age is a great one—and because you have to cobble those horrid socks. There! good-bye for the present. Don't hate me too much; I can't help the way I am made. Oh; I hear Alice. What a detestable voice she has! Now then, I'm off."

Kathleen ran up to her room, and again she locked the door. She heard Alice's step, and she felt a certain vindictiveness as she turned the key in the lock. Alice presently took the handle of the door and shook it.

"Let me in at once, Kathleen," she said. "I really can't put up with this sort of thing any longer. I want to get into my room; I want to tidy myself. I am going to supper to-night with Cassandra Weldon."

"Then you don't get in," whispered Kathleen to herself. Aloud she said:

"I am sorry, darling, but I am specially busy, and I really must have my share of the room to myself."

"Do open the door, Kathleen," now almost pleaded poor Alice. "If you want your share of the room, I want mine. Don't you understand?"

"I am not interfering, dearest," called back Kathleen, "and I am keeping religiously to my own half. I have the straight window, and you have the bay. I am not touching your beautiful half; I am only in mine."

"Let me in," called Alice again, "and don't be silly."

"Sorry, dear; don't think I am silly."

There was a silence. Alice went on her knees and peered through the keyhole: Kathleen was seated by her dressing-table, and there was a sound of the furious scratching of a pen quite audible. "This is intolerable," thought Alice. "She is the most awful girl I ever heard of. I shall be late. Mary Addersley and Rhoda Pierpont are to call for me shortly, and I shan't be ready. I don't want to appeal to mother or to be rude to the poor wild thing the first day. Stay, I will tempt her.—Kathleen!"

"Yes, darling."

"Wouldn't you like to come with me to Cassandra Weldon's? She is so nice, and so is her mother. She plays beautifully, and they will sing."

"Irish songs?" called out Kathleen.

"I don't know. Perhaps they will if you ask them."

"Thanks," replied Kathleen; "I am not going." Again there was silence, and the scratching of the pen continued. Alice was now obliged to go downstairs to acquaint her mother.

"What is it, dear? Why, my dear Alice, how excited you look!"

"I have cause to be, mother. I have come in rather late, very much fagged out from a day of hard examination work and that imp—that horrid girl—has locked me out of my bedroom. I was so looking forward to a nice little supper with Cassandra and the other girls! Kathleen won't let me in;

she really is intolerable. I can't stay in the room with her any longer; she is past bearing. Can't you give me an attic to myself at the top of the house?"

"You know I haven't a corner."

"Can't I share your bed, mummy? I shall be so miserable with that dreadful Kathleen."

"You know quite well, Alice, that that is the only really good bedroom in the house, and I can't afford to give it to one girl by herself. I think Kathleen will be all right when we really get to know her; but she is very undisciplined. Still, three guineas a week makes an immense difference to me, Alice. I can't help telling you so, my child."

"In my opinion, it is hardly earned," said Alice. "I suppose I must stay down here and give up my supper. I can't go like this, all untidy, and my hair so messy, and my collar—oh, mother, it is nearly black! It is really too trying."

"I will go up and see if I can persuade her," said Mrs. Tennant.

She went upstairs, turned the handle of the door, and spoke. The moment her voice penetrated to Kathleen's ears, she jumped to her feet, crossed the room, and bent down at the other side of the keyhole.

"Don't tire your dear voice," she said. "What is it you want?"

"I want you to open the door, Kathleen. Poor Alice wants to get in to get her clothes. It is her room as much as yours. Let her in at once, my dear."

"I am very sorry, darling Mrs. Tennant, but I am privately engaged in my own half of the room. I am not interfering with Alice's."

"But you see, Kathleen, she can't get to her half."

"The door is in my half, you know," said Kathleen very meekly, "so I don't see that she has any cause to complain. I am awfully sorry; I will be as quick as I can."

"You annoy me very much. You make me very uncomfortable by going on in this extremely silly way, Kathleen."

"I will darn some more socks for you, darling, tired pet," whispered Kathleen coaxingly. "I really am awfully sorry, but there is no help for it. I must finish my own private affairs in my own half of the room."

She retreated from the door, and the scratching of the pen continued.

Alice downstairs felt like a caged lion. Mrs. Tennant admitted that Kathleen's conduct was very bad.

"It won't happen again, Alice," she said, "for I shall remove the key from the lock. She won't shut you out another time. Make the best of it, darling. If we don't worry her too much she is sure to capitulate."

"Not she. She is a perfect horror," said Alice.

Mrs. Weldon's supper party was to begin at eight o'clock. It was now seven, and the girls were to call for Alice at half-past. If Kathleen would only be quick she might still have time.

The boys came in. They stared open-eyed at Alice when they saw her still sitting in her rough school things, a very cross expression on her face. David came up to her at once; he was the favorite, and people said he had a way with him. Whatever they meant by that, most people did what David Tennant liked. He stood in front of his sister now and said:

"What's the matter? And where's the little Irish beauty?"

"For goodness' sake don't speak about her," said Alice. "She's driving me nearly mad."

"Your sister is naturally much annoyed, David," said his mother. "Kathleen is evidently a very tiresome girl. She has locked the door of their mutual bedroom, and declines to open it; she says that as the door happens to be in her half of the room, she has perfect control over it."

David whistled. Ben burst out laughing.

"Well, now that is Irish," David said.

"If you take her part I shall hate you all the rest of my life," said Alice, speaking with great passion.

"But can't you wait just for once?" asked David. "Any one could tell she is just trying it on. She'll get tired of sitting there by herself if only you have patience."

"But I am due at Cassandra's for supper" and Mary Addersley and Rhoda Pierpont are to call for me at half-past seven."

"Oh, that's it, is it?" said David.—"Ben, leave off teasing." For Ben was whistling and jumping about, and making the most expressive faces at poor Alice,—"I will see what I can do," he said, and he ran upstairs. David was very musical; indeed, the soul of music dwelt in his eyes, in his voice, in his very step. He might in some respects have been an Irish boy himself. He bent down now and whistled very softly, and in the most flute-like manner, "Garry Owen" through the keyhole. There was a restless sound in the room, and then a cross voice said:

"Go away."

David stopped whistling "Garry Owen," and proceeded to execute a most exquisite performance of "St. Patrick's Day in the Morning." Kathleen trembled. Her eyes filled with tears. David was now whistling right into her room "The Wearing of the Green." Kathleen flung down her pen, making a splash on the paper.

"Go away," she called out. "What are you doing there?"

"The outside of this door doesn't belong to you," called David, "and if I like to whistle through the keyhole you can't prevent me;" and he began "Garry Owen" again.

Kathleen rushed to the door and flung it open. The tears were still wet on her cheeks.

"Can't you guess what you are doing?" she said. "You are stabbing me—stabbing me. Oh! oh! oh!" and she burst into violent sobs. David took her hand.

"Come, little Irish colleen," he said. "Come along downstairs. I am going to be chummy with you. Don't be so lonely. Give Alice her room; one-half of it is hers, and she wants to dress to go out."

"Let her take it all," sobbed Kathleen. "I am most miserable. Oh, Garry Owen, Garry Owen! Oh, Land of the Shamrock! Oh, my broken heart!"

She laid her head on David's shoulder and went on sobbing. David felt quite bashful. There was nothing for it but to take out his big and not too clean handkerchief and wipe her tears away.

"Whisper," he said in her ear. "There are stables at the back of the house; they are old, worn-out stables. There is a loft over one, and I keep apples and nuts there. It's the jolliest place. Will you and I go there for an hour or two after supper?"

"Do you mean it?" said Kathleen, her eyes filling with laughter, and the tears still wet on her cheeks.

"Yes, colleen, I mean it, for I want you to tell me all you can about your land of the shamrock."

"Why, then, that I will," she replied. "Wisha, then, David, it's a broth of a boy, you are!" and she kissed him on his forehead. David took her hand and led her into the dining-room. Alice was still there, looking more stormy than ever.

"It's too late now," she said; "the girls have come and gone. I can't go at all now."

"But why, darling?" said Kathleen. "Oh! I wish I had let you in.—She must go, David, the poor dear. It would be cruel to disappoint her.—What dress will you wear?" said Kathleen.

"Let me alone," said Alice.

She rushed upstairs, but Kathleen was even quicker.

"I'm not going to be nasty to you any more," she said. "I have found a friend, and I shall have more friends tomorrow. Kathleen O'Hara would have died long ago but for her friends. I shall be happy when I have got a creelful of them here. Now then, let me help you. No, that isn't the shoe you want; here it is. And gloves—here's a pair, and they're neatly mended. Which hat did you say—the one with the blue scarf round it? Isn't it a pretty one? You put that on. Aunt Katie O'Flynn is going to send me a box of clothes from Dublin, and I will give you some of them. You mustn't say no; I will give you some if you are nice. I am ever so sorry that I kept you out of your part of the room; I won't do it any more. Now you are dressed; that's fine. You won't hate me forever, will you?"

Alice growled something in reply. She had not Kathleen's passionate, quick, impulsive nature—furious with rage one minute, sweet and gentle and affectionate the next. She hated Kathleen for having humiliated and annoyed her; and she went off to Cassandra's house knowing that she would be late, and determined not to say one good word for Kathleen.

CHAPTER V.
WIT AND GENIUS: THE PLAN PROPOUNDED.

While Kathleen was locked in Alice's room, she was writing to her father:

"My Darling Daddy.—If ever there was a cold, dreary, abominable land, it is this where they wave the British flag. The ugliness of it would make you sick. The people are as ugly as the country, and they're so stiff and stuck-up. If you suppose for a moment that your wild Irish girl can stand much of this sort of thing, you are fine and mistaken, and you can tell the mother so. I mean to write to Aunt Katie O'Flynn to-morrow and give her a fine piece of my mind. Early in the day, dad, I did not think that I could stay at all; but I have got a plan in my head now, and if I succeed I may at least put up with one term of this detestable school. I won't tell you the plan, for you mightn't approve; in fact, I can guess in advance that you wouldn't approve. Anyhow, it is going to occupy the time and thoughts of your Kathleen. Now I want a good bit of money; not a pound or even five pounds, but more than that. Can you send me a ten-pound note, daddy mine, and say nothing whatever about it to the mother or the retainers at Carrigrohane? And can you let me have it as quick as quick can be? Maybe I will want more before the term is up, or maybe I won't. Anyhow, we will let that lie in the future. Oh, my broth of an old dad, wouldn't I like to hug you this blessed minute? How is everybody at home? How are the mountains? How is the sea? How is the trout-stream? Are those young cousins of mine behaving themselves, the spalpeens? And how are you, my heart of hearts—missing your Kathleen, I doubt not? Well, no more for the present. They're rattling at the door like anything, and there's a detestable boy now whistling 'Garry Owen' right into my heart. You can't imagine what I am feeling. Oh, the omadhaun! he is changing it now into 'St. Patrick's Day,'

Wisha, then, daddy! I must stop, for it's more than the heart of woman can stand. Your affectionate daughter, "Kathleen."

This letter was posted by Kathleen herself. After supper she went with David into the old loft over the tumble-down stables. It was not a very safe place of refuge, for the rafters were rotten and might tumble down at any time. Still, the sense of danger made it all, the more interesting to the children. There they sat side by side, and Kathleen told David about her old life. She was very outspoken and affectionate, and very fierce and very wild. To look at her, one would have said there never was any one less reserved; but Kathleen in her heart of hearts was intensely reserved. Her real feelings she never told; her real hopes she never breathed. She talked with high spirits all the time; and although she liked David and was much comforted by his words and his actions, he did not get at the real Kathleen at all.

When Alice came back that evening Kathleen was sound asleep in her little bed, dreaming of Carrigrohane and the old home. She was murmuring some loving words as Alice entered the room.

"Oh, daddy mine, my heart is sore for you," she was saying in a tone which caused Alice to pause and look at her attentively.

"She is the most awful girl I ever heard of," thought Alice. "I am sure she will get us into trouble. I know that those three guineas a week that mother gets for having her are not worth all the mischief she will drag us into. But still, she does look pretty when she is asleep."

Kathleen had very long and very thick eyelashes and nobly arched brows. Her forehead was broad and full and beautifully white. The mischievous, dare-devil expression of her face when awake was softened in her sleep. Alice, who had determined to come very noisily into the room and bang her things about, to take rude possession of her own half of the room—which, after all, was the better half—was softened by the look on the girl's face. She knelt for a moment at her bedside and prayed that God would keep her from quite hating Kathleen. This was a great deal from Alice, who had made up her mind never to be friends with the Irish girl. Then she got into bed and fell asleep.

The next morning, quite early, Kathleen was up. She was accustomed to getting up almost at cock-crow at Carrigrohane, and when Alice opened her eyes, it was to see an empty bed and an empty room.

"I wonder if she's up to mischief?" she thought.

She got up and went to the window. Kathleen was walking across the common. She had no hat on, and no jacket. She was stepping along leisurely, looking up sometimes at the sky, and sometimes pausing as though she was thinking hard.

"She will catch cold and be ill; that will be the next trouble," thought the indignant Alice. She sleepily proceeded with her dressing. It was only half-past seven. The Great Shirley School met at nine. Alice was seldom downstairs until past eight. When she came down this morning she saw, to her amazement, Kathleen helping the very untidy maid-of-all-work to lay the breakfast things. She was dashing about, putting plates and cups and saucers anyhow upon the board.

"Now then, Maria," she said, "shall I run down to the kitchen and bring up the hot bacon and the porridge? I will, with a heart and a half. Oh, you poor girl, how tired you look!"

Maria, whom Alice never noticed, looked with adoring eyes at beautiful Kathleen.

"It isn't right, miss. I ought to be doing my own work," she said. "I am ever so much obliged to you, miss."

"Wisha, then, it is I who like to help you," said Kathleen, "for you look fair beat."

She dashed past Alice, and appeared the next moment in the kitchen.

"Where's the bacon, cook? And where's the bread, and where's the butter, and all the rest of the breakfast? See, woman—see! Give me a tray and I will fill it up and take the things upstairs with my own hands. You think it is beneath me, perhaps; but I am a lady from a castle, and at Carrigrohane Castle we often do this sort of thing when the hands of the poor maids are full to overflowing."

The cook, a sandy-haired and sour-looking woman, began by scowling at Kathleen; but soon the girl's pretty face and merry eyes appeased her. She and Kathleen had almost a quarrel as to who was to carry up the tray, but Kathleen won the day; and when Mrs. Tennant made her appearance, feeling tired and overdone, she was amazed to see Kathleen acting parlor-maid.

"I love it," she said. "If I can help you, you dear, tired, worn one, I shall be only too glad."

"I am sure, mother," said Alice, "it is very good of Kathleen to wish to do the household work; but as she has been sent here to gain some information of another sort, do you think it ought to be allowed?"

"And who will prevent it, darling? That is the question," said Kathleen in her softest voice.

Alice was silent.

"I tell you what," said Kathleen. "When I see you beginning to help your poor, exhausted mother, and running messages for that overworked slavey—I think you call her Maria—then perhaps I'll do less. And when there's some one else to mend the boys' socks, perhaps I won't offer; but until there is, the less you say about such things the better, Miss Alice Tennant."

Ben kicked David under the table, and David kicked him back to stay quiet. Altogether the breakfast was a noisy one.

Kathleen went to school quite prepared to carry out her promise to Susy Hopkins. She had neatly packed the little Irish diamond brooch in a box, and had slipped under it a tiny note:

> "Get as many foundation girls as you can to meet me, at whatever place you like to appoint, this evening. I have a plan to propose.—Kathleen O'Hara.
>
> "P.S.—You can name the place by pinning a note under my desk. Be sure you all come. The plan is gloryious."

The thought of the note and the plan and the little brooch kept Kathleen in a fairly good humor on her walk to school. There she saw Ruth Craven. She was decidedly angry with Ruth for having, as she said to herself, "snubbed her" the day before. But beauty always had a curious effect on the Irish girl, and when she observed Ruth's really exquisite little face, clear cut as a cameo, with eyes full of expression, and watched the lips ready to break into the gentlest smiles, Kathleen said to herself:

"It is all over with me. She is the only decent-looking colleen I have met in this God-forsaken country. Make up to her I will."

She dashed, therefore, almost rudely through a great mass of incoming girls, and seized Ruth by her shoulder.

"Ruth," she said, "go and talk to Susy Hopkins during recess. She will have something to say, and I want you so badly. You won't refuse me, will you, Ruth?"

"But I don't know what you want," said Ruth.

"Go and talk to Susy Hopkins; she will know. Oh, there she is!"

"Kathleen, Kathleen!" called out Alice. "The school-bell has just rung, and they are opening the doors. Come do come."

"In a jiff," replied Kathleen.

She ran up to Susy.

"This is what I promised," she said; "and there is a note inside. Read it, and give me the answer where I have asked you."

Susy Hopkins, a most ordinary little girl, who had no position of any sort in the school, colored high with delight. Some of the paying girls looked at her in astonishment. Susy walked into the school with her head high in the air; she quite adored Kathleen, for she was making her a person of great distinction.

"We are going to have a glorious time," whispered Susy to Kate Rourke as they made their way to their respective classes.

Susy was small, rather stupid, and absolutely unimportant. Kate was big, black-eyed, impudent. She was jealous of the paying girls of the school; but she treated Susy as some one beneath contempt.

"Don't drag my sleeve," she replied crossly. "And what you do mean by a glorious time? I don't understand you."

"You will presently," said Susy. "And when all is said and done, you will have to remember that you owe it to me. But I have no time to talk now; only meet me, and bring as many of the foundationers as you can collect into the left-hand corner of the playground, just behind the Botanical Laboratory, at recess."

Kate made no answer, unless a toss of her head could have been taken as a reply. Her first impulse was to take no notice of Susy's remarks—little Susy Hopkins, the daughter of a small stationer in the town, a girl who had scarcely scraped through in her examination. It was intolerable that she should put on such airs.

The work of the school began, and all the girls were busy. Kate was clever, and she meant to try for one of the big scholarships. She would get her forty pounds a year when the time came, and go to Holloway College or some other college. She was not a lady by birth; she had not a single instinct of a true lady within her; but she was intensely ambitious. She did not care so much for beauty as for style; she made style her idol. The look that Cassandra wore as she walked quietly across the room, the set of her dress, the still more wonderful set of her head as it was placed on her queenly young shoulders—these were the things that burnt into Kate's soul and made her restless and dissatisfied. She would willingly have given all her father's wealth—and he was quite well-to-do for his class—- to have Cassandra's face, Cassandra's voice, Cassandra's figure. Cassandra was not at all a pretty girl, but her appearance appealed to all the wild ambitions in Kate's soul. She had a jealous contempt of Ruth Craven, who, although a foundation girl, managed to look like a lady; but her envy was centered round Cassandra. As to the Irish girl, she had scarcely noticed her up to the present.

Work went on that morning with much verve and vigor. It was a pleasant morning: the windows were open; the schoolrooms were all well ventilated; the teachers, the best of their kind, were stimulating in their lectures and in their conversation. There was a look of business and animation throughout the whole place: it was like a hive of bees. At last the moment of recess arrived. Kate just raised her head, looked over the shoulders of her companions, and saw Susy Hopkins darting restlessly about, catching one girl by the sleeve, another by the arm, whispering in the ear of a third, flinging her arm round the neck of a fourth; and as she spoke to the girls they looked interested, astonished, and cordial. They moved away to that lonely part of the playground which was situated at the back of the Botanical Laboratory. Kate had made up her mind not to take the least notice of Susy. She was pacing up and down alone; for, most provoking, all her chosen friends had gone off with that young lady. Suddenly she saw Ruth Craven going very quietly by. By all the laws of the foundationers, Ruth ought to speak to her companions in misfortune. Kate rushed up to her.

"What are they all doing there?" she said. "Do you happen to know Susy Hopkins?"

"No," replied Ruth gently. "She came up to me just now and asked me to join her and some other girls at the back of the Laboratory. I don't know that I want to."

"I am curious," said Kate. "Of course, I am no friend of Susy's; she is a most contemptible little wretch; but I may as well know what it is all about. Come with me, won't you?"

Ruth hesitated.

"Come along; we may as well know. There is probably some mischief on foot, and it is only fair that we should be forewarned."

"I don't want to know," said Ruth; but as Kate slipped her hand through her arm and pulled her along, she said resignedly, "Well, if I must I must."

As they strolled across the big playground, Ruth turned and glanced at Cassandra; but Cassandra was busy making friends with Florence, who was very angry with her for her desertion of the day before, and took no notice of Ruth. The Irish girl was nowhere in sight. Ruth sighed and continued her walk with Kate.

The most lonely and most dreary part of the playground was that little portion which was situated at the back of the Laboratory. Nothing grew there; the ground was innocent of grass, and much worn by the tramping of young feet. There were swings and garden-seats and preparations for tennis and other games in the rest of the big playground, but nothing had ever been done at the back of the Laboratory. When the two girls arrived they found five other girls waiting for them. Their names were, of course, Susy Hopkins, who considered herself on this delightful occasion quite the leader; a gentle and refined-looking girl of the name of Mary Rand; Rosy Myers, who was pretty and frivolous, with dark eyes and fair hair; Clara Sawyer, who was renowned for her vulgar taste in dress; and Hannah Johnson, a heavy-looking girl with a scowling brow and a very pronounced jaw. Hannah Johnson was about the plainest girl in the school. When Susy saw Kate Rourke and Ruth Craven she uttered a little scream of delight.

"Now we are complete," she said. "Listen to me, all you girls, for I haven't too long in which to tell you; that horrid bell will ring us back to lessons and dullness in less than no time. The most wonderful, delightful chance is offered to us. I met her yesterday, and she decided to do it. She is a brick of bricks. She will make the most tremendous difference in our lives. You know, although you pretend not to feel it, but you all must know how we foundationers are sat upon and objected to in the school. We bear it as meekly as we can for the sake of our so-called advantages; but if we can be snubbed, we are, and if we can be neglected, we are—although it isn't the teachers we have to complain of, but the girls. Sometimes things are past bearing, and yet we are powerless. There are three hundred paying girls, and there are one hundred foundationers. What chance has one hundred against three?"

"What is the good of bringing all that up, Susy?" said Mary Rand. "We are foundationers, and we ought to be thankful."

"The education is splendid; we ought not to forget that," said Ruth Craven.

Susy turned on Ruth as though she would like to eat her.

"It is all very fine for you," she said. "Just because you happen to be pretty, they take you up. I wonder one of your fine friends doesn't pay for you, and so save your position out and out."

"I wouldn't allow her to," replied Ruth, her eyes flashing fire. "I had much rather be a foundationer. I mean to prove that I am every bit as good as a paying girl. I mean to make you all respect me, so there!"

"That'll do, Spitfire," said Kate Rourke. "The time is passing, and we must get to the bottom of Susy Hopkins's remarkable address.—What's up, Susy? What's up?"

"This," said Susy. "You know the Irish girl who has come to live with the Tennants?"

"Can't say I do," said Kate.

"Well, you will soon. She's a regular out-and-out beauty."

"I know her," cried Ruth Craven. "She is most lovely."

"She's better," said Susy; "she's bewitching. See; she gave me this." Here she pointed proudly to the Irish diamond brooch, which she had stuck in the bosom of her dress. The diamond had been polished, and flashed brightly; the silver setting was also as good as was to be found. The girls crowded round to admire, and "Oh, my!" "Oh, dear!" "Did you ever?" and "Well, I never!" sounded on all sides.

"You will be so set up now, Susan Hopkins, that we won't be able to bear you in the same class," said Clara Sawyer.

"Go on," exclaimed Hannah Johnson—"go on and tell us what you want. Your horrid brooch doesn't interest us. What have you got to say?"

"You are mad with jealousy, and you know it," answered Susy. "Well, I am coming to the great news. The Irish girl's name is Kathleen O'Hara, and she comes from a castle over in the wild west of Ireland. Her father is very rich, and he keeps dogs and horses and carriages and—oh, everything that rich people keep. Compared to the other girls in the school, she is ten times a lady; and she has a true lady's heart. And she has taken a dislike, as far as I can see, to Alice Tennant."

"And I'm sure I'm not surprised," said Rosy Myers.

"Stuck-up thing!" said Clara Sawyer.

"Dirt beneath our feet!" exclaimed Hannah Johnson.

"Well; she doesn't like her either, though she doesn't use that kind of language," continued Susy. "Anyhow, she wants to befriend *us*—Oh, do let me speak!"—as Kate interrupted with a hasty exclamation. "She thinks that we are just as good as herself. There is no false pride about a real lady, girls; and the end of it is that she has a plan to propose—something for our benefit and for her benefit. See for yourselves; this is her letter. It is in her own beautiful Irish, handwriting. You can read it, only don't tear it all to bits."

The girls did read the letter. They pressed close together, and one peeped over the shoulder of her companion, another stood on tiptoe, while a third tried to snatch the letter from the hand of her fellow; but all managed to read the words: "Get as many foundation girls as you can to meet me, at whatever place you like to appoint, this evening. I have a plan to propose."

This letter and the end of the postscript excited the girls; there was no doubt whatever of that. "The plan is *gloryious*." They laughed at the word, smiled into each others' faces, and stood very close together consulting.

"The old quarry," whispered Rosy.

"That's the place!" exclaimed Mary.

"Let us meet her, we seven by ourselves," was Kate's final suggestion. "We will then know what she wants, and if there is anything in it. We can form a committee, and get other girls to join by degrees. Hurrah! I do say this is fun."

Susy was now quite petted by her companions. The conference hastily ended, and on entering the school Susy pinned a piece of paper under Kathleen's desk, on which she wrote: "The old quarry; nine o'clock this evening. Will meet you at a quarter to nine outside Mrs. Tennant's house."

When Kathleen received the communication her eyes flashed with delighted fire. She thrust the letter into her pocket and proceeded with her work. The Irish girl looked quite happy that day; she had something to interest her at last. Her lessons, too, were by no means distasteful. She had a great deal of quick wit and ready perception. Hitherto she had been taught anyhow, but now she was all keen to receive real instruction. Her intuitions were rapid indeed; she could come to startlingly quick conclusions, and as a rule her guesses were correct rather than otherwise. Kathleen had a passion for music; she had never been properly taught, but the soul of music was in her as much as it was in David Tennant. She had a beautiful melodious voice, which had, of course, not yet come to maturity. Just before the end of the morning she took her first lesson in music. Her mistress was a very amiable and clever woman of the name of Agnes Spicer. Miss Spicer put a sheet of music before her.

"Play that," she said.

Kathleen frowned. Her delicate white fingers trembled for an instant on the keys. She played one or two bars perforce and very badly; then she dashed the sheet of music in an impetuous way to the floor.

"I can't," she said; "it isn't my style. May I play you something different?"

Miss Spicer was about to refuse, but looking at the girl, whose cheeks were flushed and eyes full of fire, she changed her mind.

"Just this once," she said; "but you must begin to practice properly. What I call amateur music can't be allowed here."

"Will this be allowed?" said Kathleen.

She dashed into heavy chords, played lightly a delicate movement, and then broke into an Irish air, "The Harp that once through Tara's Halls." From one Irish melody to another her light fingers wandered. She played with perfect correctness—with fire, with spirit. Soon she forgot herself. When she stopped, tears were running down her cheeks.

"What is music, after all," she said, looking full into the face of her teacher, "when you are far from the land you love? How can you stand music then? No, I don't mean to learn *music* at the Great Shirley School; I can›t. When I am back again at home I shall play ‹The Harp that once through Tara›s Halls,› but I can›t do it justice here. You will excuse me; I can't. I am sorry if I am rude, but it isn't in me. Some time, if you have a headache and feel very bad, as my dear father does sometimes, I shall play to you; but I can't learn as the other girls learn—it isn't in me."

Again she put her fingers on the keys of the piano and brought forth a few sobbing, broken-hearted notes. Then she started up.

"I expect you will punish me for this, Miss Spicer, but I am sorry—I can't help myself."

Strange to say, Miss Spicer did not punish her. On the contrary, she took her hand and pressed it.

"I won't ask you to do any more to-day," she said. "I see you are not like others. I will talk the matter over with you to-morrow."

"And you will find me unchanged," said Kathleen. "Thank you, all the same, for your forbearance."

CHAPTER VI.
THE POOR TIRED ONE.

Mrs. Tennant spent the afternoon out shopping. She told the girls at dinner that she would be home for tea, that she expected to be rather tired, and hoped that they would be as good as possible. The boys were always out during the afternoon, and as a rule never returned until after tea; but Alice and Kathleen were expected to be in for this meal. When Mrs. Tennant walked down the street, Kathleen went to the window and looked after her.

"What are you going to do this afternoon?" said Alice, who was lying back in an easy-chair with an open novel in her hand.

"I don't know," replied Kathleen. "What a dull hole this is! How can you have grown up and kept well in a place like this?"

"Opinions differ with regard to its dullness," said Alice. "I think our home a very pleasant, entertaining place. I wouldn't live in your wild castle for all you could give me."

"Nobody asked you, my dear," said Kathleen, with a saucy nod of her head.

She left the room and went up to what she called her half of the bedroom on the next floor. She knelt down by the window and looked across over the ugly landscape. There were houses everywhere—not a scrap of real country, as she expressed it, to be found. She took out of her pocket the letter which the foundation girls had sent her, and opened and read it.

"The old quarry! I wonder where the old quarry is," she thought. "It must be a good way from here. We have such a place at home, too. I did not suppose one was to be found in this horrid part of the world. I am rather glad there is an old quarry; it was quite nice of little Susy to suggest it, and she will meet me, the little colleen. That is good. What fun! I shall probably have to return through the bedroom window, so I may as well explore and make all in readiness. Dear, dear! I should like David to help me. It isn't the naughtiness that I care about, but it is the fun of being naughty; it is the fun of having a sort of dangerous thing to do. That is the real joy of it. It is the ecstacy of shocking the prim Alice! Oh! there is her step. She's coming up, the creature! Now then, I had best be as mum as I can unless I want to distract the poor thing entirely."

Alice entered the room.

"Do you greatly object to shutting the window?" she said to Kathleen. "I have a slight cold, and the draught will make it worse."

"Why, then, of course, darling," said Kathleen in a hearty voice, as she brought down the window with a bang. "Would you like me to shut the ventilator in the grate?" she then asked.

"No. How silly you are!"

"Is it silly? I thought you had a cold. You are afraid of the draughts. Why are you going out?"

"I want to see a school friend."

"You will be back in time for tea, won't you?"

"Can't say."

"But your mother, the poor tired one, asked you to be back."

"I do wish, Kathleen, that you wouldn't call mother by that ridiculous name. She is no more tired than—than other women are."

"If that is the case," said Kathleen, "I heartily hope that I shall not live to be a woman. I wouldn't like us all to be as fagged as she is—poor, dear, gentle soul! She's overworked, and that's the truth."

Kathleen saw that she was annoying Alice, and proceeded with great gusto to expand her theory with regard to Mrs. Tennant.

"She's in the condition when she might drop any time," she said. "We have had old Irishwomen overworked like that, and all of a sudden they went out like snuffs: that is what happens. What are you putting on your best hat for?"

"That is no affair of yours."

"Oh, hoity-toity, how grand we are! Do you know, Alice, you haven't got at all nice manners. You think you have, but you haven't. We are never rude like that in Ireland. We tell a few lies now and then, but they are only *polite* lies—the kind that make other people happy. Alice, I should like to know which is best—to be horribly cross, or to tell nice polite lies. Which is the most wicked? I should like to know."

"Then I will tell you," said Alice. "What you call a nice lie is just a very great and awful sin; and if you don't believe me, go to church and listen when the commandments are read."

"In future," said Kathleen very calmly, "now that I really know your views, I will always tell you *home truths*. You can't blame me, can you?"

Alice deigned no answer. She went downstairs and let herself out of the house.

"And that is the sort of girl I have exchanged for daddy and the mother and the boys," thought the Irish girl. "Oh, dear! oh, dear!"

Kathleen flew downstairs. It was nearly three o'clock; tea was to be on the table at half-past four. Quick as thought she dashed into the kitchen.

"Maria," she said, "and cook, is there anything nice and tasty for tea this evening?"

"Nice and tasty, miss!" said cook. "And what should there be nice and tasty? There's bread, and there's butter—Dorset, second-class Dorset—and there's jam (if there's any left); and that's about all."

"That sort of tea isn't very nourishing, cook, is it? I ask because I want to know," said Kathleen.

"It's the kind we always have at Myrtle Lodge," replied cook. "I don't hold with it, but then it's the way of the missis."

"I have got some money in my pocket," said Kathleen. "I want to have a beautiful, nice tea. Can't you think of something to buy? Here's five shillings. Would that get her a nice tea?"

"A nice tea!" cried Maria. "It would get a beautiful meal; and the poor missis, she would like it."

"Then go out, Maria; do, like a darling. I will open the door for you if anybody calls. Do run round the corner and bring in—Oh! I know what. We'll have sausages—they are delicious—and a little tin of sardines—won't they be good?—and some water-cress, and some shrimps—oh, yes, shrimps! Be quick! And we will put out the best tea-things, and a clean cloth; and it will rest the poor tired one so tremendously when she comes in and sees a good meal on the table."

Both cook and Maria were quite excited. Perhaps they had an eye to the reversion of the tea, the sausages, the sardines, the shrimps, and the water-cress.

Maria went out, and Kathleen stood in the hall. Two or three people arrived during Maria's absence, and Kathleen went promptly to the door and said, "Not at home, ma'am," in a determined voice, and with rather a scowling face, to these arrivals. Some of the visitors left rather important messages, but Kathleen did not remember them for more than a moment after they were delivered. Maria presently came back and the tea-table was laid. Kathleen gave Maria sixpence for the washing of an extra cloth, and the well-spread table looked quite fresh and wonderfully like a school-feast.

When Mrs. Tennant returned (she came in looking very hot and tired), it was to see the room tidy, Kathleen seated in her own special chair cobbling the boys' socks as hard as she could, and an appetizing tea on the table.

"What does this mean?" said Mrs. Tennant.

"It means," said Kathleen, jumping up, "that you are to plant yourself just here, and you are not to stir. Oh, I know you are *dead* tired. I will take off your shoes, poor dear; I have brought your slippers down on purpose, and you are to have your tea at this little table. Now what will you have? Hot sausages?—They are done to a turn, aren't they, Maria?"

"That they are, miss."

"A nice hot sausage on toast, and a lovely cup of tea with cream in it."

"But—but," said Mrs. Tennant, "what will Alice say?"

"Maria and I don't care twopence what Alice says. This is my tea, and Maria fetched it. Now then, dear tired one, eat and rest."

Mrs. Tennant looked at Kathleen with loving eyes.

"Did you buy these things?" she said.

"That she did, ma'am," cried Maria. "I never did see a more thoughtful young lady."

"My dear child," said Mrs. Tennant, "you are too good."

Kathleen laughed.

"If there is one thing I am, it is not that," she said. "I am not a bit good. I am as wild and naughty and——Oh, but don't let us talk about me. I am so hungry. You know I didn't much like your dinner to-day. I am not fond of those watery stews. Of course, I can eat anything, but I don't specially like them; so if you don't mind I will have a sausage, too, and a plateful of shrimps afterwards, and some sardines. And isn't this water-cress nice? The leaves are not quite so brown as I should like. Oh, we did have such lovely water-cress in the stream at home! Mrs. Tennant, you must come back with me to Carrigrohane some day, and then you will have a real rest."

Mrs. Tennant, feeling very much like a naughty child herself, enjoyed her tea. She and Kathleen laughed over the shrimps, exclaimed at the fun of eating the water-cress, enjoyed the sausages, and each drank four cups of tea. It was when the meal had come to an end that Kathleen said calmly:

The Rebel of the School | 59

"Three or four, or perhaps five, ladies called while Maria was out."

"Who were they, dear?"

"I don't know. They left messages, and I have forgotten them. One lady was dressed in what I should call a very loud style. She was quite old. Her face was all over wrinkles. She was stout, and she wore a short jacket and a big—very big—picture-hat."

"You don't mean," said Mrs. Tennant, "that Mrs. Dalzell has called? She is one of my most important friends. She promised to help me with regard to David's future. What did she say—can't you remember?"

"I am ever so sorry, but I can't. I kept staring at her hat all the time. I don't remember anything about her except that she was old and had wrinkles and a big picture-hat—the sort of hat that Ruth Craven would look pretty in."

Mrs. Tennant began to find the remembrance of her delightful tea a little depressing, for, question Kathleen as she might, she did not remember anything about the ladies except a few fugitive descriptions. As far as Mrs. Tennant could make out, people who were of the greatest importance to her had left messages, and yet none of the messages could be attended to.

"I can't even imagine who the other ladies can be," she said. "But as to Mrs. Dalzell, she must not be neglected; I must go out and see her at once."

"Then you will be more tired than ever, and I have not done a scrap of good."

"You meant very kindly, my dear child, and have given me a delicious and strengthening tea. Only don't do it again, darling, for it is my place to give you tea, not yours to give it to me."

CHAPTER VII.
THE QUEEN AND HER SECRET SOCIETY.

Mrs. Tennant had not been out more than a minute or two before David and Ben came in. Kathleen saw them from the window; she tapped on the window with her knuckles, nodded to them, kissed her hand, and looked radiant with delight. Some boys at the opposite side of the street saw her and burst out laughing. David's face grew red.

"I wish the little Irish girl wouldn't make us figures of fun," said Ben, speaking in an annoyed tone.

The next instant David had opened the door with his latchkey, and Kathleen was waiting for them in the hall.

"Sausages," she said, bringing out the word with great gusto, "and shrimps, and water-cress, and sardines, besides bread-and-butter galore, and nice hot tea. Maria is making fresh tea now in the kitchen. Come along in—do; you must be ravenous."

The boys stared at her. Ben forgot his anger; he was schoolboy enough to thoroughly enjoy the delicious meal which Kathleen had prepared.

When it came to an end David jumped up impatiently.

"Where are you going, Dave?" asked Kathleen in an interested voice. She wanted him to help her. She had hoped that he and she would go away to the old loft together, and talk as they had done the night before. But David was firm.

"I am going to the church," he said, "to practice on the organ. I only get the chance three times a week, and I must not neglect it."

"David hopes to be no end of a swell some day," remarked Ben. "He thinks he can make the instrument speak."

"And so can I," said Kathleen. "May I come with you, Dave?"

"Some day," he replied, looking at her kindly, "but not to-day. I'll be back as soon as I can."

David did not notice her disappointed face; he went out immediately, without even going upstairs first. Ben and Kathleen were now alone. Kathleen looked at him attentively.

"I wonder—" she said slowly.

"What are you staring at me for?" said Ben.

"I have been wondering what sort you are. I have got cousins at home, and they do anything in the world I like. I wonder if you would."

Ben had been very cross with Kathleen when she had knocked to him and David from the dining-room window, but he was not cross now. He was only thirteen, and up to the present no pretty girl had ever taken the slightest notice of him. He was a plain, sandy-haired boy, with a freckled face, a wide mouth, and good-humored blue eyes.

"You make me laugh whenever I look at you," was Kathleen's next candid remark.

"I didn't know that I was so comical," was his answer.

"Perhaps you don't like it."

"I can't say I do."

"Well, this is the Palace of Home Truths," said Kathleen, laughing. "I asked your darling, saintly sister just now which was the most wicked— to tell a polite lie, or a frightfully rude home truth. She said that a polite lie was an awful sin, so in this house I must cleave to the home truths. I could tell you, you know, that you have quite a fascinating smile, and a very taking voice, and a delightful and polished manner; but I prefer to tell you that you are comical, which means that I feel inclined to burst out laughing whenever I look at you."

"Thank you," said Ben, who could be very sulky when he liked. "Then I will take my objectionable presence out of your sight. I have got my lessons to do."

Kathleen raised her brows and gave a slow smile. Ben got as far as the door.

"Benny," she said then in a most seductive whisper.

He turned.

"I am so glad you are in."

"I should not have thought so."

"But I am. It is awfully lonely for a girl like me, who has got dozens of cousins at home, and uncles and aunts and all the rest of the goodly fry, to be stranded. I like David. I am quite smitten with David; and I like you, too. You can be a *great* friend of mine.»

"Oh, I don't mind," said Ben.

He thought it would be very good fun to tell the other fellows about the charming Irish girl who liked him so much.

"I wonder if you'd help me, Ben."

"What can I do?" asked Ben.

"Sit down, and let's be cozy. I will sit in the tired one's chair, and you can sit on that little stool at my feet. Now isn't that nice?"

"Who do you mean by the tired one?"

"Your mother, silly boy, of course."

"It is a very ridiculous name to call her."

"It belongs to the Palace of Home Truths. Your mother is tired, and you—you lazy omadhauns—"

"Well, go on," said Ben. "I see by your manner that you want me to do something. I suppose it's something a little bit—a little bit not quite good."

"It is perfectly good. I'll love you ever so much if you will do it."

"What is it?"

"I am going out this evening. I may not be in until late. If the others are in bed, will you come and unlock the door for me when I throw gravel up at your window? You must tell me which is your window."

"I sleep in the north attic. It doesn't look out on to the street; and I can't—I can't possibly do it."

"You can come down and wait for me in the hall."

"How can I?"

"When the tired one goes to bed, you can come down. She goes to bed at ten, I know, and I shall not be in until about half-past ten. I don't want Dave to know—well, because I don't. I don't want Alice to know, because I dislike Alice very much."

"Really, Kathleen, you ought not to speak like that."

"Well, I do, and I can't help myself. Will you do what I want? Here, do you think you'd like this in your possession?"

As Kathleen spoke she held out a golden sovereign in the palm of her little hand.

"I don't want to be bribed."

"It isn't bribery really; it is paying you for giving me a great convenience. I must go out on important business. I want to help those who are down-trodden and distressed. Will you do what I want, Ben—will you, dear Ben? You know I like you so much. Will you—will you?"

Of course, Ben fought against Kathleen's rather wicked suggestion; of course in the end he yielded. When he finally got up to his attic to thumb over his well-worn lesson-books he had Kathleen's golden sovereign in his pocket. He took it out and looked at it; he turned it round and round and examined it all over. He rubbed it lovingly against his freckled cheek, held it until it got warm in the palm of his hand, and then put it back in his pocket and jingled it against a couple of pennies which were its only companions.

"A whole sovereign," he said to himself—"a whole sovereign, and I never had so much as five shillings of my own in the whole course of my life. Well, she is a little witch. I suppose Dave would beat me black and blue for doing a thing of this sort. But how could I—how could I withstand her?"

Supper at the Tennants' generally consisted of cold pudding, cold meat, bread-and-butter, and a little jam when there happened to be any in the house. It was not a particularly tempting meal, and those who ate it required to have good, vigorous appetites. Kathleen, although she had been brought up in a considerable amount of wasteful splendor, was indifferent to what she ate. She soon jumped up and walked across the little passage into the drawing-room. Ben, looking very red and shamefaced, would not meet her eyes. Ben's face annoyed Kathleen. It did not occur to her for a minute that he would not be faithful to her, but she was afraid that others might notice his extraordinary and perturbed expression. Once, too, he jingled the sovereign in his pocket; she heard him, and wondered why David did not ask him where he had got the money. But no remark was made, and the meal came safely to an end. Kathleen took up the first book she could find and pretended to read.

"I shall feign sleepiness at a quarter to nine," she said to herself, "and go upstairs. I shall be awfully polite and sweet to dear Alice. She never comes to bed before ten, so I shall be quite safe getting out of the house. I can drop from the window, but I should prefer going by the back door; and I don't think Maria will betray me."

Just then Alice strolled into the room. She looked rather nice; she wore a very pretty pink muslin blouse, which suited her well. Her hair was neatly arranged; her face was calm. She stood before Kathleen.

"I wish—" she said suddenly.

Kathleen raised her head.

"And I wish you wouldn't stand between me and the lamp. Don't you see that I am reading?"

"I want you to stop reading. I have something to say."

"Indeed!"

Kathleen longed to be very rude, but she thought of her delightful plan so close at hand, and refrained.

"I must humor her if I can by any possibility keep my temper," was her thought. Then aloud: "What is it you want? I hope you will be very quick, for I am rather sleepy and intend to go to bed soon."

"I hope you won't do it again, that's all."

"Do what again?" asked Kathleen.

"Spend your money on buying food for us. We are not so poor as all that. My mother is paid by your father to give you your meals; your father doesn't expect you to buy them over again."

"Dad always likes me to do what I wish," replied Kathleen calmly.

"Well, don't do it again. It's extremely displeasing both to David and me."

Kathleen laughed.

"Dave gobbled up his sausage and his sardines," she said.

"Don't do it again, that's all."

Kathleen nodded her head, and again buried herself in her book.

"And there is another thing," continued Alice, dropping into a chair by Kathleen's side. "You are very low down in the school. Two of the mistresses spoke to me about you to-day. They don't like to see a great overgrown girl like you in a class with little children; it does neither you nor the school credit. They fear that during this term you may be forced to continue in your present low position; but they earnestly hope that you will work very hard, so as to be removed into a higher form. You ought, after Christmas, to get into a class at least two removes higher up in the school. That is what I came to say. I suppose you have a certain sense of honor, and you don't want your father's money to be thrown away."

"Bedad, then! he has plenty of money, and I don't much care," replied Kathleen.

She lay back in her chair and whistled "Garry Owen" in a most insolent manner.

"If you have really made up your mind not to improve yourself in the very least, mother had better write to Squire O'Hara and suggest that you don't come back after Christmas."

"And Squire O'Hara will decide that point for himself," replied Kathleen. "There are other houses where I can be entertained and fussed over, and regarded as I ought to be regarded, besides the home of Alice Tennant. The fact is this, Alice: you aggravate me; you don't understand me; I am at my worst in your presence. Perhaps I am a bit wild sometimes, but your way would never drive me to work or anything else. I have no real dislike to learning, and if another girl spoke to me as you have done I might be very glad."

"What do you mean?" said poor Alice. "I really and truly, Kathleen, do want to help you. You and I could work every evening together; I could, and would, see you through your lessons. Thus you would very quickly get to the head of your class, and get your removes without trouble at Christmas."

"I suppose you mean to be kind," said Kathleen. "I will think it over. Let me alone now."

She gave a portentous yawn. Ben heard her, came and sat down on an ottoman not far off, and began kicking his legs.

"Benny," said his sister, "if you have done your lessons, you had better go to bed."

"I don't want to go so early. You always treat me as if I were a baby."

"Well, please yourself. I am going upstairs to fetch my books. I have a good hour and a half of hard work to get through before bedtime."

The moment Kathleen and Ben were alone, Ben rushed up to her side and began to whisper.

"It is all as right as possible," he said. "I am going up to bed as usual, and when mother and Alice and Dave are safe in their rooms I'll slip down again. I'll be in the hall. Don't ring when you come back; just walk up the steps and scratch against the door with your knuckles, and I'll hear you and let you in in a trice. I am awfully pleased about that sovereign; it will make me one of the greatest toffs in the school. I'll have more money than any of the other fellows. I'm so excited I can scarcely think of anything else. I know I'm doing wrong, but you did offer me such a tremendous temptation. Now I hear Alice's step. It will be all right, Kathleen; don't you fear."

Kathleen smiled to herself. The rest of her programme was carried out to a nicety. At a quarter to nine she complained of fatigue, bade Mrs. Tennant an affectionate good-night, nodded to Alice, and left the room.

"Be sure you don't lock the door," called Alice after her. "I sha'n't be up for quite an hour, and you will be sound asleep by that time."

"I won't lock it," replied Kathleen gently.

When Kathleen had gone upstairs, Mrs. Tennant turned and spoke to her daughter.

"You know, Alice," she said, "the child is very lovable and kind-hearted—a little barbarian in some senses of the word, but a fine nature—of that I am certain."

"I am so busy to-night, mother," replied Alice. "Can't we defer talking of the charms of Kathleen's character until after I have done my lessons?"

"Of course, dear," said her mother.

She drew her basket of mending towards her, put stitch after stitch into the shabby garments, and thought all the time of Kathleen with her bright face and beautiful, merry eyes.

Meanwhile that young lady, having arranged a bolster in her bed to look as like a human being as possible, put on her hat and jacket and ran downstairs. There was no one in the hall, and she was absolutely daring enough to go out by that door. Mrs. Tennant raised her head when she heard the door gently shut.

"Can that be the post?" she said; but as no one replied, she forgot the circumstance and went on with her mending.

A few doors down the street Susy Hopkins was waiting for Kathleen.

"Oh, there you are!" she said. "We are so excited! There will be about eight of us waiting for you in the old quarry. You are good to come. You don't know what this means in our lives. You are good—you are wonderfully good."

"Where's the quarry?" asked Kathleen. "You have chosen such a funny place. I should not have imagined that a quarry—a dear, romantic quarry—could be found anywhere in this neighborhood."

"Yes, but there is, and a good big one, too. It is about half a mile away, just at the back of Colliers' Buildings. It is the safest place you can possibly imagine, for no one will ever look for us there. Now do be quick; we will find the others before us. You can't think how excited we are."

"Oh, I'm willing to be quick," replied Kathleen. "I am doing all this for you, you know, because I am sorry for the foundationers, and think it so very ridiculous that there should be distinctions made. Why, you are quite as good as the others. They are none of them much to boast of."

"What fun this is!" cried Susy again. "I assure you the paying girls think no end of themselves. They are under the supposition that there never were such fine ladies to be found in the land before. Oh, we will take it out of them, sha'n't we?"

Kathleen made no reply. Presently they reached the opening that led into the quarry. They had to go down a narrow sloping path, and then by a doorway cut in the solid rock. After they had passed through they found themselves in a large circular cavern open to the sky. There was no moon and the night was dark; but one girl had brought a lantern. She opened it and placed it on the ground; a bright shaft of light now fell on several young figures all huddled together. Susy gave a sharp whistle; the girls started to their feet.

"Here we are, girls. See, this is our queen," and she presented Kathleen to the assembled girls.

"Does the queen mind our looking at her face in turns?" said Kate Rourke. "I have not specially noticed you before," she continued, "but after we have each had a good stare we will know what sort of girl you are."

For reply Kathleen herself lifted the lantern and flung the full light upon her radiant and lovely face and figure. The intense light made her golden hair shine, and brought out the delicate perfection of each feature; the merry eyes framed in their dark lashes, the gleaming white teeth, the rosy lips were all apparent. But beyond the mere beauty of feature Kathleen had to a remarkable degree the far more fascinating beauty of expression: her face was capable of almost every shade of emotion, being sorrowful and pathetic one moment, and brimful of irrepressible mirth and roguery the next.

There was a silence amongst the girls until Mary Rand shouted:

"Hip! hip! hurrah!"

The whole eight immediately broke into a ringing cheer.

"Welcome, Queen Kathleen," they said—"welcome;" and they held out their hands and clasped the hands of the Irish girl.

"I am glad," said Kathleen.

"What about?" said Clara Sawyer.

"Why, you have crowned me queen yourselves. Now I can do what I like with you all."

"You certainly can," said Susy Hopkins.—"We are devoted to our queen, aren't we, girls?"

"We have fallen in love with her on the spot," said Rosy Myers.

"I never saw any one quite so lovely before as the queen," said Mary Rand.

"It isn't only that she's lovely, she is so genteel," said Susy Hopkins.

"Aristocratic!" cried Kate.—"Hannah Johnson, you haven't given your opinion yet.—And, Ruth Craven, you haven't given yours."

"I reserve my opinion," said Ruth.

"And I say there's a great deal of humbug and balder-dash in the world," said Hannah Johnson.

Ruth's remark was unexpected, but the girls pooh-poohed Hannah's. Who was Hannah Johnson that she dared to speak so rudely to one so charming and beautiful as Kathleen O'Hara? There was a disconcerting pause, and then Kathleen said:

"Hannah, doubtless you are right. There is plenty of humbug in the world; but I don't think I am one. Now the question is: Shall I be on the side of the foundationers, or shall I be on the side of the paying girls in the Great Shirley School?"

"Indeed, darling," said Rosy Myers, "you shall be on our side. Those horrid, stuck-up paying girls don't want you; and we do. Nothing will induce us to give you up. It is a chance to get a girl like you, so lovely and so sweet and so rich, to be one of us."

"Well, I think I can give you a good time, and I can show those others with their snobbish ways—"

"Hear, hear!" cried the excited girls.

"I can show the others what I think of them. They won't snub me, but perhaps I shall snub them. Well, girls, as we have decided to band together, we must draw up rules; and when they are drawn up we must obey them. I, of course, will be your head; as you have made me queen, that is the natural thing to expect."

"Of course," said Susy.

Kathleen clapped her hands.

"This is going to be a real good secret society," she said. "What fun it all will be!"

The girls laughed, and clustered with more and more friendliness round Kathleen.

"You are our queen," said Kate. "There are eight of us here, and we all swear allegiance to you.—Don't we, girls?"

"Certainly," said Susy.

"Unquestionably," remarked Mary.

"With all my heart," said Rose.

"And mine," echoed Clara.

"And mine," said Kate.

"I will join the others, although I don't approve," said Hannah Johnson, with a somewhat unwilling nod.

"And I am neutral. I don't think I ought to join at all," said Ruth.

"Oh, yes, you will, Ruth. I want you to be my Prime Minister, I want you to be with me in all things."

"I don't know that I can."

"And why should she be your Prime Minister?" said Kate in an ugly voice. "She's no better than the others, and she's very new. Some of us have been at the school for some time. Ruth Craven has only just joined.

"The queen must have her way," said Kathleen, stamping her foot. "The queen must have her way in all particulars, and she wishes to elect Ruth Craven as her Prime Minister—that is, if Ruth will consent."

They were headstrong and big girls, most of them older than Kathleen, but they submitted, for her ways were masterful and her tone full of delicate sympathy.

"I will think it over and let you know," said Ruth. "Of course, I shall not betray you; but you must please understand that I have friends amongst the paying girls of the school. Cassandra Weldon is my friend, and there are others. I will not join nor advocate any plan that annoys or worries them."

The girls looked dubious, and one or two began to speak in discontented voices.

"We must meet again in a couple of days," said Kathleen finally. "By then I shall have drawn up the rules. We can't always meet at night, but we will when it is possible, for this place is so romantic, and so correct for a secret society. Those who are present to-night will be in my Cabinet. I should like if possible to have all the foundation girls on my side, but that must be decided at our next meeting. I am willing to purchase a badge for each girl who joins me; it will be made of silver, and can be worn beneath the dress in the form of a locket."

"Oh, lovely, delicious! There never was such a queen," cried Susy Hopkins.

The little meeting broke up amidst universal applause.

CHAPTER VIII.
THE BOX FROM DUBLIN AND ITS TREASURES.

Kathleen returned quite safely to Myrtle Lodge. Ben was sitting up for her; he opened the door. The hall was quite dark. He held out his hand and drew her in.

"Am not I splendid?" he said. "I have been standing here for half-an-hour, all drenched with perspiration. If mother came down" what wouldn't she say? And as to Alice, she'd be even worse. But a sov.'s worth doing something for. I say! I do feel happy! I never had all that lot of bullion in the whole course of my life before. Are you right now, Kathleen—can you slip upstairs without making any noise? Don't forget that the step just before you reach the upper landing gives a great creak like the report of a pistol; hop over it on to the landing itself, and you are safe. Alice is in bed, snoring like anything; I listened outside the keyhole."

"Thanks," said Kathleen. "I'm awfully obliged to you, Ben. See if I don't do something for you. You are a broth of a boy. What do you say to Carrigrohane in the summer, and a gun all to yourself? I'll teach you how to shoot rabbits and to bring down a bird on the wing."

She brushed her lips against his cheek, and ran lightly upstairs. She escaped the treacherous second step, and entered her bedroom without waking Alice. The bolster carefully manipulated had done its work; it had never occurred to Alice that the form in the bed was anything but the living form of Kathleen O'Hara. She had shaded the light from what she supposed to be the sleeping girl, and got into bed herself feeling tired and sulky. She had dropped asleep immediately.

Kathleen's first step, therefore, towards the formation of a secret society in the Great Shirley School was marked with success. The idea which she had formulated in the old quarry spread like wildfire amongst the foundationers; but Kathleen was determined not to have another meeting for nearly a week. She wished to hear from her father; she wanted to have money in hand.

"They are all poor," she thought. "If I appear just as poor as they are, I shall never be able to keep my exalted position as queen. We cannot have our next meeting until I have drawn up the rules, and I should like Ruth Craven to help me. She has got sense. I don't want the thing to be riotous, nor to do harm in any way. I just want us to have a bit of fun, and to teach the horrid paying girls of the school a lesson."

The thought of her secret society kept Kathleen in a fairly good humor, and she worked at her lessons so well that Alice began to have hopes of her. About a week after her arrival at Myrtle Lodge the box which Aunt Katie O'Flynn was sending from Dublin arrived. It came when the girls were at school. When they returned to early dinner they saw it standing in the front hall.

"Whatever is this, and why is it put here?" said Alice, springing forward to look at the address:

"Miss Kathleen O'Hara, care of Mrs. Tennant, Myrtle Lodge."

"Golloptious!" cried Kathleen. "It's my own. It's my clothes—my sort of a kind of a treasure. Oh, what delicious fun! Now you will see how smart I can be. Maybe there will be something here to fit you, Alice. Wouldn't you like it? We are going to tea to-night to Mrs. Weldon's, and Ruth Craven is to be there. The darling girl—I will give her something. I should love to make her look just as beautiful as she can look. I am not a bit a stingy sort of girl; you know that, Alice. I want to be quite generous with my lovely things."

"Well, do stop talking," said Alice. "I never came across such an inveterate chatterbox. I suppose you'd like to have the box taken up to our room; but I don't think you'll have any time to open it at present. You have promised to come back with me to the school this afternoon, in order that Miss Spicer may give you a special lesson in music."

"Arrah, then, my dear!" cried Kathleen, "it isn't me you'll see at school again to-day. It's gloating and fussing over my clothes I will be—portioning out those I mean to give to others, and trying on the ones that will suit me. You can go to your horrid, stupid lessons if you like, but it won't be Kathleen O'Hara who will accompany you. Perhaps the poor tired one would like to have a pleasant afternoon in my bedroom. Oh, glory be to goodness! we will have a time. Isn't it worth anything to see that blessed trunk? My eyes can almost pierce through the deal and see the lovely garments folded away inside."

Alice took no notice; she marched on to her room. Kathleen followed her.

"The boys shall bring it up for me immediately after dinner," she said. "I sha'n't be going out again until I go to Mrs. Weldon's. I expect people will open their eyes when they see me to-night."

"You must please yourself, of course," said Alice. "For my part, I am extremely sorry that the trunk has come. You were settling down a little, and were not quite so objectionable as at first."

"Thanks *awfully*, darling," said Kathleen, dropping a mock curtsy.

"Not quite so objectionable," continued Alice in a calm voice. "But now, with all these silly gewgaws, you will be worse titan ever. But please clearly understand that I do not want any of your ornaments."

"Don't trouble yourself, darling; they were not made for you. I force my treasures on nobody."

"I wouldn't wear them if you were to give them. I hope I have some proper pride."

"Pride of the *most* proper sort,» said Kathleen, dancing before her.

"And I do hope, also, that you won't make yourself a merry-andrew or a figure of fun at the Weldons' to-night. It will be in extremely bad taste. We are not going to have a large party—just one or two of the mistresses and little Ruth Craven, who, although she is a foundationer, seems to be a very nice sort of child. It would be in the worst taste possible to wear anything but the simplest clothes."

"All right," said Kathleen. "If I am a chatterbox, you are about the greatest preacher, with the most long-winded sermons, that ever entered a house. You are a perfect plague to me, and that is the truth, Alice Tennant."

Alice poured some water into her basin, washed her hands, and went downstairs.

"Mother," she said, "I am obliged to be out the whole afternoon. The scholarship examination takes place in six weeks now, and if I am to have any chance of getting through I must not idle a single moment. I grieve to say that a box of finery has arrived for Kathleen—most unsuitable, for she has plenty of clothes. I do trust, mother, you will keep her in tow a little this afternoon, and not allow her to make a show of herself."

"You are not very kind to Kathleen," said Mrs. Tennant. "Why shouldn't the child enjoy her pretty things? I like to see girls nicely dressed. It is a great trial to me to be obliged to deny you the ribbons and frills and laces which most girls of your age possess."

"Thanks, mother," answered Alice; "but if you were as Rich as Crœsus, I should not wish, while I am a schoolgirl, to dress any better than I do."

"You certainly have a great deal of sense, dear; but don't be too hard on the little girl. Ah! here she comes. Now we must sit down to dinner at once."

During dinner Kathleen's eyes sparkled so brightly, and she looked so merry and mysterious, that both the boys gazed at her in wonder.

"Don't mind me," she said, whispering to David as she bent towards him. "It's in real downright delight I am. I am expecting to have the most wonderful joy all the afternoon that was ever given a girl. Ah, then, it's illegant myself will be when you see me next, boys. And do look at her! I declare she's getting crosser each minute."

"Hush, Kathleen!" said David. "You must not say unkind things."

"Don't trouble to reprove her, David," called out Alice in a calm and lofty tone. "I assure you she doesn't annoy me in the least. Sometimes I think there is a little gnat flying about and trying to sting me, but that's all."

"And a charming metaphor, too," said Kathleen.

She ate her meal soberly, but occasionally a bubble of laughter came to the surface, and her merry eyes glanced from Mrs. Tennant's face to Alice's, and from Alice's to those of the boys. The moment the meal came to an end Kathleen jumped up.

"Now, then, my angels, you come with me," she said, and she caught David by the one hand and Ben by the other, and led her willing slaves into the hall.

"Did you ever see anything like it?" said Alice to her mother. "She will ruin the boys in addition to all her other mischief. Mother, must we keep her long? It is really most disturbing."

"If you would only take poor little Kathleen as she is, you would find her quite agreeable, Alice," was her mother's answer.

"Oh dear, mother! you seem to be just as much infatuated as the others. But never mind. I am off now, and I need not be back in the house until it is time to dress to go to Mrs. Weldon's. I declare that girl is causing me to hate my home. I don't think its fair, whatever you may say to the contrary."

Mrs. Tennant sighed. Alice had always been a little difficult; she was more than difficult at the present moment. But very soon afterwards the welcome bang of the hall door was heard, and the house was free.

"Now for a jolly time," said Kathleen. "Tired one, where are you?"

"Kathleen, you ought not to call me by that name. You ought to be more respectful."

"Arrah, then, darling, I can't; 'tain't in me. I am so fond of you—oh, worra, worra! there's nothing I wouldn't do for you; but I must be as I'm made. You do look tired, and tired you will go on looking until I take you to Carrigrohane to rest you and to feed you with good milk and good fruit and good eggs and good cream.—Now then, boys, lift up that trunk. Be aisy with it, so that you won't hurt it. Take it up to my bedroom and put it on the floor. Maybe there's something in it for you, or maybe there isn't—Mrs. Tennant, acushla! you will come along upstairs with me at once. You can bring your mending basket, and I will pop you into the arm-chair by the window, and we can consult together over the garments. It's fine I'll look when I have them on. Aunt Katie O'Flynn is a woman who has real taste, and I know she is going to dress me up as no other girl ever was dressed before in the Great Shirley School."

Mrs. Tennant could not help laughing. The boys were also in the highest good-humor; Kathleen's mirth was contagious. They went upstairs to the bedroom, and then Ben saucily perched himself on the foot of one of the beds; while David, having brought up a hammer and screwdriver, proceeded to lift the lid of the box, which was firmly nailed down. Under the lid was a lot of tissue-paper. Kathleen went on her knees, lifted it up, uttered a shout, and turned to the boys.

"You make off now," she said.

"No, indeed I won't," said Ben. "I want to see the fun."

"Go, both of you. There will be something nice for you when you come back to tea," said Kathleen.

They looked regretful, but saw nothing for it but to go. Kathleen in a breathless sort of way, scarcely uttering a word, spread out her treasures on the bed. Was there ever such a box? Skirts, bodices, blouses, shirts; an evening dress, an afternoon dress, a morning dress—they seemed simply endless. Then there were frills and ribbons and veils; there were two great, big, very stylish-looking hats, with long plumes; and there was a little toque made of crimson velvet, which Kathleen declared was quite too sweet for anything. There were also dozens of handkerchiefs, dozens of pairs of stockings, and some sweet little slippers all embroidered and fit for the most bewitching feet in the world. Kathleen's cheeks got redder and redder.

"Here's a cargo for you," she said. "Here's something to delight the heart. Now, my dear Mrs. Tennant, let us come and examine everything. Do you think I am utterly selfish, Mrs. Tennant? Do you think I want all these things for myself?"

"I am sure you don't, dear."

"It quite makes me ache with longing to give some of them away. I don't want so many frocks: there are a good dozen here all told. Aunt Katie O'Flynn's the one for extravagance, bless her! and for having a thing done in style, bless her! I should like you to see her. It's splendacious she is entirely when she's dressed up in her best—velvet and feathers and laces and jewels. Why, nothing holds her in bounds; there's nothing she stops at. I have seen her give hundreds of pounds for one little glittering gem. Ah! and here's a ring. Look, Mrs. Tennant."

Kathleen had now opened a small box which was lying at the bottom of the great trunk. There were several treasures in it: a necklet of glittering white stones, another of blue, another of red, and this little ring—a little ring which contained a solitary diamond of the purest water.

"Now I shall look stylish," said Kathleen, and she slipped the ring on the third finger of her left hand.

"My wedding finger too, bedad!" she said.

When the contents of the trunk had been finally explored, Kathleen began to sort her finery. Mrs. Tennant gave advice.

"Some of these things are a little too fine for everyday use," she said. "But some of these blouses are very suitable, and so are these white and gray and pink shirts. And this blue bodice is quite nice for the evening, and so is the skirt belonging to it; but this and this and this—I wouldn't wear these until I went home if I were you, my love."

Kathleen glanced at her. A slight frown came between her brows.

"Don't you see," she said impatiently, "that I want to give away some of these things? Do you see this dozen of blouses, all exactly alike, in this box? These are for the secret society."

"The what, Kathleen?"

"Oh, you musn't tell—it is the most profound secret—but I have joined one. Being an Irish girl, it is quite natural. I sent a line to Aunt Katie to get a dozen of the very prettiest blouses she could. Of course there are a lot more members, but our Cabinet has risen to something like a dozen, so I thought I'd have them handy. Aren't they just sweet?"

As she spoke she took out of the box the palest blue cashmere blouse, most exquisitely trimmed with blue embroidery flecked with pink silk. The blouse had real lace round the neck and cuffs, and must have cost a great deal of money.

"Don't you think Alice would look very nice in one of these?" said Kathleen, gazing with a very earnest face at Mrs. Tennant.

"Pink is more Alice's color. She is too pale for blue," was Mrs. Tennant's reply.

"Well, then, look here. Isn't this a perfect duck? See for yourself. It's a sort of cross between a coral and a rose—oh, so exquisite! And see how it is made, with all these teeny tucks and the embroidery let in between. And the sleeves—aren't they just illegant entirely? Don't you think we might make her wear it?"

"I am sorry, Kathleen, but you are not getting on very well with Alice. I wish it were different. Could you not do something to propitiate her?"

"Wisha, then, darling!" said Kathleen, pausing a moment to consider; "that's just what I can't do. Alice's ways are not my ways, and if I copied her it's kilt I'd be entirely. She never likes to see a smile on my face, and she can't abide to watch me if I dance a step, and she wouldn't take a joke out of me if it was to save her life. To please Alice I'd have to be the primmest of the prim, and always stooping over my horrid lessons, and the end of it there'd be no more of poor Kathleen O'Hara—- it's dead and in her grave she'd be, the creature. Indeed, I'm glad I'm not made on Alice's pattern, even if she is your daughter. I can't aspire to anything so fine and high up even for your sake, darling, and you are one of the sweetest women on God's earth. I couldn't do it—not by no means."

Mrs. Tennant could not help laughing as Kathleen described the sort of girl she would be if she adopted Alice's role.

"But the question is now," said the girl, "what are we to do to make her have some of these pretty things? Mightn't I give the blouse to you first, and you could give it to her? She'd look so sweet in this pink blouse when she went to tea at her chosen friends. She'd be almost pretty if she was nicely dressed. I've got this white one for little Ruth Craven, and I want Alice to have this so badly. Can't you manage it, dear Mrs. Tennant?"

Mrs. Tennant felt tempted. The blouse was very dainty and pretty, and unlike anything she could afford to buy for her only daughter. Kathleen threw her arms round her neck and kissed her.

"You will—you will, dear Mrs. Tennant," she said. "It is yours entirely. You tell her you got it at a cheap sale. Say you went to a jumble sale and bought it; you paid one-and-twopence-halfpenny for it. That's the right figure, isn't it, for the best things at a jumble sale? Tell her it's *quite* new, and was thrown in promiscuous like.»

"But, my darling child, I can't tell her what isn't true. She would wear it if she didn't know it came from you. She would not only wear it, but she would delight in it; but nothing would induce her to take it if she thought you had given it."

"Then don't let's tell her. Besides, it wouldn't be true, for I have given it to you, dear. And now, see, here is something for your sweet self. I wrote to Aunt Katie, and Aunt Katie is so clever. See! come to the glass."

Kathleen had opened a cardboard box, and out of it she took a black velvet bonnet with nodding plumes and a little pink strip of velvet fastened under the brim. This she put with trembling fingers on Mrs. Tennant's head. Mrs. Tennant was in reality not at all old, and she looked quite young and pretty in the new toque.

"You are charming, that's what you are," said Kathleen. "And I can't take it back, for you know perfectly well that it is a wee bit too old for me. You will have to wear it."

"But what will Alice say?"

"Never mind. Don't tell her; just be mum. Say, 'it is mine, and I mean to wear it.' Oh, I'd manage Alice if I happened to be her mother."

"I don't think you would, dear."

"Indeed, but I would. And now I must consider whom I am to give the other things to."

When Kathleen had finally parcelled out her treasures there was not such a great deal left for herself, for this girl and the other who had taken her fancy were all allotted a treasure out of that famous box. And there was a thick albert chain made of solid silver for Ben, and a keyless silver watch for David; and what could boys possibly want more? Kathleen had remembered all her friends, and Aunt Katie O'Flynn was more than willing to carry out her request.

Finally, at the very bottom of the trunk was a little parcel which she refrained from opening while Mrs. Tennant was present. It contained the badges of the new society. Kathleen had decided that they were to call themselves "The Wild Irish Girls," and this title was neatly engraved on the little badges, which were of the shape of hearts. Below the name was the device—a harp with a bit of shamrock trailing round it. The badges were small and exceedingly neat, and there were about sixty of them in all.

"Now then, I can go ahead," thought Kathleen. "What with the finery for my dear, darling chosen ones, and the badges for all the members, I shall do."

She was utterly reckless with regard to expense. Her father was rich, and he did not mind what he spent on his only child. The box seemed to fill up every crevice of her heart, as she expressed it, and it was a very happy girl who dressed to go to the Weldons' that evening. Kathleen was intensely affectionate, and would have done anything in the world to please Mrs. Tennant; but when it came to wearing a very quiet gray dress with a little lace round the collar and cuffs, she begun to demur.

"It can't be done," she thought. "Half of them will be in gray and half of them in brown, and a few old dowdies will perhaps be in black. But I must be gay; it isn't fair to Aunt Katie to be anything else."

She made a wild and scarcely judicious selection. She put on crimson silk stockings, and tucked into her bag a pair of crimson satin shoes. Her dress consisted of a black velvet skirt over a crimson petticoat, and her bodice was of crimson silk very much embroidered and with elbow-sleeves. Round her neck she wore innumerable beads of every possible color, and twisted through her lovely hair were some more beads, which shone as the light fell on them. Altogether it was a very bizarre and fascinating little figure that appeared that evening at the Weldons' hall door. Over her showy dress she wore a long opera-cloak, so that at first her splendors were not fully visible. This gaily dressed little person entered a room full of sober people. The effect was somewhat the same as though a gorgeous butterfly had flown into the room. She lit up the dullness and made a centre of attraction—all eyes were fastened upon her; for Kathleen in her well-made dress, notwithstanding the gayety of its color, looked simply radiant. The mischief in her dark eyes, too, but added to her charm. She glanced with almost maliciousness at Alice, who, in the dowdiest of pale-gray dresses, with her hair rather untidy and her face destitute of color, was standing near one of the windows. And as Alice glanced at Kathleen she felt that she almost hated the Irish girl.

CHAPTER IX.
CONSCIENCE AND DIFFICULTIES.

All the people who knew her were beginning to make a fuss over Ruth Craven. She who had hardly ever been noticed during the early part of her life, who was just her grandfather's darling and her grandmother's idol, was now petted and made much of and fussed over by every one. It was quite an extraordinary thing for the paying girls of the Great Shirley School to be so interested and excited about a foundationer. Cassandra Weldon was not the only girl who had taken Ruth up; some of the best and nicest girls of the school began to patronize her. The fact was that she was very modest and a perfect lady, and it was impossible to feel anything but good-will towards her. The rest of the foundation girls at first determined that they would leave her with her fine friends, but when Kathleen insisted on Ruth's joining the secret society of the Wild Irish Girls, they were obliged to submit.

"We'd do anything in the world for our queen," said Susy Hopkins, talking to another foundation girl one day as they strolled along the road. "It is to-night we are to meet again, and she says she will bring the rules all drawn up, and she will read them to us. There are about thirty of us now, and more and more offer to join every day. The difficulty is that we have got to keep the thing from the knowledge of the teachers and the paying girls of the school. Kathleen is certain that it would be suppressed if it were known; and it must not be known, for it is the biggest lark and the greatest fun we ever had in all our lives."

"Yes," said Rosy Myers; "I feel now quite honored at being a foundation girl."

"She does promise us wonderful things," said Kate Rourke. "She says when the summer comes we shall have all sorts of nice excursions. Of course, we can't do anything special in the daytime, unless sometimes on Saturday, when we have a whole holiday; but at least; she says, the nights are our own and we can do as we like. It really is grand. I suppose it is wicked, but then that makes it rather more fascinating."

"We are in the queen's Cabinet, bless her, the duck!" said Susy Hopkins. "There are a dozen of us now, and there is talk of a sort of livery or badge for the members of the Cabinet; but we'll know all about it when we meet sharp at nine to-night. We are the twelve members of the Cabinet, and there are about twenty girls who are our sort of standing army. It is really most exciting."

The girls talked a little longer and then parted. As Susy Hopkins was running home helter-skelter—for she wanted to get her lessons done in order to be fully in time for the meeting that evening—she met Ruth Craven. Ruth was walking slowly by with her usual demure and sweet expression.

"Hullo!" called out Susy. "We'll meet to-night, sha'n't we?"

"I don't know," said Ruth.

"Aren't you coming? Why, you are sort of Prime Minister to the queen."

"You don't think it right really, do you," said Ruth—"not from the bottom of your heart, I mean?"

"Right or wrong, I mean to enjoy myself," said Susy Hopkins. "I suppose, if you come to analyse it, it is wrong, and not right. But, dear me, Ruth! what fun should we poor girls have if we were too particular on these points?"

"It always seems to me that it is worth while to do right," said Ruth.

"So you say, but I don't quite agree with you. You will come to-night, in any case, won't you?"

"Yes, I will come to-night; but I am not happy about it, and I wish Kathleen—Oh, I know it is very fascinating, and Kathleen is just delightful, but I should not like our teachers to know."

"Of course not," said Susy, staring at her. "They'd soon put a stop to it."

"Are you certain? I know so little about the school."

"Certain? I'm convinced. Why, they'd be furious. I expect we'd be expelled."

"Then that proves it. I didn't know there was any strict rule about it."

"Why, what are you made of, Ruth Craven?"

"I thought," said Ruth, "that when we were not in school we were our own mistresses."

"To a certain extent, of course; but we have what is called the school character to keep up. We have, as it were, to uphold the spirit of the school. Now the spirit of the school is quite against secrecy in any form. Oh dear, why will you drag all this out of me? I'd made up my mind not to think of it, and now you have forced me to say it. Of course you will come to-night.

You have to think of Kathleen as well as the school, and she's gone to a fearful lot of expense. You could not by any possibility forsake her, could you?"

"No, of course not," said Ruth very slowly.

She bade Susy good-bye and walked on; her attitude was that of one who was thinking hard.

"Ruth is very pretty," said Susy to herself, "but I don't know that I quite admire her. She is the sort of girl that everybody loves, and I am not one to admire a universal favorite. She is frightfully, tiresomely good, and she's just *too* pretty; and she›s not a bit vain, and she›s not a bit puffed up. Oh, she is just right in every way, and yet I feel that I hate her. She has got the sort of conscience that will worry our queen to distraction. Still, once she joins she'll have to obey our rules, and I expect our queen will make them somewhat stringent."

A clock from a neighboring church struck the half-hour. Susy looked up, uttered an exclamation, put wings to her feet, and ran the rest of the way home. Susy's home was in the High Street of the little town of Merrifield. Her mother kept a fairly flourishing stationer's shop, in one part of which was a post-office. Some ladies were buying stamps as Susy dashed through the shop on her way to the family rooms at the back. Mrs. Hopkins was selling stationery to a couple of boys; she looked up as her daughter entered. Susy went into the parlor, where tea was laid on the table. It consisted of a stale loaf, some indifferent butter, and a little jam. The tea, in a pewter teapot, was weak; the milk was sky-blue, and the jug that held it was cracked.

Susy poured out a cup of tea, drank it off at a gulp, snatched a piece of bread-and-butter from the plate, and sat down to prepare her lessons at another table. She had two hours' hard work before her, and it was already nearly six o'clock. The quarry was a little distance away, and she must tidy herself and do all sorts of things. Just then her mother came in.

"Oh, Susy," she said, "I am so glad you have come! I want you to attend to the shop for the next hour. I am sent for in a hurry to my sister's; she has a bad cold, and wants me to call in. I think little Peter is not well; your aunt is afraid he is catching measles. Run into the shop the moment you have finished your tea, like a good child. You can take one of your lesson-books with you if you like. There won't be many customers at this hour."

"Oh, mother, I did really want to work hard at my lessons. They are very difficult, you know, and you promised that when I went to the Great Shirley School you'd never interfere with my lesson hours."

"I did say so, and of course I don't mean to interfere; but this is a special case."

"Can't Tommy go and stand in the shop? If any special customers come in I will attend to them."

"No, Tommy can't. He has a headache and is lying down upstairs. You must oblige me this time, Susy. You can sit up a little longer to-night to finish your lessons if you are much interrupted while I am away."

"You are sure you will not be more than an hour, mother?"

"Oh, certain."

"And I suppose in any case I may shut up the shop at seven o'clock, mayn't I?"

"Shut the shop at seven o'clock!" said Mrs. Hopkins. "You forget that this is Wednesday. We always keep the shop, except the post-office part, open until past nine on Wednesdays; such a lot of people come in for odds and ends on this special night. But I will be back long before nine. Don't on any account shut the shop until I appear."

Susy, feeling cross and miserable, all her bright hopes dashed to the ground, took a couple of books and went into the shop and sat behind the counter. The days were getting short and cold, and as the shop door was opened there was a thorough draught where she was sitting. Her feet grew icy cold; she could scarcely follow the meaning of her somewhat difficult lessons. No customers appeared.

"How stupid I am!" thought the little girl. "This will never do."

She roused herself, and bending forward, propped her book open before her. Presently she heard the clock outside strike seven.

"Mother will be back now, thank goodness!" she thought. "If I work desperately hard, and stop my ears so that I needn't hear a sound, I may have done by nine o'clock."

Just at that moment two ladies came in to ask for a special sort of stationery. Susy, who was never in the least interested in the shop, did not know where to find it. She rummaged about, making a great mess amongst her mother's neat stores; and finally she was obliged to say that she did not know where it was.

"Never mind," said one of the ladies, kindly; "I will come in again next time I am passing. It doesn't matter this evening."

Susy felt vexed; she knew her mother would blame her for sending the ladies away without completing a purchase. And they had scarcely left before she found the box which contained the stationery. She pushed it out of sight on the shelf, and sat down again to her book. Her mother ought to be coming in now. Susy would have to do a lot of exercises; these she could not by any possibility do in the shop. She had also some mathematical work to get through or she would never be able to keep her place in class. Why didn't Mrs. Hopkins return? Half-an-hour went by; three-quarters. It was now a quarter to eight. Susy felt quite distracted. With the exception of the two ladies, there had been no customer in the shop up to the present. The fact was, they did not begin to appear until soon after eight on Wednesday evenings. Then the schoolgirls and schoolboys and many other people of the poorer class used to drop in for penn'orths and ha'p'orths of stationery, for pens, for ink, for sealing-wax, &c.

"Mother must be in soon. I know what I will do," said Susy. "I will open the door of the parlor and sit there. If any one appears I can dash out at once."

No sooner had the thought come to her than she resolved to act on it. She turned on the gas in the parlor—it was already brightly lighted in the shop—and sat down to her work.

"An hour and a quarter before the meeting of the Wild Irish Girls," she said to herself. "Strange, is it not, that I should call myself a Wild Irish Girl when I am a Cockney through and through? Well, whatever happens, I shall be at the meeting."

CHAPTER X.
THE WILD IRISH GIRLS' SOCIETY IS STARTED.

While Susy sat in the parlor a tramp happened to pass the brightly lighted shop. He was weather-beaten and slipshod, and altogether made a most disreputable appearance. A hand was thrust into each of his pockets, and these pockets were destitute of coin. The tramp was hungry and penniless. The little shop with its gay light and tempting articles of stationery, and books and sealing-wax displayed in the window, were quite to the man's taste. He could not see the parlor beyond, nor the peep-hole where Susy was supposed to be able to watch the shop; he only noticed that no one was within. The tramp was in the humor to do something desperate; he entered the shop under the pretense of begging; made straight for the till, pulled it open, and took out a handful of money. He had no time to count his spoils, but leaving the till-drawer still open, he dashed out of the shop.

Now it so happened that Susy, just when the tramp stole in, had gone upstairs to fetch a fresh exercise-book. She noticed nothing amiss on her return, and went tranquilly on with her work. Eight o'clock struck. Susy was in despair.

"I can't possibly fail Kathleen," she said to herself. "She started this splendid idea in order to help me and give me pleasure. I must be at the quarry whatever happens to-night. Something very unusual is detaining mother. I know what I'll do: I'll shut up the shop at half-past eight, leave a little note for mother, and then go to the quarry as fast as I can. I will tell mother that I am due at an important meeting, and she is sure not to question me; mother is always very kind, and gives me as much liberty as she can."

Susy made a great struggle to keep her mind centered on her books, but with all her efforts her thoughts would wander. They wandered to Kathleen and the Wild Irish Girls' Society; they wandered to her other schoolfellows; they wandered to the hardship of having to take care of the shop when she wished to be otherwise employed; and finally they settled themselves on Ruth Craven. She could not help wondering what Ruth would do—whether she would continue to be a valuable aid to the queen of the new society, or whether she would give them up altogether.

"I'd almost like her not to stay with us," thought Susy; "for then perhaps Kathleen would make me her Prime Minister. I'd like that. Kathleen is the dearest, truest, greatest lady I ever came across. She doesn't think anything of birth, nor of those sort of tiresome distinctions; she thinks of you for what you are worth yourself. And she is so splendid to look at, and has such a gallant sort of way. I do admire her just!"

The shop-bell rang. Susy was out in a moment. A woman had called for a penn'orth of paper and an envelope. She put down her penny on the counter, and Susy supplied her from a special box.

"I was in such a taking," said the woman. "I just remembered at the last moment that all the shops were shut. I don't know what I should have done if I hadn't recalled that Mrs. Hopkins kept hers open until nine o'clock. I am obliged to you, little girl. I have to send this letter to my son in India, and I'd miss the mail if it wasn't posted to-night. You couldn't now, I suppose, oblige me with a stamp."

"Of course I can," said Susy, cheerfully. "Mother always keeps a supply of stamps in the till."

She turned to the till as she spoke, and for the first time noticed that the drawer was open.

"How careless of me not to have shut it!" she thought.

It did not occur to her to examine its contents, or to suppose for a single moment that any one had taken money out of it. She provided the woman with a stamp, and then, shut the drawer of the till. It was now half-past eight, and Susy determined to take the bull by the horns and to close the shop without further ado. She sent for the little maid in the kitchen to put up the shutters, and in a minute or two the shop was in darkness and Susy was racing through the remainder of her lessons. It would take her a quarter of an hour, running most of the way, to reach the old quarry, and she must have three or four minutes to dress. She stood up, therefore, at her work, in order, as she expressed it, to save time. She was so occupied when her mother came in.

"Why have you shut the shop?" said Mrs. Hopkins in an annoyed voice. "It is only a very little past half-past eight, and I saw two poor women outside. They wanted a penn'orth of paper each. They said, 'We thought you always kept open until nine o'clock,' Now it will spread all over the place that I shut at half-past eight. Why did you do it, Susy? It's hard enough to make ends meet without adding any more difficulties."

Mrs. Hopkins stood, looking very pale and perplexed, in the parlor. Susy glanced at her mother, and could not help reflecting that the poor woman was fit to drop.

"Do sit down, mother," she said. "I was so distracted; I have to be a good way from here at nine o'clock, I couldn't think whatever kept you. I was obliged to shut the shop. I am sorry."

"Well, never mind. You didn't tell me that you were going out. I wish you wouldn't go out so much in the evening, Susy; it does make it so hard for me. There's no one now to help me with a bit of mending, and all your things are getting so racketed through."

"What kept you, mother?" said Susy, ignoring her mother's speech.

"Oh, it was your aunt. She's in such a taking about little Peter; she's quite certain he's in for measles or something worse. I'm persuaded that it's nothing but a cold. I never saw such a muddle-headed woman as your aunt Bessie. She hadn't a thing handy in the place. I had to stay and see the doctor, and then to fetch the medicine myself, and then put the child to bed. I assure you I haven't sat down since I left."

"And I suppose she never thought of giving you as much as a cup of tea?" said Susy.

"No," answered her mother; then catching sight of the teapot, she added, "You might have had the tea-things removed, Susy. I will make myself a fresh cup."

Susy stood still for a moment. Temptation tugged at her heart. Her mother certainly required if ever a mother did require a daughter. But the Wild Irish Girls—surely they were pining for her in the distance!

"I wish I could help you, mother. I would if I hadn't promised to go out. If you will give me the latchkey I can let myself in. You needn't wait up; I promise to lock up carefully."

"Very well, dear," said Mrs. Hopkins.

She did not reproach Susy; that was not her way. She put a little kettle on the gas-stove, fetched a clean cup and saucer, and presently sat down to her belated meal.

Susy dashed upstairs. She put on her hat and jacket, snatched up a pair of gloves, and the next moment was out of the house.

"Free at last," she thought. "But, oh, what an evening I have had! I must say it is horrid to be poor. Now, if I was rich like Kathleen, wouldn't I have a gay time of it? Poor dear mother should drive in a carriage, and I'd ride on my pony by her side; and Tom should be a public school boy. There'd be no horrid shop then, and no horrid women coming in for ha'p'orths and penn'orths of paper."

But as she ran through the autumn night-air she felt that, after all, there was something good in life. Her pulses, which had been languid enough in the stuffy little parlor at the back of the shop, now galloped fiercely. She arrived two or three minutes after nine, but still in fairly good time to see a number of dark heads surrounding a bright light. This light was caused by two lamps which had been placed on the ground in the old quarry; Kathleen had brought them herself in a hamper. She had managed to buy them that day, and had smuggled them off without any one being the wiser. A large bottle of crystalline oil accompanied the lamps. Kathleen, who had dressed lamps for pleasure at home, knew quite well how to manage them, and when Susy appeared they stood at each end of a wide patch of light. Kathleen herself was in the midst of the light, and the other girls clustered round the edge.

"Isn't it scrumptious?" said Kate Rourke.—"Oh, is that you, Susy Hopkins? You are late."

"Yes, I know I am. It's a wonder I could come at all," said Susy.

"Ruth Craven hasn't come yet," said another voice.

"Yes, here she is," cried a third, and Ruth came and stood at the edge of the patch of light.

Kathleen flung off her hat, and the light from the lamps lit up her brilliant hair. Her cheeks were flaming with color, and her very dark-blue eyes looked as black as night. She faced her companions.

"Well," she said, "here we are, and we call ourselves the Wild Irish Girls. I really wonder if you English girls who are assembled here in the old quarry to-night have the least idea what it means to be a wild Irish girl. If you don't know, I'd like to tell you."

"Yes, do tell us," cried several.

"The principal thing that it means," continued Kathleen, raising her voice to a slightly theatrical pitch, and extending her arm so that the lamplight fell all over it—"the chief thing that it means is to be free—yes, free as the air, free as the mountain streams, free as the dear, darling, glorious, everlasting mountains themselves. Oh, to know freedom and then to be torn away from it! Girls, I will tell you the truth. I feel in your dull old England as though I were in prison. Yes, that's about it. I don't like England. I want you girls to join me in loving Ireland."

"But we can't hate England," said Kate Rourke; "that is quite impossible. If Ireland is your native land, England is ours, and we cannot help loving her very, very much."

"You have never known Ireland," continued Kathleen. "You are not cramped up in that favored spot; you are allowed to get up when you like and to go to bed when you like, to eat what you like, to read what books you like, to row on the lake, to shoot in the bogs, to gallop on your pony over the moors, and—and—oh, to live the life of the *free*."

It was Ruth Craven who now interrupted the eager words of the queen of the new society.

"Can't you tell us, Kathleen," she said, "how to get Ireland into England—how to introduce what is good of Ireland into England? That is the use of the society as far as I am concerned. With the exception of yourself we are all English girls."

"Yes," said Susy suddenly; "and we have very bad times most of us. I wish you knew what a dull evening I have just been living through—taking care of a tiny, very dull little shop. Mother was out looking after a sick child, and I had to mind the shop. Poor women came in for penn'orths of paper. I can tell you there wasn't much freedom about that; it was all horrid."

"Well, we have shops in Ireland too," continued Kathleen, "and I suppose people have to mind them. But what I want to say now is this. I have been sent over to this country to learn. My aunt Katie O'Flynn—she's the finest figure of a woman you ever laid eyes on—thought that I ought to have learning; mother thought so too, but the dad didn't much care. However, I needn't worry you about that. I have been sent here, and here I am. When I came to your wonderful school and looked all around me, I said to myself, 'If I'm not to have companions, why, I'll die; the heart of Kathleen O'Hara will be broken. Now, who amongst the schoolgirls will suit me? I saw that very dull Cassandra Weldon, and I noticed a few companions of hers who were much the same sort. Then I observed dear, pretty little Ruth Craven, and some one said to me, 'You won't take much notice of Ruth, for she's only a foundation girl.' That made me mad. Oh yes, it did—Give me your hand, Ruth.—That made my whole heart go out to Ruth. Then I was told that a lot of the girls were foundation girls, and they weren't as rich as the others, and they were somewhat snubbed. So I thought, 'My time has come. I am an Irish girl, and the heritage of every Irish girl, handed down to her from a long line of ancestors, is to help the oppressed,' So now I am going to help all of you, and we are going to found this society, and we are going to have a good time."

Kathleen's somewhat incoherent speech was received with shouts of applause.

"We must make a few rules," she continued when her young companions had ceased to shout—"just a few big rules which will be quite easy for all of us to obey."

"Certainly," said Kate. "And I have brought a note-book with me, and if you will dictate them, Kathleen, I will jot them down."

"That is easy enough," said Kathleen. "Well, I am queen."

"Certainly you are!" "Who else could be?" "Of course you are queen!" "Darling!" "Dear!" "Sweet!" "Duck!" fell from various pairs of lips.

"Thank you," said Kathleen, looking round at them, her dark-blue eyes becoming dewy with a sudden emotion. "I think," she added, "I love you all already, and there is nothing on earth I wouldn't do for you."

"Hear her, the dear! She is bringing a fine change into our lives, cried a mass of girls who stood a little out of the line of light.

"Well," said Kathleen, "I am queen, and I have my Cabinet. Now the girls of my Cabinet are the following: Ruth Craven is my Prime Minister; Kate Rourke comes next in importance; then follow Susy Hopkins, Clara Sawyer, Hannah Johnson, Rosy Myers, and Mary Rand. Now all of you girls whom I have named are expected to uphold order—such order as is alone necessary for the Wild Irish Girls. You are expected on all occasions to uphold the authority of me, your queen. You are never under any circumstances to breathe a word against dear old Ireland. The other girls who join the society will be looked after by you; you will instruct them in our rules, and you will help them to be good members of a most important society. I believe there are a great many girls willing to join. If so, will they hold up their hands?"

Immediately a great show of hands was visible.

"Now, Kate Rourke," cried Kathleen, "please take down the names of the girls who intend to become members of the Wild Irish Girls."

The girls came forward one by one, and Kate took down their names; and it was quickly discovered that, out of the hundred foundationers who belonged to the Great Shirley School, sixty had joined Kathleen's society.

"We shall soon get the remaining forty," said Mary Rand. "They will be all agog to come on. Their positions are not so very pleasant as it is, poor things!"

"Perhaps sixty are about as many as we can manage for the present," said Kathleen. "Now, girls, I intend to present you each with a tiny badge.

I have a bag full of them here. Will you each come forward and accept the badge of membership?"

Kathleen's badges were very much admired, the eager girls bending down towards the light of the lamps in order to examine them more thoroughly. She had strung narrow green ribbon through each of the little silver hearts, and the girls could therefore slip them over their heads at once.

"You must hide them," said Kathleen. "The thing about these badges is that you will always feel them pressing against your hearts, and nobody else will know anything about them. They belong to Ireland and to me—to the home of the free and to Kathleen O'Hara. They seal you as my loving friends and followers for ever and ever."

Girls are easily impressed, and Kathleen's words were so fervent that some of them felt quite choky about the throat. They received their badges with hands that very nearly trembled. Kathleen next handed a slightly handsomer badge, but with exactly the same device, to the members of her Cabinet. Finally, she took the box of pale-blue cashmere blouses and opened it in the light of the lamps. The enthusiasm, which had been extremely keen before the appearance of the blouses, now rose to fever-height. Whom were these exquisite creations meant for? Kathleen smiled as she handed one to Mary Rand, another to Ruth Craven, another to Kate Rourke, and finally to each member of her Cabinet.

"I wish I could give you all a blouse apiece," she said to the other girls of the society, "but I am afraid that is not within my means. I chose these sweet blouses on purpose, because I know you could wear them at any time, girls," she added, turning to the members of her Cabinet. "Outsiders won't know. They will wonder at the beauty of your dress, but they won't know what it means; but *we* will know," she shouted aloud to her companions—"we will know that these girls belong to us and to old Ireland, and in particular to me, and they will be faithful to me as their queen."

"Oh dear," said little Alice Harding, a pale-faced girl, who loved fine dress and never could aspire to it, "what means can I take to become a member of the Cabinet?"

"By being a very good outside member, and trusting to your luck," laughed Kathleen. "But the time is passing, and we must proceed to what little business is left for to-night."

Each member of the Cabinet took possession of her own blouse, wrapped it up tenderly, and tucked it under her arm. Kathleen desired some one to throw the tell-tale box away, and then she collected her followers round her.

"Now," she said, «*Rule One*. To stick through thick and thin each to the other."

"Yes!" cried every voice.

"*Rule Two*. If possible, never to quarrel each with the other.»

This rule also was received with acclamations.

"*Rule Three*. To have a bit of fun all to ourselves at least once a week."

This rule quite "brought down the house." They shouted so loud that if the spot had been less lonely some one would certainly have taken cognizance of their proceedings.

"*Rule Four*. That as far as possible we hold ourselves aloof from the paying members of the Great Shirley School."

This rule was not quite as enthusiastically received. The foundationers were not altogether without friends amongst the other girls of the school. Ruth Craven in particular had several.

"I don't think that is a very fair rule," she said. "I am fond of Alice Tennant, and I am fond of Cassandra Weldon."

"And I care for Lucy Sharp"; "And I am devoted to Amelia Dawson," said other members of the Cabinet.

Nevertheless Kathleen was firm.

"The rule must be held," she said. "In a society like ours there are always rules which are not quite agreeable to every one. My principal object in starting this society is to put those horrid paying girls in their proper places. There must not be friendship—not real friendship, I mean—between us and them."

"You are a paying girl yourself," suddenly exclaimed Mary Rand.

"I know. I wish I were not, but I can't help myself. You must allow me to stand alone; I am your queen."

"That you are, and I love you," said Mary.

"This rule must hold good," repeated Kathleen. "I must insist on my society adhering to it.—Ruth Craven, why are you silent?"

"Because I earnestly wish I had not joined. I cannot give up Cassandra, nor Alice, nor—nor other girls."

"Nonsense, Ruth! You dare not fail me now," said Kathleen, with enthusiasm. "I will make it up to you. You shall come with me to Ireland in the summer. You shall. Oh Ruth, don't fail me!"

"I won't; but I hate that rule."

"And, girls, I think we must part now," said Kate Rourke. "It is getting late, and it would never do for our secret meetings to be discovered."

"Whatever happens, we must stick together," said Kathleen. "Well, good-night; we meet again this day week."

There was quite a flutter of excitement along that lonely road as the Wild Irish Girls returned to their different homes. Susy Hopkins felt quite the happiest and most light-hearted of any. By-and-by she and Ruth Craven found themselves the only girls who were walking down the road called Southwood Lane. This road led right into the centre of the shops where Susy's mother lived.

"What a good thing," said Susy, "that I took the latchkey with me! It is past ten o'clock. Mother would be wild if she had to sit up so late."

Ruth was silent.

"Aren't you happy, Ruthie? Don't you think it is all splendid?" cried Susy.

"Yes and no," said Ruth. "You see, I am a foundationer, and when she pressed me to join I hated not to; but now I am sorry that I have joined. What am I to do about Cassandra and about Alice?"

"You think a great deal about Cassandra, don't you?"

"Oh, yes; she is quite a splendid girl, and she has been so very good to me."

"I suppose you are quite in love with her?"

"No, I don't think I am. It isn't my way to fall violently in love with girls, like some of the rest of you. But I like her; and I like Alice Tennant."

"All the same," said Susy, "it is worth sacrificing a little thing to belong to the Wild Irish Girls. Did you ever in all your life see any one look more splendid than Kathleen as she stood with the light of those big lamps upon her? She is a wonderful girl—so graceful, and with such a power of eloquence. And she has such a way of just taking you by storm; and her language is so poetic. Oh, I adore her! She is the sort of girl that I could die for. If all Irish girls are like her, Ireland must be a wonderful country to live in."

"But they are not," said Ruth. "Half of them are quite commonplace. She happens to be rich and beautiful, and to have a taking way; but all the others are not like her, I am certain of it."

"Anyhow, whether they are or not, I am glad to belong to the society," said Susy. "It will give us great fun, and we need not mind now whether the paying girls are disagreeable to us or not. Then, too, think of the blouses we have got. Oh dear! oh dear! when I put mine on on Sunday mother will gape. I shall feel proud of myself in it. It was just sweet of her to get things like this to give us. And she knew we weren't well off. Oh, I do think she's one in a thousand! She must have thought of you, Ruth, when she ordered these sweet pale-blue colors, for that color is yours, isn't it?"

"I suppose so," said Ruth. "Well, all the same, I feel rather anxious. I like her, of course, but I think she is mistaken. I must go on now, but I feel somehow——"

"What?" said Susy, with some impatience.

"As though I had not done right—as though I had something to conceal. Well, I can't help myself, only I won't hate the girls who are good to me. Good-night, Susy. We won't be in time for school in the morning if we stay talking any longer."

CHAPTER XI.
THE BLOUSE AND THE ROBBERY.

Susy Hopkins shared none of Ruth Craven's scruples. To her the Wild Irish Girls' Society was all that was lovely. She trod on air as she went down the street, and when she finally let herself into her mother's little shop, locked the door after her, and went softly upstairs, her heart was beating so loud that she hardly knew herself. She slept in a tiny room just at the back of her mother's; it was sparsely furnished, and had a sloping roof at one side. The chest of drawers also did duty as a dressing-table, and there was a small square of looking-glass placed on the top. Susy had secured a candle in a tin candlestick, with which she had lighted herself to her bedroom, but when she got there she had no intention of putting up with such feeble illumination. She first of all drew the bolt to secure herself against intrusion, and then stepping on tiptoe, she unlocked a drawer and took from it several ends of candle which she had collected from time to time. These she stuck on the dressing-table, and when she had made her little garret almost as bright as day she unfolded her pale-blue blouse. She bent low over her treasure, examining the blue embroidery, which was rendered still more fascinating with small stitches of pink silk, looking with ecstacy at the real lace round the neck and cuffs and finally pressing the delicate color against her blooming cheek.

Susy Hopkins was quite an ordinary-looking little girl. Her nose was decidedly snub, her mouth wide; but her eyes were dark and bright, and she had fairly good eyebrows. She had a low forehead, rather nice curly hair, and a high color in her cheeks.

"In this blouse I shall look a positive beauty," she thought. "Won't Tom respect me when he sees me in it on Sunday? I must try it on now; I really must."

Accordingly she slipped off her bodice, and substituted the pale-blue cashmere blouse for the ugly and threadbare garment she had removed. Whether the blouse was becoming to Susy Hopkins or not remains to be proved, but it certainly delighted its wearer, causing her eyes to sparkle and the color in her cheeks to grow brighter.

"It is the most beautiful thing I ever saw in my life," she thought. "Why, Kathleen is like a fairy godmother. And how well it fits! And what a perfect cut about the neck! And, oh! these darling little cuffs at the end of the sleeves, and this sweet pink embroidery and this little ruffle of lace round the neck. Oh! there never, never was anything made so beautifully before. I am in luck; I am—I am."

Her mother's hand knocking on the wall brought her down from the clouds.

"Go to bed, dear," called out her parent. "It is very late, and you are disturbing me."

"Yes, mother," called back Susy.

She removed the blouse, folded it in tissue-paper, put it into her drawer, blew out the candles, and got into bed. But all through the remainder of the night Susy dreamt of her blouse. The blouse filled her thoughts, otherwise she might have been in raptures over her pretty silver locket and its green ribbon. But as this was for private wear, and must on no account be shown to any one who was not a member of the society, it did not give her the amount of rapture it would otherwise have done.

"It is lovely too. It is a badge, and means a great deal," she said to herself, and she closed her hand over it as she lay in bed. "It is tiresome that I cannot show it. It is a sweet little locket, and I might save up money enough to have it gilded over. People would think I had a gold locket. I have always nearly died to have one; but of course I couldn't do that, for it would displease our queen, the darling, and I wouldn't for all I am worth do anything to annoy her. Oh dear, things are turning out lovely! I am twice as happy a girl as I was before Kathleen O'Hara came to the school."

At school next day the members of the new society looked a little conscious. Their eyes often met, and those eyes spoke volumes. Sometimes a girl would put her hand up to her neck in a somewhat significant way, and another girl would respond with a similar signal. There was a sort of suppressed excitement in the school; but the teachers remarked nothing. On the contrary, they were pleased with the way lessons were done, exercises gone through, and work accomplished. The girls were so completely in league with each other, so full of delight over the new amusement which Kathleen had started in their midst, that they had no time to be supercilious or disagreeable to the paying girls, who were left in peace. They were usually a good deal tormented by the foundationers, who took their revenge by small spiteful ways—by taking the ink when they did not want it, by removing good pens and putting bad ones in their places, by spilling ink on the blotting paper. In short, they had many ways of rendering the life of a paying girl anything but happy. To-day, however, all was peace and quiet. Kathleen walked in her radiant fashion through her lessons; her beautiful face could not but be an attraction. She was very bright and very smart, and even Alice gave her an approving glance.

"Mother is right," she thought. "She is a little better than she was. If only she would take a real interest in her work I should have hopes of her."

Now Cassandra Weldon had come to the school that day with the intention of asking Ruth Craven to come home with her. She had a suggestion to make to Ruth. She knew that the little girl was very poor and very clever. Cassandra was working very hard for one of the big scholarships, and her mother had gone to the expense of getting a special coach to help her at home. Cassandra had spoken to her mother, and her mother had agreed that Ruth might come back with her each evening and also take advantage of the services of Miss Renshaw. If Ruth got a scholarship she would indeed be a happy girl, and it was Cassandra's, opinion that, although she had been such a short time in the school, she would have a very good chance if she got a little outside help.

Accordingly Cassandra waited for Ruth outside the school when lessons were over. During the morning her eyes had travelled in Ruth's direction pretty often, and her eyes had conveyed to the little girl all sorts of kind and friendly messages. But Ruth had avoided Cassandra's eyes. She had made up her mind.

"I can't be two things," she said to herself. "I have elected to go with the foundationers and with Kathleen O'Hara, although I don't care for the society, and I don't want to belong to the girls who band themselves together against the paying girls. But if I do this I certainly can't take advantage of Cassandra's kindness. I do love her—I am sure I should love her dearly—but I can't have much to say to her now."

Accordingly, while Cassandra waited for Ruth, hoping that she would appear at any moment, and that she could tell her what a good thing she had arranged on her behalf, Ruth avoided Cassandra. Presently Kathleen O'Hara, dressed somewhat extravagantly, and with her blue velvet cap perched upon the back of her golden hair, strolled out of school. She had a crimson sash round her black velvet dress, and a wide lace collar encircled her neck. She was fastening a heavily embroidered coat of blue cashmere when Cassandra accosted her.

"How do you do, Miss O'Hara?" she said.

"How are you?" replied Kathleen, just raising her brows, and then turning to say something to Susy Hopkins.

Cassandra frowned.

"How can Kathleen, who with all her eccentricities is a lady, waste her time talking to an insignificant little girl like Susy?" thought Cassandra.

Kathleen seemed to read her neighbor's thoughts, for she slipped her hand inside Susy's arm.

"I will walk with you a little way," she said; "I have something I want to say."

"One moment first," said Cassandra. "Have you seen Ruth Craven anywhere?"

"Oh yes; Ruth has left the school. Didn't you see her go? There she is, crossing the field. I suppose she is in a hurry to get home."

"Thank you," said Cassandra.

She caught up her books and started running in the direction of Ruth Craven.

"How tiresome of her to have gone so fast!" she said to herself?

Presently she shouted Ruth's name, and Ruth was obliged to stop.

"Why, Ruth," said Cassandra, "what is the matter with you? You generally wait to talk to me after school is over. Why are you in such a hurry?"

"I am not," said Ruth, who was not going to get out of her difficulty by telling an untruth.

"Well, if you are not in a hurry, why are you running across this field at the rate of a hunt? It looks as if you were—" Cassandra paused, and the color came into her cheeks—"as if you were running away from me."

Ruth was silent. Cassandra came close to her and looked into her face.

"What is the matter, Ruth?" she repeated.

"I have promised granny that I would help her with some darning this afternoon."

"Your granny must do without you, for you have got to come back with me."

"Oh, indeed, I can't!"

"But you must, my little girl. I have got the most heavenly plan to suggest to you."

Cassandra laid her hand on Ruth's shoulder. Ruth started away.

"What is it, Ruth? How queer you look! What is the matter?"

"I must get home. I promised granny."

"But listen before you decide. You know Miss Renshaw, don't you?"

"Miss Maria Renshaw, the coach. Yes, I do."

"Don't you remember my pointing her out to you?"

"Of course I remember it, Cassandra; and she looked—oh, lovely!"

"She is far more lovely than she looks—that is, if you mean she is clever and taking and all the rest. She is just perfectly splendid. She makes you see a thing at the first glance. She has a way of putting information into you so that you cannot help knowing. Oh, she is delightful! And mother says that I may have her to coach me for the big scholarship—the sixty-pounds-a-year scholarship. You know there are two of them. There is one quite in your line, and there is one in mine; and there is no earthly reason why you should not get one and I the other."

"Well?" said Ruth.

Her beautiful, fair, delicately chiselled face had turned pale. She stood very upright, and looked full at Cassandra.

"It could be easily done, dear little Ruth. Miss Renshaw would just as soon coach two girls as one, and mother has arranged it. Yes, she has arranged it absolutely. Miss Renshaw will coach you and me together. You are to come home with me every evening. She will give us both an hour. Isn't it too splendid?"

Ruth did not speak.

"Aren't you pleased, Ruth? Don't you think it is very nice of me to think of my friends? You are my friend, you know."

"Oh no," said Ruth.

"But what is it? What is the matter?"

"I—I can't."

"You can. It will be madness to refuse. Think what a chance is offered you. If you get Miss Renshaw's instruction you are safe to get that scholarship; and it is for three years, Ruth. It would send you, with a little help from your grandfather, perhaps to Holloway College, perhaps to Somerville or Newnham, or even Girton. Perhaps you could try for a scholarship in one of these great colleges afterwards. You daren't refuse it. It means—oh, it means all the difference in your whole life."

"I know," said Ruth. "Cassandra, I will write to you. I can't decide just now. I am awfully obliged to you; I can't express what I feel. You are good; you are very, very good."

Ruth caught one of Cassandra's hands and raised it to her lips.

"You are very good," she said again.

Meanwhile Kathleen O'Hara, after walking a very short way with Susy Hopkins, gave her an abrupt good-bye and started running in the direction of the Tennants' house. She did not care a bit for Susy; but being a member of the Wild Irish Girls, and not only a member, but one of the Cabinet, she must on all occasions be kind to her. Nevertheless a commonplace little girl like Susy Hopkins had not one thing in common with Kathleen.

"Everything is going splendidly," she said to herself. "No fear now that I shall not have plenty of excitement in the coming by-and-by. I mean to write to father and ask him whether I may not invite some of the members of the Cabinet to Carrigrohane. Wouldn't they enjoy it? Kate Rourke, of course, must come; and dear little Ruth Craven. How pale and sweet Ruth looked to-day! She is far and away the nicest girl in the school. I am so glad I have taken steps to prevent that horrid friendship with Cassandra coming to anything! Ruth mustn't love anybody in the school very, *very* much except me. Oh, things are going well, and Alice little guesses what she is driving me to by her extraordinary behavior."

Kathleen entered the house, banging the door loudly after her, as was her fashion.

Another little girl had also reached home, but she did not bang the door. She entered her mother's shop to encounter the flushed and much-perturbed face of her parent.

"Well, Susy," said Mrs. Hopkins, "I wouldn't have thought it of you."

"Why, what is it, mother?"

"There's nineteen-and-sixpence taken out of the till," said Mrs. Hopkins. "Some one must have come into the shop, for the accounts are nineteen-and-sixpence short. When I left the house yesterday there were three pounds in the till—three pounds and fivepence-halfpenny. You sold, according to your own showing, a penn'orth of paper, which makes an extra penny; but when I went into the accounts this morning I found that the whole amount was only two pounds one shilling and a halfpenny. Nineteen-and-sixpence is missing. Susy, what does this mean?"

"I am sure, mother, I can't tell you. No one came into the shop; certainly no one stole the money."

"My dear child, seeing is believing. I assure you there are only two pounds one shilling and a halfpenny in the till. I scarcely took a penny this morning, and that nineteen-and-sixpence makes it impossible for me to pay my rent, as I meant to do, to-day. Who can have come in and stolen very nearly a pound's worth of my hard-earned money?"

"Nobody, mother dear. Do let me examine the till."

"Are you quite positive that no one came into the shop?"

"Nobody, mother."

"You did not leave the shop even for a moment?"

"Yes; I went to sit in the parlor."

"Oh, Susy? there you are! I trust you with my house and property, and you leave the shop without any one in it Did you lock the till?"

Susy had an unpleasant memory of having found the till open when she returned to attend to a customer.

"No" she said, hanging her head.

Mrs. Hopkins uttered a heavy sigh.

"Oh, dear!" she said. "And as you sat in the parlor you could see the shop. You did not leave the parlor, did you?"

For one minute Susy remembered that she had gone upstairs for an exercise-book, but she determined not to tell her mother of this further enormity.

"I was either in the shop or in the parlor all the time. I only went into the parlor because I could not do my exercises in the shop. But I sat where I could see everything."

"You couldn't have done so. This money would not have gone without hands. How am I to manage I don't know. I have lost a large sum for such a poor woman."

Susy pitied her mother, tried to assure her that the fault was not hers, was convinced that the money would be found, and went on talking a lot of nonsense until Mrs. Hopkins fairly lost her temper.

"Examine the drawer for yourself" she said. "I tell, you what it is, Susy, I won't be able to buy you a new winter frock at all this year; and you will have to have your boots patched, for I can't afford a new pair. I was trying to collect a pound towards your winter things, but this puts a stop to everything."

"Mother doesn't know what a lovely blouse I've got," thought Susy. "When she sees me in that she'll be quite cheered up."

The moment she thought of the blouse the little girl felt a frantic desire to run upstairs to look at it.

"Mother," she said, "I don't mind a bit about the winter dress; and if my boots are neatly patched and well blacked every day, I dare say I can do with them a little longer. And I will sit with you this afternoon, mother, and help you to sew. I can't understand who could have stolen the money. Perhaps it is a practical joke of Tom's; you know he is fond of doing things of that sort now and then."

"No, it isn't, for I asked him. Who can have come into the shop? Do you think you fell asleep over your work?"

"Oh, no."

"Then it is a mystery past bearing. If nobody came in, and you never left either the shop or the parlor, that money was taken out of the till as though by magic."

"We will find it, mother; we are sure to find it," said Susy; and the way she said these words aggravated poor Mrs. Hopkins, as she said afterwards, more than a little.

CHAPTER XII.
TOM HOPKINS AND HIS WAY
WITH AUNT CHURCH.

It was quite true that Mrs. Hopkins could ill afford to lose so large a sum as nineteen-and-sixpence out of her small earnings. During her husband's lifetime the stationer's shop had gone well and provided a comfortable living for his wife, son, and daughter. But unfortunately, in an evil moment he had been induced to put his hand to a bill for a friend. The friend had, as usually is the case, become bankrupt. Poor Hopkins had to pay the money, and from that moment the affairs in the stationer's shop were the reverse of flourishing. In fact, the blow killed the poor man. He lingered for a time, broken-hearted and unable to rouse himself, and finally died about about three years before the date of this story. For a time Mrs. Hopkins was quite prostrate, but being a woman with a good deal of vigor and determination, she induced one of her relatives to lend her one hundred pounds, and determined to keep on with the shop. She could not, of course, stock it as fully as she would have liked; she could never extend her connection beyond mere stationery, sealing-wax, pens, and a very few books, and Christmas cards in the winter. Still, she managed to support herself and Tom and Susy; but it was a scraping along all the time. She had to count every penny, and, above all things, to avoid going in debt. She was only in debt for the one hundred pounds, which had been lent to her by an aunt of her husband's, an old woman of the name of Church, who lived in a neighboring village about four miles away.

Mrs. Church was quite rich, according to the Hopkinses' ideas of wealth. She lived alone and hoarded her money. She had not been at all willing to lend Mrs. Hopkins the hundred pounds; but as she had really been fond of Mr. Hopkins, and had at one time meant to make him her heir, she had listened to Mrs. Hopkins's lamentations, and desired her to send Tom to her to inspect him, and had finally handed over the money, which was to be paid back by monthly installments within the space of three years.

Mrs. Hopkins was so relieved to get the money that she never thought at all of the terrible tax it would be to return it. Still, by working hard morning, noon, and night—she added to her gains by doing fine needlework for several ladies, who said that no one could embroider like Mrs. Hopkins—she managed to make two ends just meet together, and she always continued to send Mrs. Church her two pounds fifteen shillings and sevenpence on the first of every month. Tom was the one who generally ran across to the old lady's with the money; and so fond was she of him that she often gave him a piece of cake, and even on one or two rare occasions kept him to dinner. Tom enjoyed his visits to Mrs. Church, and Mrs. Hopkins was sure to encourage him to go to her, as she hoped against hope that when the old lady died Tom would be left some of her money.

It was on a Wednesday that Susy sat in the parlor and forgot all about the interests of the shop; it was on that very night that the tramp had come in and helped himself to a ten-shilling-piece and some silver out of the till; and it was on the following Saturday that Mrs. Hopkins, for the first time since she had borrowed the hundred pounds from Aunt Church, as she called the old lady, found that she could not return even a portion of what had just fallen due. She called Tom to her side.

"Tom," she said, "you must go and see Aunt Church this afternoon as soon as ever you come in. You must go, and you must tell her."

"Of course I'll go, mother," answered the boy. "I always like going to Aunt Church's; she is very kind to me. She said next time I came along she'd show me things in her microscope. She has got a beetle's wing, mother, mounted on glass, and when you gaze down at it it seems to be covered with beautiful feathers, as long as though they were on a big bird. And she has got a drop of water full of wriggly things all alive; and she says we drink it by the gallon, and it is no wonder we feel bad in our insides. I'll go, right enough. I suppose you have the money ready?"

"No, Tom, that's just what I have not got. I told you how that night when I had the misfortune to go and see your aunt and look after her sick child, some one came into the shop and stole nineteen-and-sixpence out of the till. I am so short from the loss of that money that I can't pay Aunt Church for at least another week. Ask her if she'll be kind enough to give me a week's grace, Tom; that's a good boy. I can't think how the money was stolen."

"Why don't you put it into the hands of the police?" said Tom.

"Why, Tom," said his mother, looking at him with admiration, "you are a smart boy. Do you know, I never thought of that. I will go round to the police-station this very afternoon and get Police-Constable Macartney to take it up."

"But, mother, the thief, whoever he is, has left the place long before now. The money was stolen on Wednesday, and this is Saturday morning."

"Well, Tom, there's no saying. Anyhow, I will go round to the police-station and lodge the information."

Accordingly, while Susy was again trying on her lovely pale-blue cashmere blouse behind locked doors upstairs, Tom and his mother were plotting how best to cover the loss of the nineteen-and-sixpence. Naughty Susy, having made up her mind to deny herself a new frock and new boots, had given the matter no further consideration. She was accustomed to the fact that her mother was always in money difficulties. As long as she could remember, this was the state of things at home. She had come to the conclusion that grown-up persons were always in a frantic state about money, and she had no desire to join these anxious ones herself. As she could not mend matters, she did not see why she should worry about them.

Tom had a scrap of dinner and then ran off to see Aunt Church. He found the old lady sitting at her parlor window looking out as usual for him. She was dressed in rusty black; she had a front of stiff curls on her forehead, a white widow's-cap over it, and a small black crape handkerchief crossed on her breast. Mrs. Church was a little woman; she had very tiny feet and hands, and was very proud of them. She never thought of buying any new clothes, and her black bombazine dress was more brown than black now; so was her shawl, and so was the handkerchief which she wore round her neck. Her cap was tied with ribbons which had been washed so often that they were no longer white, but yellow.

She came to the door to greet Tom when he arrived, and called him in.

"Ah, Tom!" she said, "I have got a piece of plumcake waiting for you; and if you are a really good boy, and will shoo the fowls into my backyard and shut the gate on them, you may look into my microscope."

"Thank you, Aunt Church," said Tom. "Shall I go at once and shoo the fowls?"

"You had best give me my money first. Here is the box; you drop it in: two pounds in gold—I hope to goodness your mother has sent the money in gold—two pounds in gold and the rest in silver. Now then, here is the box. Drop it in like a good child, and then you shall shoo the fowls, and have your plumcake, and look in the microscope."

"But, Aunt Church—" said Tom. He planted himself right in front of the old lady. He was a tall boy, well set up, with a sandy head, and a face covered with freckles. He had rather shallow blue eyes and a wide mouth, but his whole expression was honest and full of fun. "I am desperately sorry, and so is mother."

"Eh! What?" said the old lady. She put her hand to her ear. "I am a bit hard of hearing, my dear; come close to me."

"Mother's awfully sorry, but she can't pay you to-day."

"Oh!" said Mrs. Church; "can't pay me to-day! But it's the first of the month, and she was never behindhand—I will say that—in her payments before."

"She's fretting past bearing," said Tom. "She'd give all the world to be able to pay you up, but she ain't got the money, and that's a fact. We have had a robbery in the shop, Aunt Church, and mother has took on dreadful."

"A burglary?" said Mrs. Church. "Now tell me all about it. Stand here and pour your words into my ear. I am very much interested about burglaries. Was there attempted murder? Speak up, boy—speak up."

Tom quite longed to say that there was. Had he been able to assure Mrs. Church that burglars with masks on their faces had burst into the shop at dead of night and penetrated to his mother's bedroom, and had held pistols to her throat and Susy's throat, and a great bare, glittering knife to his; and had he been further able to tell her that he himself, unaided, had grappled with the enemy, had wrested the knife from the hand of one, and knocked the loaded pistols from the hands of the others—then, indeed, he would have felt himself a hero, and the mere fact of not being able to return the money on the appointed day would not have signified.

But Tom was truthful, and he had but a lame story to tell. Nineteen-and-sixpence had been abstracted from the till. Nobody knew how it had been done, and nobody had the least idea who was the thief. Mrs. Church, who would have given her niece unlimited time to return the money had there been a real, proper, bloodthirsty burglary, was not at all inclined to show mercy when the affair dwindled down into an unknown thief taking a small sum of money out of the till.

"Why didn't you get it back?" she said. "Why didn't you send for the police? My word, this is a nice state of things! And me to be out of my money that I counted upon. Why, Tom, boy, I spend that money on my food, rent, and the little expenses I have to go to. I made up my mind when I drew that hundred pounds from my dear husband's hard-earned savings that, whatever happened, I'd make that sum last me for all expenses for three years. And I have done it, Tom—I have done it. I am in low water, Tom. I want the money; I want it just as much as your poor mother does."

"But you have money in the bank, haven't you?"

"That is no affair of yours, Tom Hopkins. Don't talk in that silly way to me. No, I don't want you to shoo the fowls into the yard, and I don't mean to give you any plumcake. I shall have to eat it myself, for I have no money to buy anything else. And I won't show you the beautiful wings of the beetle in the microscope. You can go home to your mother and tell her I am very much annoyed indeed."

"But, Aunt Church," said Tom, "if you were to see poor mother you wouldn't blame her. She looks, oh, so thin and so tired! She's terribly unhappy, and she will be certain sure to pay you next week. It was silly of her, I will own, not to think of the police sooner; but she's gone to them to-day, ordered by me to do that same."

"That was thoughtful enough of you, Tom, and I don't object to giving you a morsel of the stalest cake. I always keep three cakes in three tin boxes, and you can have a morsel of the stalest; it is more than two months old, but you won't mind that."

"Not me," said Tom, "I like stale cakes best," he added, determined to show his aunt that he was ready to be pleased with everything. He was a very knowing boy, and spoke up so well, and was so evidently sorry himself, and so positive that as soon as ever the police were told they would simply lay their hands on the thief and the thief would disgorge his spoils, that Aunt Church was fain to believe him.

In the end she and he made a compact.

"I tell you what it is," he said. "You haven't been to see mother for a long time, and if you ain't got any money to buy a dinner for yourself, it is but fair you should have a slice off our Sunday joint."

"Sunday joint, indeed!" snapped Mrs. Church.

"You couldn't expect us not to have a bit of meat on Sunday," said Tom. "Why, we'd get so weak that mother couldn't earn the money she sends you every month."

"And you couldn't do your lessons and be the fine big boy that I am proud of," said Mrs. Church. "Now, to tell the truth, I can't bear that sister of yours—Susy, you call her—but I have a liking for you, Tom Hopkins. What is it you want me to do?"

"If you will let me come here to-morrow, I'll push you all the way to Merrifield in time for our dinner. Wouldn't you like that? And I'd bring you back again in the evening. There's your own old bath-chair that Uncle Church used to be moved about in before he died."

"To be sure, there is," said Mrs. Church, her eyes brightening. "But the lining has got moth-eaten."

"Who minds that?" said Tom. "I'll go and clean it after you have given me that bit of cake you promised me."

Everything ended quite satisfactorily as far as Tom was concerned, for Mrs. Church forgot her anger in the interest that the boy's visit gave her. She consulted him about her fowls, and gave him a new-laid egg to slip into his pocket for his own supper. Later on she allowed him to munch some very poor and very stale plumcake. Finally she gave him his heart's delight, for he was allowed to peer into the old microscope and revel in the sight of the beetle's wings with thin, sweeping plumes, as he afterwards described them.

It was rather late when Tom returned home. He burst into the parlor where his mother and Susy were sitting.

"Mother," he said, "I have done everything splendidly; and she's coming to dine with us to-morrow."

"She's what?" said Mrs. Hopkins.

"Aunt Church is coming to dine with us. She was mad about the money, and nobody could have been nastier than she might have turned out but for me. But it's all right now. We must have a nice dinner for her. She is very fond of good things, and as she never gives them to herself, she will enjoy ours all the more."

"She'll think that I am rich, when I am as poor as a church mouse," said Mrs. Hopkins. "But I suppose you have done everything for the best, Tom, and I must go around to the butcher's for a little addition to the dinner."

Mrs. Hopkins left the house, and Tom sank into a chair by his sister.

"It's golloptious for me," he said. "She's taking no end of a fancy to me. See this egg? She gave it to me for my supper. Mother shall have it. Mother is looking very white about the gills; a new-laid egg that she hasn't to pay for will nourish her up like anything."

"So it will," said Susy. "We'll boil it and say nothing about it, and just pop it on her plate when she's having her supper. All the same, Tom, I wish you hadn't asked old Aunt Church here. She is such a queer old body; and the neighbors sometimes drop in on Sundays. And I have asked Miss Kathleen O'Hara to come in to-morrow, and she has promised to."

"What?" said Tom. "That grand beauty of a young lady, the pride of the school? Why, everybody is talking about her. At the boys' school they've caught sight of her, and there isn't a boy that hasn't fallen in love with her.

They all slink behind the wall, and bob up as she comes by. You don't mean that *she's* coming here?»

"Yes; why not? She's very fond of me."

"But she's no end of a howler. They say she's worth her weight in gold, and that her father is a sort of king in Ireland. Why should she take up with a little girl like you?"

"Well, Tom, some people like me, although you think but little of your sister. Kathleen is very fond of me. I invited her to have tea with us to-morrow, and she is coming."

"My word!" said Tom. "To think that I shall be sitting at the same table with her! I'll be able to make my own terms now with John Short and Harry Reid and the rest of the chaps. Why, Susy, you must be a genius, and I thought you weren't much of a sort."

"I am better than you think; and she is fond of me."

"And you really and truly call her by her Christian name?"

"Of course I do."

Susy longed to tell Tom about the wonderful society; but its strictest rule was that it was never to be spoken about to outsiders. Susy, as a member of the Cabinet, must certainly be one of the last to break the rules.

Mrs. Hopkins came back at that moment. She had added a pound of sausage and a little piece of pork to their usual Sunday fare. She had also brought sixpennyworth of apples with her.

"These are to make a pudding," she said. "I think we shall do now very well."

Susy and Tom quite agreed with their mother. Susy rose and prepared supper, and at the crucial moment the new-laid egg was laid on Mrs. Hopkins's plate. It takes, perhaps, a great deal of poverty to truly appreciate a new-laid egg. Mrs. Hopkins was delighted with hers; she thought Tom the noblest boy in the world for having denied himself in order to give it to her. Tears filled her tired eyes as she thanked God for her good children.

Susy and Tom watched her as she ate the egg, and thought how delicious it must taste, but were glad she had it.

The following day dawned bright and clear, with a suspicion of frost in the air. It was, as Tom expressed it, a perfect day. Susy went to church with her mother in the morning, the dinner being all prepared and left to cook itself in the oven. Tom started at about eleven o'clock on his walk to the tiny village where Mrs. Church lived.

As soon as Susy returned from her place of worship she helped her mother to get the little parlor ready. She put some autumn leaves in a jug on the center of the table. Her mother brought out the best china, which had not been used since her husband's death. The best china was very pretty, and Susy thought that no table could look more elegant than theirs. The best china was accompanied by some quite good knives and forks. The forks were real silver; Mrs. Hopkins regarded them with pride.

"If the worst—the very worst—comes," she said to Susy, "we can sell them; but I cling to them as a piece of respectability that I never want to part from. Your dear father gave them to me on our wedding-day—a whole dozen of beautiful silver forks with the hall-mark on them, and his initials on the handle of each. I want them to be Tom's some day. Silver should always be handed on to the eldest son."

Susy felt that she was almost worthy of Kathleen's friendship as she regarded the silver forks.

"You must never part with them, mother," she said—until Tom is married. Then, of course, they will belong to him."

"You are a good little girl, Susy," said her mother. "Of course, there never was a boy like Tom. It was sweet of him to give up his egg to me last night."

Having seen that the table was in perfect order, and that the dinner was cooking as well as dinner could in the oven, Mrs. Hopkins went upstairs to put on a lace collar and a neat black silk apron.

Meanwhile Susy had locked herself into her own room. The crowning moment of her life had arrived. She had made up her mind that she would wear her new blouse at dinner that day. Susy's stockings were coarse, and showed darns here and there; Susy's shoes were rough, and could not altogether hide the disfiguring patches on the toes of each; Susy's skirt was dark-blue serge, fairly neat in its way. Altogether Susy from her waist down was a very ordinary little girl—the little daughter of poor people; but from her waist up she was resplendent.

"Oh! if I could only show my sweet, sweet little badge," she thought, "it would make me perfect. But I daren't. The queen commands that it should be hidden, and the queen's commands must be obeyed."

Susy slipped into her blouse. She fastened it; she put a belt round her waist. She curtsied before her little glass. She bobbed here; she bobbed there. She looked at herself front view, then over her shoulder, then, with a morsel of glass, at her back; she surveyed herself, as far as the limited accommodation of her room afforded, from every point of view. Finally, with flushed cheeks and a very proud expression on her face, she tripped downstairs. The pale-blue cashmere blouse, with its real lace and embroidered trimmings, might have been worn by any girl, even in the highest station of life.

Mrs. Hopkins was busy in the kitchen. She called to Susy:

"Come and hold the vegetable dish, child. I hear Tom pushing Aunt Church in at the gate; I know he is doing it by the creak of the bath-chair. There never was a bath-chair that creaked like that. Hold this while I—Why, sakes alive, Susy! wherever did you get—"

"Oh, it's my new blouse, mother."

"Your new what?"

"What you see, mother—my new blouse. Don't you admire it?"

Mrs. Hopkins was so stunned that she could not speak for a moment. Her face, which had been quite florid, turned pale. She suddenly put up her hand and caught Susy by the arm.

"Oh, mother, don't!" said the little girl. "Your hand isn't clean. Oh, you have made a stain! Oh, mother, how could you?"

"Run upstairs at once, child, and take it off. For the life of you don't let *her* see it; she›d never forgive me. It isn›t fit for you, Susy; it really isn›t. Wherever did you get it from? Where did you buy it?»

Now Susy had really no intention of making a secret with regard to the blouse. She meant to tell her mother frankly that it was a present from Miss Kathleen O'Hara, but Mrs. Hopkins's manner and words put the little girl into a passion, and she was determined now not to say a word.

"It is my secret," she said. "I won't tell you how I got it, nor who gave it to me. And I won't take it off."

Just then there were voices, and Aunt Church called out:

"Where are you, Mary Hopkins? Why don't you show yourself? Fussing over fine living, I suppose. Oh, there is your daughter. My word! Fine feathers make fine birds.—Come over and speak to me, my dear, and help me out of this chair. Now then, give me your hand. Be quick!"

Susy put out her hand and helped Mrs. Church as well as she could out of the bath-chair. Tom winked when he saw the splendid apparition; then he stuck his tongue into his cheek, and coming close to his sister, he whispered:

"Wherever did you get that toggery?"

"That's nothing to you," said Susy.

Mrs. Church glanced over her shoulder and looked solemnly at Susy.

"It's my opinion," she said, speaking in a slow, emphatic, rather awful voice, "that you are a very, very bad little girl. You will come to no good. Mark my words. I prophesy a bad end for you, and trouble for your unfortunate mother. You will remember my words when the prophecy comes true. Help me now into the parlor. I cannot stay long, but I will have a morsel of your grand dinner before I leave."

CHAPTER XIII.
AUNT CHURCH AT DINNER AND THE CONSEQUENCES THEREOF.

When Mrs. Church was comfortably established in the easy-chair in the little parlor, with her feet on the fender, and a nice view of the street from the window near by—when her best widow's-cap was perched upon her head, and her little black mitts were drawn over her delicate, small hands—she looked around her and gave a brief sigh of satisfaction.

"Upon my word," she said, "I'm not at all sorry I came. There's nothing like seeing things for yourself. Most elegant damask on the table. Mary Hopkins, where did you get that damask?"

Mrs. Hopkins, whose cheeks were flushed, and who looked considerably worried, replied that it had been left to her by her own mother.

"My mother was a housekeeper in a nobleman's family," she said, "and she was given that cloth and two or three more like it. I have 'em in the linen-chest upstairs, and I wouldn't part with 'em to anybody."

"I admire your pride," said Mrs. Church. "Next door to pride comes honesty. I am sometimes inclined to believe that it comes afore pride; but we needn't dispute that delicate point at present. And the silver forks. My word!—Tom, my boy, pass me a fork to examine."

Tom took up a fork and handed it to Mrs. Church.

"Hall-marked and all!" she said.

She laid it down with emphasis.

"Perhaps you know," she said, fixing her beady black eyes upon Mrs. Hopkins's face, "that I'll be very low as regards victuals for the rest of this week. But never mind; I am never one to press what it ain't convenient to return. Ah! and here comes the dinner. Well, I will say that I have a good appetite.—You can push me right up to the table, Tom, my boy."

Tom did push the old lady into the most comfortable seat. She now removed her mittens, put a napkin on her lap, and bent forward with a look of appetite to regard the different dishes which Ellen, the tiny twelve-year-old servant, brought in. Ellen trembled very much in the company of the old lady, and Mrs. Hopkins trembled still more. But Susy, who saw no reason why she should bow down before Aunt Church, ate her good dinner with appetite, tossed her little head, and felt that she was making a sensation. Tom was very attentive to Mrs. Church, and helped her to a large glass of ginger-wine. She thoroughly enjoyed her dinner, and, while she was eating it, forgot all about Susy and the pale-blue cashmere blouse.

But when the meat had been followed by the apple-pudding, and the apple-pudding by some coffee which was served in real china cups, and Mrs. Church had folded her napkin and swept the crumbs from her bombazine dress, and Mrs. Hopkins, assisted by Susy, had removed the cloth, and the little maid had swept up the hearth, Mrs. Church began to recollect herself. It is true she was no longer hungry nor cold, for the fire was plentiful, and the sun also poured in at the small window. But Mrs. Church had a memory and, as she believed, a grievance. In her tiny house on the common four miles away firing was scarce, and food was scarcer. The owner of the house did not care to spend more than a very limited sum of money on coals and food. There was nothing in the cottage for Mrs. Church's supper except a bit of stale cake, a hunch of brown bread, and a little tea. The tea would have to be drunk without milk, and with only a modicum of brown sugar, for Mrs. Church was determined to spend no money, if possible, until Mrs. Hopkins paid the debt which had been due on the previous day. It was one thing, therefore, for Mrs. Church's debtors to eat good roast beef and good boiled pork and good apple-pudding, but it was another thing for Mrs. Church to tolerate it. She fixed her eyes now on Susy in a very meaning way. Susy had never appealed to the old lady's fancy, and she appealed less than ever to-day.

"Come right over here, little girl," said Mrs. Church, waving a thin arm and motioning Susy to approach.

Susy Hopkins, remembering her blouse and her proud position as a member of the Cabinet of the Queen of the Wild Irish Girls, felt for a moment inclined to disobey; but Mrs. Church had a certain power about her, and she impelled Susy to come forward.

"Stand just in front of me," she said, "and let me look at you. My word! I never did see a more elegant figure. Don't you think that you are something like a peacock—fine above and ugly below?"

"No, I don't, Aunt Church," said Susy.

"Tut, tut, child! Don't give me any of your sauce, but just answer a straight question. Where did you get that bodice? It is singularly fine for a little girl like you. Where did you get it?"

"I don't think it is any business of yours, Aunt Church."

"Susy!" said her mother in a voice of terror. "Don't talk like that. You know very well you mustn't be rude to Aunt Church.—Don't mind her, aunt; she is a very naughty girl."

"I am not, mother," said Susy; "and it's awfully unkind of you to say it of me. I am not a bit rude. But it is not Aunt Church's affair. I didn't steal the blouse; I came by it honestly, and it wasn't bought out of any of Aunt Church's money."

"That remains to be proved," said Mrs. Church. "Susan Hopkins, I don't like you nor your ways. When I was young I knew a little girl, and you remind me of her. She had a face summat like yours, no way pretty, but what you'd call boastful and conceited; and she thought a sight of herself, and put on gay dress that she had no call to wear. She strutted about among the neighbors, and they said, 'Fine feathers make fine birds,' and laughed at her past bearing. But she didn't mind, because she was a little girl that was meant to go to the bad—and she did. She learned to be a thief, and she broke her mother's heart, and she was locked up in prison. In prison she had to wear the ugly convict-dress with the broad-arrow stamped on all her clothes. Afterwards, when she came out again, her poor mother had died, and her grandmother likewise; and her brother, who was the moral image of Tom there, wouldn't receive her in his house. I haven't heard of her for a long time back, but most likely she died in the work-house. Well, Susan, you may take my little story for what it is worth, and much good may it do you."

"I think you are very rude indeed, Aunt Church," said Susy. "I don't see that I'm bound to submit to your ugly, cruel words. I like this blouse, and I'll wear it whenever I wish."

"Oh, hoity-toity!" said the old lady; "impudent as well as everything else. That I should live to see it!—Mary Hopkins, can it be convenient to you to let me have the remainder of my hundred pounds? There wasn't any contract but that I could demand it whenever I wanted it, and it is about convenient to me that I should have it back now. You owe me between thirty and forty pounds, and I'd like, I will say, to see the color of my money. It can't be at all ill-convenient to you to give it to me when you can afford blouses of that quality for your impudent young daughter. Real lace, forsooth! I know it when I see it. We'll say Wednesday week to receive the money, and I will come over in my bath-chair, drawn by Tom, to take it; and I will give Tom a whole shilling for himself the day I get it back. That will be quite convenient to you, Mary Hopkins, won't it?"

"Susy," said poor Mrs. Hopkins, "for goodness' sake, leave the room.— Aunt Church, you know perfectly well that I am not responsible for the naughty ways of that naughty little girl. It's apologize to you she shall, and that before you leave this house. And you know that if you press me now to return the money in full I'll have to sell up the shop, and the children won't have anything to eat, and we'll all be ruined. You wouldn't be as cruel as that to your own flesh and blood, would you?"

"Well, Mary, I only said it to frighten you. I ain't at all a cruel woman. On the contrary, I am kind-hearted; but I can't stand the sauce of that little girl of yours. It's my opinion, Mary, that the lost money of yours is on the back of your Susan, and the sooner you get her to confess her sin the better it will be for us all."

Now, before Mrs. Hopkins had time to utter a word with regard to this preposterous and appalling suggestion of Aunt Church's, there came a loud knock on the little street-door, and, listening in the parlor, the people within could distinctly hear the rustle of silk petticoats.

"Who in the world can that be?" said Mrs. Hopkins.

Tom turned first red and then white, and rushed into the passage. Susy, who had been crying in the shop, also appeared on the scene.

"I'll open the door," said Tom. "Do wipe your eyes, Susy; don't let her see you crying. It's herself, of course."

The knocker was just going to be applied to the door again, when Tom opened it with a flourish, and there stood, waiting on the steps, a very brilliant apparition. This was no less a person than Miss Kathleen O'Hara, in her Sunday best.

Now, Kathleen tried to bear with Mrs. Tennant's advice with regard to her clothes in the week, but on Sundays she was absolutely determined that her love of finery should find full vent. Accordingly, from her store of rich and beautiful garments, she chose the gayest and the most likely to attract attention. On the present occasion she wore a crimson velvet toque. Her jacket was bright blue, and she had a skirt to match. On her neck she wore a rich necklet of flaming beads, which was extremely becoming to her; and thrown carelessly round her neck and shoulders was a boa of white fur, and she had a muff to match. Altogether her radiant dress and radiant face were quite sufficient to dazzle Tom. But Susy pushed past Tom and held out her hand.

"Oh, Kathleen," she said, "I am glad you have come. You'd best come into the shop with me; there's company in the parlor, and I don't think you'd care about it."

Kathleen, of course, was just as pleased to stay in the shop with Susy as to go into any other part of the house; but just then Mrs. Hopkins put a sad, distressed face outside the door, and Mrs. Church's voice was heard in high and grating accents:

"I want to see the person who is talking in the passage."

"Oh! don't go in," said Susy. "It's Aunt Church, and she's dreadful."

"An old lady?" cried Kathleen. "I love old ladies."

She pushed past Susy and made her appearance in the parlor.

Now, Mrs. Church was a person of discernment. She strongly objected to gay dress on the person of little Susy Hopkins; but, as she expressed it, she knew the quality. Had she not lived all her earlier days as housekeeper to a widowed nobleman? Could she ever forget the fine folk she helped to prepare for in his house? Now, Kathleen, standing in the tiny room, had a certain look of wealth and distinction about her. Mrs. Church seemed to sniff the fine quality air in a moment; she even managed to rise from her chair and drop a little curtsy.

"If it weren't for the rheumatics," she said, "I wouldn't make so bold as to sit before you, miss."

"But why shouldn't you? I'm sorry you suffer from rheumatism. May I bring a chair and come and sit near you? Are you Mrs. Hopkins—Susy Hopkins's mother?"

"Indeed, my dear, I'm truly thankful to say I am not. And what may your name be, my sweet young lady?"

"Kathleen O'Hara."

"Oh, dear, but it's a mouthful."

"I'm not English," said Kathleen; "I'm Irish. Do you know, in our country we have old ladies something like you. A good many of them have dresses like you; and they live in little cottages, and we bring them up to the castle and give them good food very, very often. There are twelve of them, and they all live in their tiny cottages close to each other. We make a great fuss about them. They love to come to the castle for tea."

"The castle!" said Mrs. Church, more and more impressed. "I should think they would like it. Who wouldn't like it? It's a very great honor for an old lady to be entertained to her tea in a castle. And so you live in a castle, my bonny young lady?"

"Yes; my father owns Carrigrohane Castle."

"Eh, love! it is a mouthful of a word for me to get round my lips. But never mind; it is but to look at you to see how beautiful and good you are."

"And you are beautiful, too," said Kathleen. "I mean, you are beautiful for an old lady. I love the beauty of the old. But I want to see Mrs. Hopkins, and I want to see Susy. Susy is a great friend of mine."

Mrs. Church opened her eyes very wide; her mouth formed itself into a round O. An eager exclamation was about to burst from her lips, but she restrained herself.

"And a very good little girl Susan Hopkins is," she said, after a moment's pause; "and a particularly great friend of mine, being, so to speak, my grand-niece.—Mary, my dear, call your little girl in."

Mrs. Hopkins, in some trepidation, crossed the room and called to Susy, who was still sulking in the shop.

"My visitor and all," she kept saying. "And I wanted to have her all to myself; I had such a lot to say to her. I never saw anybody quite so horrible as Aunt Church is to-day."

"Never mind, Susy; never mind," said her mother. "The young lady is pleasing your aunt like anything, and she has sent for you."

"Come along in, Susan, this minute," called out Mrs. Church. "Come, my pet, and let's have a little talk."

"Go, Susy, and be quick about it," said her mother.

By the aid of Tom and Mrs. Hopkins, who pushed Susy from behind, she was induced to re-enter the little parlor. There, indeed, all things had changed. Kathleen called to her, made room for her on the same chair, and held her hand. Mrs. Church glanced from one to the other. Only too well did she see the difference between them. One was a rather plain little girl, the daughter of her own relation; the other was a lady, beautiful, stately, and magnificently dressed.

"I know her kind," thought Aunt Church. "I have aired beds for quality of that sort, and I have watched them when they danced in the big ballroom, and watched them, too, when their sweethearts came along, and seen—oh, yes, many, many things have I seen, and many, many things have I heard of those fair young ladies of quality. She belongs to them, and she likes that good-for-nothing, pert little Susy Hopkins! Yet it don't matter to me. Susy shall have my good graces if she has secured those of Miss Kathleen O'Hara."

Accordingly, Mrs. Church changed her tactics. She praised Susy in honeyed words to the visitor.

"A good little girl, miss, and deserving of anything that those who are better off can do for her. She is a great help to her mother.—Mary Hopkins, come nigh, dear. You are very fond of your Susy, aren't you?"

"Of course I am," said Mrs. Hopkins in an affectionate voice.

Susy longed to keep up her anger, but she could not. She was soon smiling and flushing.

"And what a neat little bodice my Susy is wearing!" said Mrs. Church. "And bought with her own hard-earned savings. You wouldn't think so, would you, miss?"

"It gives her great credit," said Kathleen in a calm voice. "I like people to wear smart clothes, don't you, Mrs. Church? If you lived on our estate, I would dress you myself. I love to see our old ladies gaily dressed. On Christmas Day they come to the castle and have dinner as well as tea. It is wonderful how smart they look."

"They are very lucky ladies—very lucky," said Mrs. Church. "They don't wear old bombazine like this, do they?"

"Your dress suits you very well, indeed," said Kathleen; "but my old ladies wear velveteen dresses. They save them, of course. We don't want them to be extravagant; but they always come up to the castle in velveteen dresses, with white caps, and white collars round their necks; and they look very nice. They have a happy time."

"I am sure they have, miss."

"Yes, they have a very happy time. They want for nothing. There was an old lady belonging to our house who left a certain sum of money, and the old ladies get it between them. They get six shillings a week each, and a dear little house to live in. We are obliged to supply them with as much coal as they want, and candles, and a new pair of blankets on the first of every November, and a bale of unbleached calico on the first of May. You can't think how comfortable they are. And then, of course, we throw in a lot of extra things—the black velveteen dresses, and other garments of the same quality."

"It must be a wonderful place to live in. Is it very difficult to get into one of these houses, missy?"

"I don't know. Would you like to come?"

"That I would."

"I'll write to father and ask him if you may."

"Miss, it would be wonderful."

"You'd be very picturesque amongst them," said Kathleen, gazing at Mrs. Church with a critical eye. "And you'd have so much to tell them; because all the rest are Irish, and they have never gone beyond their own country. But you have seen such a lot of life, haven't you?"

"Miss, I can't express all the tales I could tell. I lived with the quality for so long. I lived with Lord Henshel until he died; I was housekeeper there. Oh, I could tell them lots of things."

"It would be very nice if you came over; and I am almost sure there is a cottage vacant," said Kathleen in a contemplative voice. "It seems unfair to give the cottages entirely to Irish people. We might have one English old lady. You would enjoy it; you'd have such a lovely view! And you might keep your own little pig if you liked."

Mrs. Church was not enamored with the idea of keeping a pig.

"Perhaps fowls would do as well," she said. "I have a great fancy for birds, and I am fond of new-laid eggs."

"Fowls will do just as well," said Kathleen, rising now carelessly from her seat. "Well, Mrs. Church, I will write to father and let you know if there is a vacancy; and you could come back with me in the summer, couldn't you?"

"Oh, miss, it would be heaven!"

"Can't we go out and have a walk now, Susy?" said Kathleen, who found the small parlor a little too close for her taste.

Susy rushed upstairs, put on her outdoor jacket and a cheap hat, and, trying to hide the holes in her gloves, ran downstairs. Kathleen, however, was the last girl to notice any want in her companion's wardrobe. She had all her life been so abundantly supplied with clothes that, although she loved to array herself in fine garments, the want of them in others never attracted her attention.

"Susy," she said the moment they got out of doors, "what is the matter with Ruth Craven?"

"With Ruth Craven?" said Susy, who was by no means inclined to waste her time over such an uninteresting person.

"Yes. You must go to her house; you must insist on seeing her, and you must find out and let me know what is wrong. She has written me a most mysterious letter; she has actually asked me to let her withdraw from our society. Ruth, of all people!"

"It is very queer of her," said Susy, "not to be grateful and pleased, for she is no better than the rest of us."

"No better than the rest of you, Susy?" said Kathleen, raising her brows in surprise. "But indeed you are mistaken. The rest of you are not a patch on her. She is my Prime Minister. I can't allow her to resign."

"Oh, well," said Susy, "if you think of her in that way—"

"Of course I think of her in that way, Susy. I like you very much, and I want to be kind to everybody; but to compare you or Mary Rand or Rosy Myers, or any of the others, with Ruth Craven—"

"But she is no better."

"She is a great deal better. She is refined and beautiful. She mustn't go; I can't allow it. But she has written me such a queer letter, and implored and besought of me not to come to see her, that I am forced to accede to her wishes. So you will have to go to her to-night and tell her that she must meet me on my way to school to-morrow. Tell her that I will go a bit of the way towards her house; tell her that I will be at the White Cross Corner at a quarter to nine. You needn't say more. Oh, Susy, it would break my heart if Ruth did not continue to be a member of our society."

"I will do what you want, of course," said Susy. "I'd do anything in the world for you, Kathleen. It was so kind of you to come to see us this afternoon. You will keep your promise and come and have tea with us, won't you?"

"I am very sorry, but I am afraid I can't. I do wish I had a home of my own, and then I'd ask you to have tea with me. But, Susy, how funnily you were dressed to-day, now that I come to think of it! You did look odd. That blouse is too smart for the coarse blue serge skirt you were wearing."

"I know it is; but I can't afford a better skirt. Mother is rather worried about money just now. I know I oughtn't to tell you, but she is. And, do you know, before you came in Aunt Church was so horrid. She got quite dreadful about the blouse, and she tried to make out that I had stolen the money from mother to buy it. Wasn't it awful of her? I can tell you it was a blessing when you came in. You changed her altogether. What did you do to her?"

"Well," said Kathleen, "I rather like old ladies, and she struck me as something picturesque."

"She's a horrid old thing, and not a bit picturesque. I hate her like poison."

"That is very wrong of you, Susy. Some day you will get old yourself, and you won't like people to hate you."

"Well, that's a long way off; I needn't worry about it yet," cried Susy. "I do hate her very much indeed. And then, you know, when you appeared she began to butter me up like anything. I hated that the worst of all."

"I am sorry she is that sort of old lady," said Kathleen after a pause; "but I have promised to try and get her into one of our almshouses. It would be rare fun to have her there."

"But she is not a bit poor. She oughtn't to go into an almshouse if she is rich," said Susy.

"Of course she mustn't go into an almshouse if she is rich; but she doesn't look rich."

"She is quite rich. I think she has saved three hundred pounds. You must call that rich."

"I'm afraid I don't," said Kathleen.

Susy was silent for a moment.

"There are so many different views about riches," she said at last. "I am glad you are so tremendously rich that you think nothing of three hundred pounds. Mother and I often sigh and pine even for *one* pound. For instance, now—But I mustn›t tell you; it would not be right. Perhaps Aunt Church will be a little nicer to me now that you have taken her up. I'll threaten to complain to you if she doesn't behave."

Here Susy laughed merrily.

"That's all right, Susan," said Kathleen. "I must go back now, for I have promised to go for a walk with Mrs. Tennant. No one ever thinks about her as she ought to be thought of; so I have some plans in my head for her, too. Oh, my head is full of plans, and I do wish—yes, I do, Susy—that I could make a lot of people happy."

"You are a splendid girl," said Susy. "I wish there were others like you in the world."

"No, I am not splendid," said Kathleen, her lovely dark eyes looking wistful. "I have heaps and lashons of faults; but I do like to make people happy. I always did since I was a little child. The person I am most anxious about at present is Ruth: I love Ruth so very much. You will be sure to see her this evening, won't you?"

"Sure and certain," said Susy. "I am very much obliged to you, Kathleen; you have made a great difference in my life."

The two girls parted just by the turnstile. Kathleen passed through on her way across the common to Mrs. Tennant's house, and Susy went slowly back to the High Street and the little stationer's shop.

She found Mrs. Church in the act of being deposited in her bath-chair, and Tom, looking proud and flushed, attending on her. Mrs. Hopkins was also standing just outside the shop, putting a wrap round the old lady and tucking her up. When Susy appeared her mother called out to her:

"Come along, you ungrateful girl. Here's Aunt Church going, and wondering why you have deserted her during the last hour."

"That's just like you, Mary Hopkins," said old Mrs. Church. "You scold when there's no occasion to, and you withhold scolding when it's due. I don't blame your daughter Susan for going out with that nice young lady. I am only too pleased to think that any daughter of yours should be taken notice of by a young lady of the Miss Kathleen O'Hara type. She's a splendid girl; and, to tell you the honest truth, none of you are fit for her to touch you with a pair of tongs."

"Dear, dear!" said Susy. "But she has touched me pretty often. I don't think you ought to say nasty things of that sort, Aunt Church, for if you do I may be able to—"

Aunt Church fixed her glittering black eyes on Susan.

"Come here, child," she said.

Susy went up to her somewhat unwillingly.

"My bark is worse than my bite," said old Mrs. Church. "Now look here; if you bring that charming young lady to see me, and give me notice a day or so before—Tom can run over and tell me—if you and Tom and Miss Kathleen O'Hara would come and have tea at my place, why, it's the freshest of the plumcakes we'd have, not the stalest. And the microscope should be out handy and in order, and with some prepared plates that my poor husband used, which I have never shown to anybody from the time of his death. I have a magnifying-glass, too, that I can put into the microscope; it will make you see the root of a hair on your head. And I will—Whisper, Susy!"

Susy somewhat unwillingly bent forward.

"I will give you five shillings. You'd like to trim your hat to match that handsome blouse, wouldn't you?"

Susy's eyes could not help dancing.

"Five shillings all to yourself; and I won't press your mother about the installment which was due to me yesterday. I'll manage without it somehow. But I want to see that beautiful young lady in my cottage, and you will get the money when you bring her. That's all. You are a queer little girl, and not altogether to my taste, but you are no fool."

Susy stood silent. She put her hand on the moth-eaten cushion of the old bath-chair, bent forward, and looked into Mrs. Church's face.

"Will you take back the words you said?"

"Will I take back what?"

"If not the words, at least the thought? Will you say that you know that I got this blouse honestly?"

"Oh, yes, child! I'd quite forgotten all about it. Now just see that you do what I want; and the sooner the better, you understand. And, oh, Susy, mum's the word with regard to me being well off. I ain't, I can tell you; I am quite a poor body. But I could do a kindness to you and your mother if—if certain things were to come to pass. Now that's about all.—Pull away, Tom, my boy. I have a rosy apple which shall find its way into your pocket if you take me home in double-quick time."

Tom pulled with a will; the little bath-chair creaked and groaned, and Mrs. Church nodded her wise old head and she was carried over the country roads.

Meanwhile Susy entered the house with her mother.

"What a blessing," said Mrs. Hopkins, "that that pretty young lady happened to call! I never saw such a change in any one as what took place in your aunt after she had seen her."

"Well, mother, you know what it is all about," said Susy. "Aunt Church wants to get into one of those almshouses."

"Just like her—stingy old thing!" said Mrs. Hopkins.

"I don't want her to get in, I can tell you, mother; and when Kathleen and I were out I told Kathleen that she was a great deal too rich. She asked me what her means were, and I said I believed she has three hundred pounds put by. Now, mother, don't you call that riches?"

"Three hundred pounds!" said Mrs. Hopkins. "That depends, child. To some it is wealth; to others it is a decent competence; to others, again, it is poverty."

"Kathleen didn't think much of it, mother."

"Well," said Mrs. Hopkins, "I have notions in my head. Maybe this very thing can be turned to good for us; there's no saying. I think if your aunt was sure and certain to get into one of those almshouses she might do a good turn to you, Susy; and she's sure and certain to help Tom a little. But there! we can't look into the future. I am tired out with one thing and another. Susan, my dear child, where did you get that beautiful pale-blue blouse?"

"I didn't get it through theft, mother, if that's what you are thinking of. I got it honestly, and I am not obliged to tell; and what's more, I won't tell."

Mrs. Hopkins sighed.

"Dear, dear!" she said, and she sat down in the easy-chair which Mrs. Church had occupied and stared into the fire.

"I am not nearly as low-spirited as I was," she said after a pause. "If Miss Kathleen will do something for Aunt Church, it stands to reason that Aunt Church won't be hard on us."

Susy made no answer to this. She stood quiet for a minute or two, and then she went slowly upstairs. She removed the beautiful blouse and put on a common one. She then wrapped herself in an old waterproof cloak—for the sunshiny morning had developed into an evening of thick clouds and threatening rain—and went downstairs.

"Where in the world are you going?" said her mother in a fretful tone. "I did think you'd sit quietly with me and learn your collect. If you are going out, it ought to be to church. I don't see what call you have to be going anywhere else on Sunday evening."

"I want to see Ruth Craven. Don't keep me, please; it is very important."

"But I don't know who Ruth Craven is."

"Oh, mother, I thought every one knew her. She is the very, very pretty little granddaughter of old Mr. Craven, who lives in that cottage close to the station."

"A handsome old man, too," said Mrs. Hopkins, "but I confess I don't know anything about him."

"Well, he and his old wife have got this one beautiful grandchild, and she has joined the foundationers at the Great Shirley School. Miss Kathleen O'Hara has taken up with her as well as with me and other foundation girls, and instead of having a miserable, dull, down-trodden life, we are extremely likely to have the best life of any girls in the school. Anyhow, I have a message for Ruth and I promised to deliver it."

"All right, child; don't be longer away than you can help."

Susy left the house. The distance from her mother's shop to the Cravens' cottage was a matter of ten minutes' quick walking. She soon reached her destination, walked up the little path which led to the tiny cottage, and tapped with her fingers on the door. The door was opened for her by old Mrs. Craven. Mrs. Craven was in her Sunday best, and looked a very beautiful and almost aristocratic old lady.

"Do you want my grandchild?" she said, observing Susy's size and dress.

"Yes; is she within?" asked Susy.

"No, dear; she has gone to church. Would you like to wait in for her, or would you rather go and meet her? She has gone to St. James the Less, the church just around the corner; you know it?"

"Yes, I know it," said Susy.

"They'll be coming out now," said Mrs. Craven, looking up at the eight-day clock which stood in the passage. "If you go and stand by the principal entrance, you are safe to see her."

"Thank you," said Susy.

"You are sure you wouldn't rather wait in the house?"

"No, really. Mother expects me back. My name is Susan Hopkins. My mother keeps the stationer's shop in the High Street."

"To be sure," said Mrs. Craven gently. "I know the shop quite well."

Susy said good-bye, and then stepped down the little path. What a humble abode the prime favorite, Ruth Craven, lived in! Susy's own home was a palace in comparison. Ruth lived in a cottage which was little better than a workman's cottage.

"There can't be more than two bedrooms upstairs," thought Susy. "And I wonder if there is a sitting-room? Certainly there can't be more than one. The old lady looked very nice; but, of course, she is quite a common person. I should love to be Prime Minister to Kathleen O'Hara. And why should there be such a fuss made about Ruth? I only wish the post was mine— shouldn't I do a lot! Couldn't I help mother and Tom and all of us? And there is that stupid little Ruth—oh, dear! oh, dear! Well, I suppose I must give her the message."

She hurried her steps as these last thoughts came to her, and presently she stood outside the principal entrance of the little church. St. James the Less was by no means remarkable for beauty of architecture or adornment of any sort; nevertheless the vicar was a man of great eloquence and earnestness, and in the evenings it was the custom for the little church to be packed.

By-and-by the sermon came to an end, the voluntary rolled forth from the organ, and the crowd of worshippers poured out. Susy stretched out her hand and clutched that of a slim girl who was following in the train of people.

"Ruth, it is me. I have something to say to you."

Ruth's face, until Susy touched her, had been looking like a piece of heaven itself, so calm and serene were the eyes, and so beautiful the expression which lingered round her lips. Now she seemed to awaken and pull herself together. She did not attempt to avoid Susy, but slipping out of the crowd of people who were leaving the church, she found herself by the girl's side.

"Come just a little way home with me," said Susy. "It won't take me long to say what I want to say."

She linked her hand in her companion's as she spoke. Yes, there was little doubt of it, Ruth was lovable. One forgot her low birth, her low surroundings, when one looked at her. Susy had heard of those few people of rare character and rare natures who are, as it is expressed, "Nature's ladies." There are Nature's gentlemen as well, and Nature's ladies and Nature's gentlemen are above mere external circumstances; they are above the mere money's worth or the mere accident of birth. Now, Ruth belonged to this rare class, and Susy, without quite understanding it, felt it. She forgot the humble little house, the lack of rooms, and the workmanlike appearance of the whole place. She said in a deferential tone:

"I have come to you, from Kathleen O'Hara. You have done something which has distressed her very much. She wants you to meet her to-morrow at the White Cross Corner on your way to school; she wants you to be there at a quarter to nine. That is all, Ruth. You will be sure to attend? I promised Kathleen most faithfully that I would deliver her message. She is very unhappy about something. I don't know what you have done to vex her."

"But I do," said Ruth. "And I can't help going on vexing her."

"But what is it?" said Susy, whose curiosity was suddenly awakened. "You might tell me. I wish you would."

"I can't tell you, Susan; it has nothing to do with you. It is a matter between Kathleen and myself. Very well, I will meet her. There is no use in shirking things. Good-night, Susan. It was good of you to come and give me Kathleen's message."

CHAPTER XIV.
RUTH RESIGNS THE PREMIERSHIP.

The next morning Kathleen O'Hara was downstairs betimes. She ran into the kitchen and suggested to Maria that she should help her to toast the bread. Maria, who was somewhat lazy, and who had already begun to appreciate Kathleen's extreme good-nature, handed her the toasting-fork and pointed to a heap of bread which lay cut and ready for toasting on the deal table in the center of the kitchen.

"Dear me, Miss Kathleen!" she said; "if only Miss Alice was as good-natured as you, why, the house would go on wheels."

"I often helped the servants at home," said Kathleen. "Why isn't Alice good-natured?"

"She's made contrary, I expect, miss."

"Cut on the cross, I call it," said cook, who came forward at this juncture and offered a chair to Kathleen.

"Well, if that's the case I'm sorry for her," said Kathleen. "It must be very unpleasant to feel sort of peppery-and-salty and cross-grained all the time."

"It isn't what you ever feel, miss," said cook with an admiring glance at the young lady.

Kathleen fixed her deep-blue roguish eyes on the good woman's face.

"No," she said, "I don't think I am cross-grained. By the way, cook, wouldn't you like a black silk apron embroidered with violets to wear when you have done all your dirty work in the kitchen?"

"Cooks don't wear black silk aprons embroidered with violets," was the good woman's answer.

"But this cook might, if a nice Irish girl, who has plenty of money, gave it to her. I have it in the bottom of my trunk. I asked Aunt Katie O'Flynn to send it to me for your mistress, but your mistress doesn't care for it. I will give it to you, cook.—And, Maria, I've got a little toque for you. It is sky-blue with forget-me-nots. Have you a young man, Maria? Most girls have, haven't they? Wouldn't you like to walk out with him in a sky-blue toque trimmed with forget-me-nots?"

"It puts me all in a flutter to think of it, miss," said Maria. "I am sure a sweeter young lady never came into this house."

Kathleen chatted on to the retainers, as she called cook and Maria, until she had toasted enough bread. She then went into the dining-room. Alice was there, looking pale and headachy. The day was a very cold one, and the fire was by no means bright. Kathleen's intensely rosy cheeks—for the fire had considerably scorched them—attracted Alice's attention.

"I do wish you wouldn't do servant's work," she said. "You annoy me terribly by the way you go on."

"Oh, don't be annoyed, darling," said Kathleen softly. "Just regard me as a necessary evil. You see, Alice, however cross you are, I'd have the others all on my side. There's your mother and David and Ben and the two servants. It isn't worth while, Alice. If they all like me, why shouldn't you?"

Alice made no reply. Kathleen stood still for a moment; then she glanced at the clock. It was a quarter past eight. She must be out of the house in a little over a quarter of an hour if she was to meet Ruth Craven at the White Cross Corner. She sat down to the table, helped herself to a piece of toast, and spread some butter on it.

"A cup of tea, please, Alice," she said.—"Oh, what letters are those? Any for me? David, if you give me a letter I'll—I'll love you ever so much. Ah, two! Dave, you are a treasure; you are a darling; you are everything that is exquisite."

It was Alice's place to pour out the tea. She poured some out now, very unwillingly, for Kathleen, who drew the cup towards her, stirred it absently, and began to read her letters. Presently she uttered a little shriek.

"It is from Aunt Katie O'Flynn, and she is crossing the Channel, the darling colleenoge. She is coming to London, and she wants me to see her. Oh, golloptious! What fun I shall have! Boys, aren't you delighted? It was Aunt Katie O'Flynn who sent me that wonderful trunk of clothes. Won't she give us a time now? I declare I scarcely know whether I'm on my head or my heels.—Alice, you'd best make yourself agreeable and join in the fun, for I can assure you it's theaters and concerts and teas and dinners and—oh! shopping, and every conceivable thing that can delight the heart of man or woman, boy or girl, that will be our portion while Aunt Katie—the duck, the darling, the treasure!—is in London. Let me see; what hotel is she going to? Oh, the Métropole. Where is the Métropole?"

"In Northumberland Avenue. But, of course, we are not going up to London," said Alice. "We are only schoolgirls. We are at school and must mind our lessons. I am trying for my scholarship, and I mean to get it. And I don't suppose, even if your aunt is coming at a most inopportune time, that she is going to upset everything."

"That remains to be proved," said Kathleen. "I am not going to have Aunt Katie so close to me without having my bit of fun. Oh, dear, dear! look at the time. I must be off."

"Why are you going so early? It is only half-past eight."

"I have business, darling—a friend to meet. Have you any objection?"

Kathleen did not wait for Alice's answer. She dashed upstairs, and on the first landing she met Mrs. Tennant, who had been suffering from headache, and was in consequence a little late for breakfast.

"Mrs. Tennant," shouted Kathleen, "I have the top of the morning as far as news is concerned. It is herself that is crossing the briny. She'll be in London to-night. Oh, did you ever hear of anything quite so scrumptious? But what's the matter, dear?"

"Kathleen, I wish you wouldn't wear that really good dress going to school."

"Is it my old lavender, and my old satin blouse?" said Kathleen, looking down at herself with a momentary glance. "Ah, then, my dear tired one, it isn't dresses I'll be thinking of when Aunt Katie is in London. She'll get me more than I can wear. She'll fig you all out, every one of you, if you like— you and Alice and David and Ben and cook and Maria. Maria is keeping company, she tells me, and would like a few fine clothes—naturally, the creature! Well, Mrs. Tennant, it's herself that is crossing, as I said; even now she is in the big steamer, coming nearer and nearer to England. Shan't we have fun when she arrives?"

"You haven't told me who it is yet, dear."

"Oh, darling, you haven't been listening. It is the dear woman who sent me the box full of new clothes—Aunt Katie O'Flynn, at your service. But there! I must be off. I'll think of it all day, and it will make me so happy."

Kathleen dashed away to her own room, put on her outdoor things, and a moment or two later was running as fast as she could in the direction of the White Cross Corner. There she saw a silent, grave-looking girl, very quietly dressed, standing waiting for her.

"Here I am," said Kathleen; "and here you stand, Ruth. And now, what have you got to say for yourself?"

"I am sorry," said Ruth. "I thought when you sent Susy to me with your message that I might as well come here this morning; but I haven't changed my mind—not a bit of it."

Kathleen's eyes, always extraordinarily dark for blue eyes, now grew almost black. A flash of real anger shot through them.

"Don't you think it is rather mean," she said, "to give me up when you promised to belong to me—to give me up altogether and to go with those dreadful, proud paying girls?"

"It isn't that," said Ruth, "and you know it. It is just this: I can't belong to two sides. Cassandra Weldon offers me an advantage which I dare not throw away. It is most essential to me to win the sixty-pounds scholarship. If I win it I shall be properly educated. When I leave school I'll be able to take the position my dear father, had he lived, would have wished for me. I shall be able to support granny and grandfather. You see for yourself, Kathleen, that I can't refuse it. It isn't a question of choice; it is a question of necessity. I love you. Kathleen—I will always love you and be faithful to you—but I can't give up the scholarship."

"I don't want you to," said Kathleen; "but why shouldn't you belong to me and yet take the scholarship? I don't want you to be with me all the time. You can go to that horrible, detestable girl when it is necessary, and have your odious coach to post you up. But I want you more than anybody else. Don't you know how I love you? Can't you do both? Think it over, Ruth."

"I have thought it over, and I can't do it. I would if I could, but it isn't to be done. It wouldn't be right to you, nor right to Cassandra."

"Well, I think you are very mean; I think I hate you."

Kathleen turned aside. She was impulsive, high-spirited, and defiant, but where her passions were concerned her heart was very soft. She burst into tears now and flung her arms around Ruth's neck.

"I like a lot of people," she said—"I like Mrs. Tennant, and even Susy, although she's not up to much, and two or three other girls—but I only *love* you. In the whole of England I only love you, and you are going to give me up.»

"No; I will still be your friend."

"But you have refused to join my society; you have refused to belong to the Wild Irish Girls."

"I can't help myself."

"But you promised."

"I know I did. I made a mistake. Kathleen, there is no help for it. I shall love you even if I don't belong to the society. Now there is nothing more to be said."

Ruth disentangled herself from Kathleen's embrace, and putting wings to her feet, ran in the direction of the school. Kathleen stood just where she had left her; over her face was passing a rapid and curious change.

"Do I love her any longer?" she said to herself. "Oh, I think—I think I love her still. But she has slighted me. She will be sorry some day. Oh, dear! The only girl in the whole of England that I love has slighted me. She has thrown ridicule upon me. She said that she would be my Prime Minister, and she has resigned everything for that horrible Cassandra. She will be sorry yet; I know she will."

CHAPTER XV.
THE SCHOLARSHIP: TROUBLE IS BREWING.

Over some of the girls of the Great Shirley School there passed that morning a curious wave of excitement. Those girls who had joined Kathleen's society were almost now more or less in a state of tension. Once a week they were to meet in the quarry; once a week, whatever the weather, in the dead of night, they were to meet in this sequestered spot. They knew well that if they were discovered they would run a very great chance of being expelled from the school; for although they were day scholars, yet integrity of conduct was essential to their maintaining their place in that great school which gave them so liberal an education, in some cases without any fees, in all other cases with very small ones. One of the great ideas of the school was to encourage brave actions, unselfish deeds, nobility of mind. Those girls who possessed any talent or any specially strong characteristic had every chance offered to them in the Great Shirley School; their futures were more or less assured, for the governors of the school had powers to give grants to the clever girls, to award scholarships for which all might compete, and to encourage industry, honesty, and charitable ideas as far as possible.

Kathleen, when she entered the school and started her society, had not the slightest idea that, while she was trying to help the foundationers, she was really leading them into very grave mischief. But several of the foundationers themselves knew this; nevertheless the fun of the whole thing, the particular fascination which Kathleen herself exercised over her followers, kept them her undeniable slaves, and not for the world would any of them have left her now that they had sworn fealty to her cause. So Kathleen had thought when she left the house that morning; but as she entered the school she knew that one girl, and that the girl whom she most cared for, had decided to choose the thorny path which led far from Kathleen and her company.

"In addition to everything else, she is quite mean," thought the little girl, and during that morning's lessons she occupied herself far more in flashing angry glances in the direction of Ruth one minute, and at Cassandra the next, than in attending to what she was about. Kathleen had been given much by Nature. Her father was a very rich man; she had been brought up with great freedom, but also with certain bold liberal ideas as regards the best in life and conduct. She was a very beautiful girl, and she was warm-hearted and amiable. As for her talents, she had a certain charm which does more for a woman than any amount of ordinary ability; and she had a passionate and great love for music. Kathleen's musical genius was already spoken of with much approbation by the rest of the school. The girls used to ask her to improvise. Kathleen could improvise in almost any style, in almost any fashion. She could make the piano sob with her heart-rendering notes; and again she could bring forth music clear and fairy-like. Again she would lead the tender and solemn strains of the march; and again she would dance over the keys so lightly, so ravishingly, that the girls kept time with their feet to her notes. The music mistress was anxious that Kathleen should try for a musical scholarship, and she had some ideas of doing so herself. But to-day she felt cross, and even her music was at fault.

"I can't do it," she said, looking Miss Spicer full in the face. "It means such drudgery, and I don't believe I'd play a bit better if I did."

"That is certainly not the case, Kathleen," said Miss Spicer. "Knowledge must be of assistance. You have great talent; if you add to that real musical knowledge you can do almost anything."

"But I don't think I much care to. I can play on the piano to imitate any birds that ever sung at home, and father loves that. I can play all the dead-marches to make mother cry, and I can play—oh, such dance music for Aunt Katie O'Flynn! It doesn't matter that I should know more, does it?"

"I can't agree with you. It would be a very great pleasure to me if I saw you presented with a musical scholarship."

"Would it?" said Kathleen, glancing at the thin and careworn face of the music teacher.

"You don't know what it would mean to me," answered Miss Spicer. "It is seldom that one has the pleasure of teaching real talent, and I can't say how refreshing it is to me to hear you play as you do. But I want you to improve; I want you to be a credit to me."

"I'd like to please you, of course," said Kathleen. She spoke gently, and then she added: "But there is only one piano at the Tennants', and that is in the drawing-room, and Alice or the boys or Mrs. Tennant are always there. I have not many opportunities to practice."

"I live in the same terrace," said Miss Spicer eagerly, "and my piano is hardly ever used. If you only would come and make use of it. There is a fire in my sitting-room, and you could come at any hour whenever you have a fancy. Will you? It would be a great pleasure to me."

"You are very kind. Yes, I will come."

Kathleen bent towards the music mistress and, somewhat to that lady's astonishment, printed a kiss on her forehead. The kiss went right down into Miss Spicer's somewhat frozen heart.

Immediately after school that day Cassandra held out her hand to Ruth. Ruth went up to her gravely.

"Well, Ruth," she said, "have you decided? I hope you have. You told me you would let me know to-day."

"I have, Cassandra," said Ruth.

Kathleen, who was standing not far away, suddenly darted forward and stood within a foot of the two girls.

"Have you really decided, Ruth?" she said. Her tone was imperious. Ruth felt her gentle heart beat high. She turned and looked with dignity first at Kathleen and then at Cassandra.

"I will join you, Cassandra," she said.—"Kathleen, I told you this morning what my decision was."

"And I hate you!" said Kathleen. She tossed her head and walked away.

Cassandra waited until she was out of hearing.

"You look very pale, dear Ruth," she said. "Come home with me, won't you?"

Ruth did not speak. Cassandra laid her hand on her arm.

"Why, you are trembling," she said. "What has that horrid girl done to you?"

"Nothing—nothing."

"But she has."

"Please, Cassie, she is not horrid."

"Oh, well, we won't discuss her. She is not my sort. Won't you come and have lunch with me, and we can arrange everything? You are going to take advantage of mother's offer?"

"I can't help myself. It is much too good to be refused. It means—I can't tell you what it means to me, Cassie. If I can only get a scholarship I shall be able to help grandfather. And yet—I must tell you the truth—I was very nearly declining it."

"I don't think I should ever have spoken to you again if you had."

"Even so, I was very nearly declining it; for you know I could not have accepted your offer and been friends with Kathleen O'Hara in the way she wants me to be. Now I am very fond of Kathleen, and if I could please myself I would retain her friendship. But you know, grandfather has lost some more money. He heard about it two nights ago, and that made me make up my mind. Of course I love you, Cassie. I have loved you ever since I came to the school. You have been so very, very kind to me. But had I the choice I would have stayed with Kathleen."

"Well, it is all a mystery to me," said Cassandra. "I don't like Kathleen; I will frankly say so. I don't think she has a good influence in the school. That sort of very rich popular girl always makes mischief. It is far better for the school not to have anybody like her in its midst. She has the power of attracting people, but she has also the power of making enemies. It is my opinion she will get into very serious trouble before she leaves Great Shirley School. I shall be sorry for her, of course."

"But what do you mean? What sort of trouble can she get into?"

"There are whispers about her that I don't quite understand. But if it were known that she does lead other girls astray, she would be had up before the governors, and then she would not find herself in a very pleasant position."

Ruth did not say anything. Her face turned white. Cassandra glanced at her, uttered a quick sigh, and resumed:

"Whether you like it or not, I am glad you are out of the whole thing. I should hate you to get into trouble. You are so clever, and so different from the others, that you are certain to succeed. And now let us hurry home. I must tell you all about our scheme. You must come to me every day; Miss Renshaw will be with us each evening from six to seven. Oh! you don't know how happy you are making me."

Ruth smiled and tried to look cheerful.

Mrs. Weldon came out to meet the two girls as they entered the pretty little cottage. Her face was smiling.

"Ah, Cassandra!" she said, "now you will be happy."

"Yes; Ruth has accepted our offer."

"Indeed I have, Mrs. Weldon," said Ruth; "and I scarcely know how to thank you."

"Come in, dear, and have some dinner.—Cassandra, I have just heard from Miss Renshaw, and she is coming this afternoon.—You can either stay, Ruth, when dinner is over, or come back again."

"I will come back," said Ruth. "Granny is not very well, and I ought not to have left her, even to have dinner here; but I couldn't help myself."

Cassandra brought her friend into the house. They had a pleasant meal together, and Ruth tried to forget that she had absolutely quarrelled with Kathleen, and that Kathleen's heart was half-broken on her account.

But Kathleen herself was determined not to give way to any real feelings of misery on account of Ruth's desertion.

"I have no time to think about it," she said to herself.

When she returned to the house she found a telegram waiting for her. She tore it open. It was from Aunt Katie O'Flynn:

"I have arrived. Come and have dinner with me to-night at the Métropole, and bring any friend you like."

"What a lark!" thought Kathleen. "And what a chance for Ruth if only she had been different! Oh, dear! I suppose I must ask Alice to come with me."

"Whom is your telegram from, dear?" asked Mrs. Tennant, coming up to her at that moment.

Alice was standing in the dining-room devouring a book of Greek history. She held it close to her eyes, which were rather short-sighted.

"It's from Aunt Katie O'Flynn. She has come, the darling!" said Kathleen. "She wants me to go to London to dine with her to-night. Of course I'll go.—- You will come with me, won't you, Alice? She says I am to bring some one."

"No, I can't come," said Alice; "and for that matter no more can you. It takes quite thirty-five minutes to get to Charing Cross, and then you have to get to the Métropole. We girls are not allowed to go to London by ourselves."

"As if that mattered."

"It matters to me, if it does not to you. Anyhow, here is a note for you. It is from Miss Ravenscroft, our head-mistress. I rather fancy that will decide matters."

Kathleen tore open the note which Alice had handed to her. She read the following words:

"Dear Miss O'Hara,—I should be glad if you would come round to see me at six o'clock this evening. I have something of importance to say to you."

"What can she mean?" said Kathleen. "I scarcely know Miss Ravenscroft. I just spoke to her the first day I went to the school."

"She has asked me too. What can it be about?" said Alice.

"Then you can take a message from me; I am not going," said Kathleen.

"What?" cried Alice. "I don't think even you will dare to defy the head-mistress. Why, my dear Kathleen, you will never get over it. This is madness.—Mother, do speak to her."

"What is it, dear?" said Mrs. Tennant, coming forward.

Alice explained.

"And Kathleen says she won't go?"

"Of course I won't go, dear Mrs. Tennant. On the contrary, you and I will go together to see Aunt Katie O›Flynn. She is my aunt, and I wouldn›t slight her for all the world. She›d never forgive me.—You can tell Miss Ravenscroft, Alice, that my aunt has come to see me, and that I have been obliged to go to town. You can manage it quite easily.»

Kathleen did not wait for any further discussion, but ran out of the room.

"I do wish, mother, you'd try and persuade her," said Alice. "I am sure, whatever her father may be, he can't want her to come to school here to get into endless scrapes. There is some mystery afoot, and Miss Ravenscroft has got wind of it. I know she has, because I have heard it from one or two of the girls."

"But what mystery? What can you mean?" said Mrs. Tennant.

"I don't know myself," said Alice, "but it has something to do with Kathleen and a curious influence she has over the foundation girls. I know Kathleen isn't popular with the mistresses."

"That puzzles me," said Mrs. Tennant, "for I never met a more charming girl."

"I know you think so; but, you see, mere charm of manner doesn't go down in a great school like ours. Of course I am sorry for her, and I quite understand that she doesn't want to disappoint her aunt, but she ought to come with me; she ought, mother. I haven't the slightest influence over her, but you have. I don't think she would willingly do anything to annoy you."

"Well, I will see what I can do. She is a wayward child. I am sorry that Miss Ravenscroft expects her to go to see her to-day, as she is so devoted to her aunt and would enjoy seeing her."

Mrs. Tennant left the room, and Alice went steadily on with her preparations. She wondered why her mother did not come back. Presently she looked at the clock. It wanted a quarter to six.

"Dear me! I must go upstairs now and fetch Kathleen. She will have to tidy herself, and I must try to persuade her not to put on anything *outre*," thought Alice.

She rushed upstairs. She opened the bedroom door. The bedroom was empty.

"Where can she be?" thought Alice.

There were signs of Kathleen's late presence in the shape of a tie flung on the bed, a hat tossed by its side, an open drawer revealing brushes and combs, laces and colored ties, and no end of gloves, handkerchiefs, &c.; but not the girl herself.

"She really is a great trial," thought Alice. "I suppose she has gone with mother to town. I wonder mother yields to her. Kathleen will get into a serious scrape at the school, that's certain."

Alice went to her own part of the room, which was full of order and method. She opened a drawer, substituted a clean collar for the one she had been wearing during the day, brushed out her satin-brown hair neatly, put on her sailor-hat and a small black coat, snatched up a pair of gloves, and ran downstairs. On the way she met Mrs. Tennant.

"Oh, mother," cried the girl, "where is Kathleen? I didn't find her in her room, and I wondered what had become of her."

"Where is she?" said Mrs. Tennant. "I thought she was going with you. I had a long talk with her. She did not say much, but she seemed quite gentle and not at all cross. I kissed her and said that I would go with her to London to see her aunt to-morrow, or that she might ask Miss O'Flynn here."

"I am sorry you did that, mother."

"Well, darling, it seemed the only thing to do; and the child took it very well. Isn't she going with you? She said she wouldn't be at all long getting ready."

"She is not in her room, mother. I can't imagine what has happened to her."

Mrs. Tennant ran upstairs in some alarm. Kathleen had certainly flown. The disordered state of the room gave evidence of this; and then on a nearer view Mrs. Tennant found a tiny piece of paper pinned in conventional fashion to the pin-cushion. She took it up and read:

"Gone to London to Aunt Katie O'Flynn."

"Well, she is a naughty girl. How troublesome! I must follow her, of course," said Mrs. Tennant. "Really this is provoking."

"Oh, mother, it isn't worth while fretting about her. She is quite hopeless," said Alice. "But there! I must make the best of it to Miss Ravenscroft, only I am sure she will be very angry with Kathleen."

Alice flew to the school. She was met by a teacher, who asked her where she was going.

"To see Miss Ravenscroft," replied Alice. "I had a note asking me to call at six o'clock. Do you know anything about it, Miss Purcell?"

"Perhaps she wants to question you about Miss O'Hara. There is some commotion in the school in connection with her. She seems to be displeasing some of those in authority."

"Kathleen had a note too, asking her to call."

"Then it must be about her. But where is she? Isn't she going with you?"

Alice threw up her hands.

"Don't ask me," she said; "perhaps the less I say the better. I am late as it is. I won't keep you now, Miss Purcell."

Alice ran the rest of the way. She entered the great school, and knocked at the front entrance. This door was never opened except to the head-mistress and her visitors. After a time an elderly servant answered her summons.

"I am Alice Tennant," said the young girl, "and I have come at Miss Ravenscroft's request to see her."

"Oh yes, miss, certainly. She said she was expecting two young ladies."

"Well, I am one of them. Can you let her know?"

"Step in here, miss."

Alice was shown into a small waiting-room. A moment later the servant returned.

"Will you follow me, miss?" she said.

They went down a passage and entered a brightly and cheerfully furnished sitting-room. There was a fire in the grate, and electric light made all things as bright as day. A tall lady with jet-black hair combed back from a massive forehead, and beautifully dressed in long, clinging garments of deep purple, stood on the hearth. Round her neck was a collar of old Mechlin lace; she wore cuffs of the same with ruffles at the wrist. Her hands were small and white. She had one massive diamond ring on the third finger. This lady was the great Miss Ravenscroft, the head of the school, one of the most persuasive, most fascinating, and most influential teachers in the whole realm of girlhood. Her opinion was asked by anxious mothers and fathers and guardians. The girls whom she took into her own house and helped with her own counsel were thought the luckiest in England. Even Alice, who was reckoned a good girl as good girls go, had never before come in personal contact with Miss Ravenscroft. The head-mistress superintended the management of every girl in the school, but she did not show herself except when she read prayers in her deep musical voice morning after morning, or when something very special occurred. Miss Ravenscroft did not smile when Alice appeared, nor did she hold out her hand. She bowed very slightly and then dropped into a chair, and pointed to another for the girl to take.

"You are Alice Tennant?"

"Yes, madam."

"You are in the upper fifth?"

"Yes," said Alice again.

"I have had very good reports of you from Miss Purcell and Miss Dove and others; you will probably be in the sixth next year."

"I hope so; it will be a very great delight to me."

Alice trembled and colored, looked down, and then looked up again. Miss Ravenscroft was regarding her with kindly eyes. Hers was a sort of veiled face; she seldom gave way to her feelings. Part of her power lay in her potential attitudes, in the possibilities which she seldom, except on very rare occasions, exhibited to their fullest extent. Alice felt that she had only approached the extreme edge of Miss Ravenscroft's nature. Miss Ravenscroft was silent for a minute; then she said gently:

"And your friend, Kathleen O'Hara? I wrote to her also. Why isn't she here?"

"I am very sorry indeed," said Alice; "it isn't my fault."

"We won't talk of faults, if you please, Alice Tennant. I asked you why your friend isn't here."

"I must explain. She isn't my friend. She lives with mother—I mean she boards with mother."

"Why isn't she here?"

"She got your letter. I suppose she didn't understand; she is so new to schools. She is not coming."

"Not coming? But I commanded."

"I know, I tried to explain, but she is new to school and—and spoilt."

"She must be."

Miss Ravenscroft was silent for a minute.

"We will defer the subject of Kathleen O'Hara until I have the pleasure of speaking to her," she said then. "But now, as you are here, I should like to ask you a few questions."

"Yes."

"What you say, Alice Tennant, will not be—I speak in judicial phrase"—here Miss Ravenscroft gave vent to a faint smile—"used against you. I should like to have what information you can give me. There is a disturbing element in this school. Do you know anything about it?"

"Nothing absolutely."

"But you agree with me that there is a disturbing element?"

"I am afraid I do."

"It has been traced to Kathleen O'Hara."

Alice was silent.

"It is influencing a number of girls who can be very easily impressed, and who form a very important part of this school. Special arrangements were made more a hundred years ago by the founders of the school that they should receive an education in every way calculated to help them in life; the influence to which I allude undermines these good things. It must therefore be put a stop to, and the first way to put a stop to anything of the sort is to discover all about it. It is necessary that I should know all that is to be known with regard to the unruly condition of the foundationers of the Great Shirley School. The person who can doubtless tell me most is Kathleen O'Hara. The mere fact of her defying my authority and refusing to come to see me when she is summoned, shows that she is insubordinate as far as this school is concerned."

Alice sat very still.

"She has not chosen to appear, and I wish to take quick and instant steps. Can you help me?"

"I could," said Alice—"that is, of course, I live in the same house with her—but I would much rather not."

"You will in no way be blamed, but it is absolutely essential that you should give me your assistance. I am authorized to ask for it. I shall see

Kathleen O'Hara, but from what you say, and from what I have heard, I am greatly shocked to have to say it, but I think it possible that she may not be induced to tell the exact truth. If, therefore, you notice anything—if anything is brought to your ears which I ought to know—you must come to me at once. Do not suppose that I want you to be a spy in this matter, but what is troubling the school must be discovered, and within the next few days. Now you understand. Remember that what I have said to you is said in the interest of the school, and absolutely behind closed doors. You are not to repeat it to anybody. You can go now, Alice Tennant. Personally I am pleased with you. I like your manner; I hear good accounts of your attention to lessons. In pleasing me you will please the governors of the school, and doubtless be able to help yourself and your mother, a most worthy lady, in the long run."

"I am very much obliged to you," said Alice. "You have spoken kind words to me; but what you have set me to do is not at all to my taste. It seems scarcely fair, for I must say that I don't like Kathleen. She and I have never got on. It seems scarcely fair that I should be the one to run her to earth."

"The fairness or the unfairness of the question is not now to be discussed," said Miss Ravenscroft.

She rose as she spoke.

"You are unfortunately in the position of her most intimate friend," she continued, "for you and she live in the same house. Regard what you have to do as an unpleasant duty, and don't consider yourself in any way responsible for being forced into the position which one would not, as a rule, advocate. The simplest plan is to get the girl herself to make a full confession to me; but in any case, you understand, *I must know.*"

CHAPTER XVI.
KATHLEEN TAKES RUTH TO TOWN.

When Kathleen ran upstairs her heart was bubbling over with the first real fierce anger she had almost ever felt in her life. She was a spirited, daring girl, but she also had a sweet temper. Now her anger was roused. Her heart beat fast; she clenched one of her hands.

"Oh, if I had Alice here, wouldn't I give it to her?" she said to herself. "If I had that detestable Miss Ravenscroft here, wouldn't I give her a piece of my mind? How dare she order me about? Am I not Kathleen O'Hara of Carrigrohane? Is not my father a sort of king in old Ireland? And what is she? I'll prove to her that I defy her. I will go to see Aunt Katie O'Flynn; nothing shall keep me back."

Carried away by the wild wave of passion which consumed her, Kathleen dressed hastily for her expedition. She was indifferent now as to what she wore. She put on the first head-dress which came to hand, buttoned a rough, shabby-looking jacket over her velvet dress, snatched up her purse which lay in a drawer, and without waiting for either gloves or necktie, ran downstairs and out of the house.

"I will go. I haven't the slightest idea how I am to get there, but I will go to Aunt Katie O'Flynn. I shall be in the train and far enough away before they have discovered that I have gone," was her thought.

From Mrs. Tennant's house to the station was the best part of a mile, but Kathleen was fleet of foot and soon accomplished the distance. She was just arriving at the station when she saw Ruth Craven coming to meet her. Ruth had enjoyed her hour with Miss Renshaw, and was altogether in high spirits. Kathleen stopped for a minute.

"Oh, Ruth," she said, "will you come to town with me? It would be so nice if you would. I am going to meet Aunt Katie O'Flynn. It would not be a bit wrong of you to come. Do come—do, Ruthie."

"But I can't in this dress," said Ruth, who felt suddenly very much tempted.

"Of course you can. Why, Aunt Katie is such a darling she'll take us out if we want things and buy them on the spot. And what does dress matter? We'll be back in no time. What time does your grandmother expect you home?"

"Oh, I don't know. I told granny I did not exactly know what time I should be back, but she certainly wouldn't expect me to be out late."

"Never mind; you are doing me a kindness. I must go to see Aunt Katie, and it isn't convenient for the Tennants to go with me. If we go together it won't be a bit remarkable. Do come, Ruthie. You hurt my feelings awfully this morning; you needn't hurt them again."

"Very well," said Ruth. "I don't know London at all, and I should like to go with you."

The two girls now turned into the railway station. Kathleen gave a puzzled glance around her for a minute, then walked boldly up to a porter, asked him to direct her to the proper place to book for London. He showed her the right booking-office, and she secured two first-class single tickets for herself and Ruth. The girls were directed to the right platform, and in process of time found themselves in the train. It so happened that they had a compartment to themselves. Kathleen had now quite got over her burst of anger, and was in the highest spirits.

"This is fun," she said. "It is so awfully nice to have met you! Do you know that Miss Ravenscroft—the Great Unknown, as we Wild Irish Girls call her—had the cheek to send me a letter?"

Ruth looked attentive and grave.

"She wanted me to go and see her at six o'clock. Well, it is half-past six now, and she will have to whistle for me. Ruth, darling, you don't know how pretty you look; and even though you have deserted me, and won't join my darling, beloved society, yet I shall always love you."

Here Kathleen seated herself near Ruth and flung one arm around her waist.

"But," said Ruth, disentangling herself from Kathleen's embrace, "you don't mean that Miss Ravenscroft—Miss *Ravenscroft*—wanted you to go and see her and you didn't go?"

"No, I didn't go. Why should I go? Miss Ravenscroft has nothing whatever to do with me."

"Oh, Kathleen! she is your mistress—the head-mistress of the Great Shirley School."

"Well, and what about that? Aunty—my darling, my own dear, sweet aunt Katie O'Flynn—sent me a telegram to meet her in town. She is at the Hôtel Métropole. Ruth, do you know where it is?"

"I haven't the most remote idea."

"Oh, well, we'll get there somehow. Never mind now; don't look so worried. I shall be sorry I asked you to come with me if you look any graver."

"But you make me feel grave, Kathleen," said Ruth. "Oh, Kathleen, I can't tell how you puzzle me. Of course, I know that you are very pretty and fascinating, and that lots and lots of girls love you, and will always love you. You are a sort of queen in the school. Perhaps you are not the greatest queen, but still you are a queen, and you could lead the whole school."

"That would be rather fun," said Kathleen.

"But you'd have to change a good bit. You'd have to be just as fascinating, just as pretty, but different somehow—I mean—"

"Oh, do tell me what you mean, and be quick. We'll be in London before long."

"You wouldn't disobey Miss Ravenscroft if you were to be our real queen."

"Then I'll not be your queen, darling, for I shall disobey Miss Ravenscroft when it comes to a case of obliging her or dear, darling, precious aunty."

Ruth said no more. In her heart of hearts she was very much distressed. She was sorry for her own sake that she had met Kathleen, and that she was going with her to London; but on the other hand she was glad that she was with the girl, who by herself might have got into a serious scrape.

Finally the two found themselves standing, very forlorn and slightly frightened, on one of the big platforms at Charing Cross.

"Now what are we to do?" said Kathleen.

"We must ask the way, of course," was Ruth's answer. "Here is a porter who looks kind."

She went up to the man.

"Have you any luggage in the van, miss?" was the immediate inquiry.

"No," she answered.

Ruth was quietly although shabbily dressed; but she had on gloves, a neat hat, and a neat necktie. Kathleen had on a very shabby coat, a most unsuitable cap of bright-blue velvet on her clustering masses of curls, and no necktie and no gloves.

"What could be the matter with the pretty young lady?" thought the man.

Ruth spoke in her gentle tones.

"We want to go to see a lady at the Hôtel Métropole," she said. "Which is the Hôtel Métropole?"

"Oh, miss, it is quite close. You have only to go out of the station, take the second turning to your left, walk down Northumberland Avenue, and you'll be there."

"But where is Northumberland Avenue? We don't know anything about London," interrupted Kathleen.

"If you will allow me to put you two ladies into a cab, the cabman will take you to the Hôtel Métropole. It's only a step away, but you'd better drive if you don't know your London."

"We have never been in our London before," said Kathleen in a voice of intense pleasure.

They now tripped confidently along by the side of the porter. He took them into the yard outside the station, and called a four-wheeler.

"No, no; one of those two-wheeled things," said the little girl.

A hansom was summoned, and the children were put in. The driver was directed to take them to the Métropole, and they started off.

"Ah!" said Kathleen, looking with great appreciation around her—"ah! the lights—aren't they just lovely? And see—see that water. That must be the Thames. Oh, Ruth, mayn't we stand up in the hansom? We could see ever so much better standing."

"No; sit down," implored Ruth.

"Why? Surely you are not frightened. There never was any sort of conveyance that would frighten me. I wish I might drive that horse instead of the stupid old Jehu on the box. Isn't London a perfect place? Oh, this is lovely, isn't it, Ruth?"

"Thank goodness I'm not always bothered by that dreadful speaking voice inside me that you seem to have got," said Kathleen.

Here the cab drew up with a jerk at the Métropole.

"How much are we to pay you?" asked Kathleen.

The man was honest, and asked the customary shilling. A porter was standing on the steps of the hotel. He flung the doors wide, and the two entered. Presently a man came up and asked Kathleen what she wanted.

The hour was just before dinner, and the wide hall of the hotel was full. Both men and women turned and stared at the children. Both were extremely pretty, Kathleen almost startlingly so. But what about the gloveless little hands and the untidy neck and throat?

"Please," said Kathleen, "we have come to see my aunt, Miss O'Flynn. She is here, isn't she?"

The man said he would inquire, and went to the bureau.

"Yes," he said after a minute's pause. "Will you come to the drawing-room, young ladies?"

He conducted the children down some wide passages covered with thick Turkey carpets, opened the folding doors of a great drawing-room, and left them to themselves. There was a minute or two of agonized terror on the part of Ruth, of suspense and rapid heart-beating as far as Kathleen was concerned, and then a deep, mellow, ringing voice was heard, and Miss Katie O'Flynn entered the apartment.

"Why, I never!" she cried. "The top of the morning to you, my honey! God bless you, my darling! Oh, it is joy to kiss your sweet face again!"

A little lady, all smiles and dimples, all curls and necklaces and gay clothing, extended two arms wide and clasped them round Kathleen's neck.

"Ah, aunty!" said Kathleen, "this is good. And I ran away to see you. I did, darling; I did. I have got into the most awful scrape; nobody knows what will happen. See me—without gloves and without a necktie. And this dear little girl, one of my chosen friends, Ruth Craven, has come with me."

"Ah, now, how sweet of her!" said Miss O'Flynn, turning to Ruth.— "Kiss me, my darling. Why, then, you are as welcome as though you were the core of my heart for being so kind to my sweet Kathleen.—Come to the light, Kathleen asthore, and let me look at you. But it isn't as rosy you are as you used to be. It's a bit pale and pulled down you look. Do you like England, my dear? If you don't like it all at all, it's home you will come with me to the old castle and the old country. Now then, children, sit by me and let's have a talk. We'll have a good meal presently, and then I have a bit of a thought in the back of my head which I think will please you both. Sit here anyway for the present, and let us collogue to our hearts' content."

Miss Katie O'Flynn and her two young charges, as she told the girls she considered them, drew a good deal of attention as they sat and talked together. The little lady was not young, but was certainly very fascinating. She had a vivacious, merry smile, the keenest, most brilliant black eyes in the world, and a certain grace and dignity about her which seemed to contrast with her rapid utterances and intensely genial manner.

Dinner was announced, and the three went into the great dining-room. Miss O'Flynn ordered a small table, and they sat down together. Ruth felt unhappy; she keenly desired to go home again. She was more and more certain that she had done wrong to listen to Kathleen's persuasions. But Kathleen was enjoying herself to the utmost. She was an Irish girl again, sitting close to one of her very own. She forgot the dull school and the dreadfully dreary house where she now lived; she absolutely forgot that such a person as Miss Ravenscroft existed; she ceased almost to remember the Society of the Wild Irish Girls. Was she not Kathleen O'Hara, the only daughter of the House of O'Hara, the heiress of her beloved father's old castle? For some day she would be mistress of Carrigrohane Castle; some day she would be a great lady on her own account. Now Kathleen's ideas of what a great lady should be were in themselves very sensible and noble. A great lady should do her utmost to make others happy. She should dispense *largesse* in the true sense of the word. She should make as many people as possible happy. Her retainers should feel certain that they dwelt in her heart. She should love the soil of her native land with a passion which nothing could undermine or weaken. The sons of the soil should be her brothers, her kinsmen; the daughters of the soil should be her sisters in the best sense of the word. But not only should the great lady of Carrigrohane love her Irish friends, but men and women, both youths and children, but she should love others who needed her help. There never was a more affectionate, more generous-hearted girl than Kathleen; but of self-control she had little or no knowledge, and those who crossed her will had yet to find that Kathleen would not obey, for she was fearless, defiant, resolute— in short, a rebel born and bred.

Ruth sat silent, perplexed, and anxious in the midst of the gay feast. Kathleen and Aunt Katie O'Flynn laughed and almost shouted in their mirth. Occasionally people turned to glance at the trio—the grave, refined, extremely pretty, but shabbily dressed girl; the radiant child, and the vivacious little lady who might be her mother but who scarcely looked as if she was. It was a curious party for such a room and for such surroundings.

"I think—" said Ruth suddenly. "Forgive me, Kathleen, but I think we ought to be looking out a train to go back by."

"Indeed, and that you won't," said Miss O'Flynn. "You are going to stay with me to-night. Why, do you think I'd let this precious darling child back again in the middle of the night? And you must stay here too—what is your name? Oh, Ruth. I can get you a room here, and you shall have a fire and every comfort."

"I at least must go home," said Ruth. "My grandfather and grandmother will be sitting up for me."

"Oh, nonsense, child!" said Miss O'Flynn. "I can send a commissionaire down to tell your grandfather that I am keeping you for the night."

"Of course, Ruth," said Kathleen. "Don't be silly; it is absurd for you to go on like that. And for my part I should love to stay."

"I am sorry, Kathleen," said Ruth, "but I must go home. Perhaps one of the porters can tell me when there is a train to Merrifield. I must go back, for grandfather would be terrified if I didn't go home. You, of course, must please yourself."

"My dear child, leave it to me," said Miss O'Flynn. "You can't possibly go back—neither you nor my sweet pet Kathleen. Oh, I'll arrange it, dear; don't you be frightened. You couldn't go so late by yourself; it wouldn't be right."

Miss O'Flynn, however, had not come in contact with a character like Ruth's before. She could be as obstinate as a mule. It was in that light Miss O'Flynn chose to consider her conduct.

"I must go," she said. "I can't by any possibility stay."

"Do, Ruth, for my sake," pleaded Kathleen, tears in her eyes.

"No, Kathleen, not even for your sake. And I think," added Ruth, "that you ought to come with me. It would be much better for you to see Miss Ravenscroft in the morning and explain matters to her."

"Nonsense!" said Kathleen, now speaking with decided temper. "That is my affair. I like you very much, Ruth, but you really need not interfere with me."

"I should think not indeed," said Miss O'Flynn. "I know nothing about you, Miss Craven, but you don't understand what a person of consequence my niece is considered in Ireland."

"That may be," replied Ruth; "but at school Kathleen, sweet and dear as she is, has to obey the rules just like any other girl.—Please, Kathleen, do be persuaded and come back with me.—Indeed, Miss O'Flynn, if you will only believe me, it is considered a very grave offence to miss morning school or to be late when nine o'clock strikes; and Kathleen can't be at school in time unless she returns home now."

"I'm not going, so there!" said Kathleen.

"Perhaps some one would tell me when the next train for Merrifield leaves Charing Cross," was Ruth's next remark.

Before any one could reply to her, however, a servant entered and said something in a low tone to Miss O'Flynn.

"Well, now," she said, speaking with eagerness, her face all smiles and dimples, "the way is made plain for you at least, Miss Craven.—Who do you think has come, Kathleen? Why, the lady who has charge of you."

"Mrs. Tennant? Oh, the dear tired one!" cried Kathleen. "She can never be cross, and I like her very much.—Where is the lady?" she added, turning to the waiter.

"She is in the hall, miss."

Kathleen flew out, and before Mrs. Tennant, who was really feeling very angry, could prevent her, had flung her arms round her neck.

"Thank goodness it is you!" said the young girl. "Now don't be angry, for you don't know how to manage it. If it was Alice, wouldn't she be in a tantrum? But you are all right; you haven't an idea of scolding me. I arrived here as safely as a girl could. And what do you think? I brought pretty Ruth Craven with me. She didn't much like it, but here she is; and she's on tenter-hooks to get home, so she can return with you, can't she?"

"You must come too, Kathleen. You annoyed me very much indeed. You gave me a terrible fright. I did not know what might have happened to you, knowing how ignorant you are of London and its ways."

"But I have got a head on my shoulders," laughed Kathleen. "And now that you have come we must have a bit of fun. I want to introduce you to aunty. It is Aunt Katie O'Flynn, you know, the lady who sent me the beautiful, wonderful clothes."

But here Miss O'Flynn herself appeared on the scene. Kathleen did the necessary introducing, and the two ladies moved a little apart to talk together. By-and-by Miss O'Flynn called the two girls to her side.

"Mrs. Tennant is not angry with you now, Kathleen. On the contrary, she loves you very much; and she will take Miss Ruth Craven back with her. I have been trying to induce her to stay here herself, but she won't; and as Ruth is anxious to return home, her escort has come very opportunely. As to you, darling, nothing will induce me to part with you until to-morrow morning."

"But what will you do about school?" said Ruth.

"That can be managed," said Miss O'Flynn. "It isn't the first time that Kathleen and I have got up with the sunrise. We'll get up to-morrow before it, I'm thinking, and take a train, and be in time to have a good breakfast at Mrs. Tennant's. — Then if you, my dear lady, will put up with me until lunch-time, I can see more of my Kathleen, and propound some plans for your pleasure as well as hers. If you must go, Mrs. Tennant, I am afraid you must, for the next train leaves Charing Cross for Merrifield at ten minutes past nine."

Mrs. Tennant looked grave, but it was difficult to resist Miss O'Flynn, and the time was passing. Accordingly she and Ruth left the Hôtel Métropole, and the aunt and niece found themselves alone.

CHAPTER XVII.
MISS KATIE O'FLYNN AND HER NIECE.

"Now, Kathleen," said Miss O'Flynn, "you come straight up to my bedroom, where there is a cosy fire, and where we will be just as snug as Punch. We'll draw two chairs up to the fire and have a real collogue, that we will."

"Yes, that we will," said Kathleen. "I have a lot of things to ask you, and a lot of things to tell you."

"Come along then, dear child. My room is on the second floor; we won't wait for the lift."

Kathleen took Miss Katie O'Flynn's hand, and they ran merrily and as lightly as two-year-olds up the stairs. People turned to look at them as they sped upwards.

"Why, the little old lady seems as young and agile as the pretty niece," said one visitor to another.

"Oh, they're both Irish; that accounts for anything," was the answer. "The most extraordinary and the most lively nation on the face of the earth."

The two vivacious Irishwomen entered their bedroom. Aunt Katie flung herself into a deep arm-chair; Kathleen did likewise, and then they talked to their heart's content. It is good to hear two Irishwomen conversing together, for there is so much action in the conversation—such lifting of brows, such raising of hands, such emphasis in tone, in voice, in manner. Imagery is so freely employed; telling sentences, sharp satire, wit—brilliant, overflowing, spontaneous—all come to the fore. Laughter sometimes checks the eager flow of words. Occasionally, too, if the conversation is sorrowful, tears flow and sobs come from the excited and over-sensitive hearts. No one need be dull who has the privilege of listening to two Irishwomen who have been parted for some time talking their hearts out to each other. Kathleen and her aunt were no exception to the universal rule. Kathleen had never been from home before, and Aunt Katie had things to tell her about every person, man and woman, old and young, on the Carrigrohane estate. But when all the news had been told, when the exact number of dogs had been recounted, the cats and kittens described, the fowls, the goats, the donkeys, the horses, the cows enumerated, it came to be Aunt Katie's turn to listen.

"Now my love, tell me, and be quick, about all you have been doing. And first and foremost, how do you like school?"

"Not at all, aunty; and I'm not learning anything."

"My dear, that is sad hearing; and your poor father pining his heart out for the want of you."

"I never wished to go to school," said Kathleen.

"You will have to bear it now, my pet, unless you have real cause for complaint. They're not unkind to you, acushla, are they?"

"Oh, not really, Aunt Katie; but they're such dull people. The teachers are dull. I don't mind Miss Spicer so much; she's the music teacher. As to Miss Ravenscroft, I have never even seen her."

"And who is she, darling?"

"The head-mistress, and no end of a toff."

"What's a toff, dear?"

"It's a slang word they use in stupid old England."

"I don't admire it, my love. Don't you demean yourself by bringing words of that sort home to Carrigrohane."

"Not I. I shan't be a minute in the old place before the salt breezes will blow England out of my memory. Ah! it's I who pine to be home again."

"It will broaden your mind, Kathleen, and improve you. And some of the English people are very nice entirely," said Miss O'Flynn, making this last statement in what she considered a widely condescending manner. "So your are not learning much?"

"I am getting on with my music. Perhaps I'll settle down to work. I should not loathe it so much if it was not for Alice."

"Ah! she's the daughter of Mrs. Tennant. I rather took to Mrs. Tennant, the creature! She seemed to have a kind-hearted sort of face."

"She's as right as rain, aunty; and so are the two boys. But Alice—she is—"

"What, darling?"

"A prig, aunty. Detestable!"

"I never took to that sort," said Miss O'Flynn. "Wouldn't you like some oyster-patties and some plumcake to munch while you are talking, deary?"

"I shouldn't mind."

"I'll ring and order them."

A servant appeared. Miss O'Flynn gave orders which resulted in a rich and most unwholesome supper being placed upon the table. Kathleen and her aunt ate while they talked.

"And what occupies you, love, at all at all?" said Miss O'Flynn as she ate her second oyster-patty. "From your description it seems to be a sort of death in life, that town of Merrifield."

"I have to make my own diversions, aunty, and they are sprightly and entertaining enough. Don't you remember when I told you to have all those little hearts made for me?"

"To be sure, dear—the most extraordinary idea I ever heard in my life. Only that I never cross you, Kathleen, I'd have written to know the meaning of it."

"It doesn't matter about you knowing."

Here Kathleen briefly and in graphic language described the Society of the Wild Irish Girls.

"It is the one thing that keeps me alive," she said. "However, I'm guessing they are going to make a fuss about it in the school."

"And what will you do then, core of my heart?"

"Stick to them, of course, aunty. You don't suppose I'd begin a thing and then drop it?"

"No; that wouldn't be at all like you, you young rebel.".

Kathleen laughed.

"I am all in a puzzle," she said, "to know where to hold the next meeting, for there is no doubt that some of the girls who hate us because they weren't asked to join spied last time; so I want the society to meet the night after next in a new place."

"And I'll tell you what I've been thinking," said Aunt Katie; "that I'll be present, and bring a sparkle of old Ireland to help the whole affair. So you'll have to reckon with me on the occasion of the next meeting."

Kathleen sat very still, her face thoughtful.

"Nothing will induce me to give them up," she said, or to betray any girl of my society. Oh, aunty, there's such a funny old woman! I met her last Sunday. She's a certain Mrs. Church, and she lives in a cottage about four miles from Merrifield. We could have our meetings there—I know we could—and she'd never tell. Nobody would guess. She is the great-aunt of one of the members of the society, Susy Hopkins, a nice little girl, a tradesman's daughter."

"Oh, dear me, Kathleen! You don't mean to say you demean yourself by associating with tradesmen's daughters?"

"I do so, aunty; and I find them very much nicer than the stuck-up girls who think no end of themselves."

"Well, well," said Miss O'Flynn, "whatever you are, you are a lady born and bred, and nothing can lower that sort—nothing nor nobody. You must make your own plans and let me know."

"I am sure I can manage the old lady, and I will tell you why. She wants to join our alms-women."

"What?"

"You know what a snug time our dear old alms-women have. I was telling Mrs. Church about it last Sunday. She took a keen desire to belong to us, and I sort of half, in a kind of a way, promised her. Is there likely to be a vacancy soon, Aunt Katie?"

"Well, dear, there is a vacancy at the present moment. Mrs. Hagan breathed her last, poor soul! and was waked not a fortnight ago. We'd better wire to your father to keep the little cottage vacant until we know more. This is going to be interesting, and you may be quite sure that if there is going to be a lark that I'm the one to help you, my colleen bawn."

Kathleen and her aunt talked until late into the night, and when the young girl laid her head on her pillow she was lost immediately in profound slumber.

It was not at all difficult for Kathleen to wake early, and accompanied by Miss O'Flynn, she arrived at Merrifield at half-past eight on the following morning. She had no time, however, to change her dress, but after washing her hands and smoothing out her tangled hair, and leaving Miss O'Flynn in the care of Mrs. Tennant—who, to tell the truth, found her considerably in the way—Kathleen, accompanied by Alice, started for school.

"You'll catch it," said Alice.

"Oh, that's very likely, darling," said Kathleen; "but I don't think I much care. Did you see Miss Ravenscroft last night, and was she very, very angry?"

"I saw her, and she was more than angry—she was astonished. I think you will have to put up with a rather serious conversation with her this morning. She asked me questions with regard to you and your doings which, of course, I could not answer; but you will have to answer them. I don't think particularly well of you, Kathleen; your ways are not my ways, nor your ideas mine; but I don't think, bad as you are, that you would tell a lie. You will have to speak out the truth to Miss Ravenscroft, Kathleen, and no mistake about it."

"Thank you," replied Kathleen. "I think I can manage my own affairs," she added, and then she was silent, not exactly cross, but lost in thought.

The girls reached the school without any further adventure. Prayers were held as usual in the great hall, and then the members of the different classes went to their places and the work of the morning began. The work went on, and to look at those girls, all steadfast and attentive and studious-looking, it was difficult to realize that in some of their hearts was wild rebellion and a naughty and ever-increasing sense of mischief. Certainly it was difficult to realize that one at least of that number was determined to have her own way at any cost; that another was extremely anxious, resolved to tell the truth, and hoping against hope that she would not be questioned.

School had very nearly come to an end when the dread summons which both Ruth Craven and Alice Tennant expected arrived for Kathleen. She was to go to speak to Miss Ravenscroft in that lady's parlor.

"Miss Ravenscroft is waiting," said the mistress who brought Kathleen the message. "Will you be quick, Kathleen, as she is rather in a hurry?"

Kathleen got up with apparent alacrity. Her face looked sunshiny and genial. As she passed Ruth she put her hand on her shoulder and said in her most pleasant voice:

"Extraordinary thing; Miss Ravenscroft has sent for me. I wonder what for."

Ruth colored and looked down. One or two of the girls glanced round at Kathleen in amazement. She did not say anything further but left the room. When she got into the passage she hummed a little air. The teacher who had summoned her had gone on in front. Kathleen followed her at a respectful distance, and still humming "The wearing of the Green," she knocked at Miss Ravenscroft's door.

Miss Ravenscroft was standing by her window. She turned when Kathleen appeared, and desired her to sit down. Kathleen dropped into a chair. Miss Ravenscroft did likewise. Then Miss Ravenscroft spoke gently, for in spite of herself Kathleen's attractive face, the wilful, daring, and yet affectionate glance in the eyes, attracted her. She had not yet had a full and perfect view of Kathleen. She had seen, it is true, the pretty little girl in a crowd of others; but now she saw Kathleen by herself. The face was undoubtedly sweet—sweet with a radiance which surprised and partly fascinated Miss Ravenscroft.

"Your name?" she said.

"Kathleen O'Hara," replied Kathleen.

She rose to her feet and dropped a little bobbing curtsy, then waited to be asked to sit down again. Miss Ravenscroft did not invite her to reseat herself. She spoke quietly, turning her eyes away from the attractive little face and handsome figure.

"I sent for you last night and you did not obey my command. Why so?"

"I did not mean to be rude," said Kathleen. "You see, it was this way. My aunt from Ireland (Miss O'Flynn is her name—Miss Katie O'Flynn) was staying at the Métropole. I had a telegram from her desiring me to go to her immediately in town. I got your note after I had read the telegram. It seemed to me that I ought to go first to my aunt. She is my mother's own sister, and such a darling. You couldn't but love her if you saw her. You might think me a little rude not to come to you when you sent for me, but Aunt Katie would have been hurt—terribly, fearfully hurt. She might even have cried."

Kathleen raised her brows as she said the last word; her face expressed consternation and a trifle of amazement. Miss Ravenscroft felt as though smiles were very near.

"Even suppose your aunt had cried," she said, "your duty was to me as your head-mistress."

"Please," said Kathleen, "I did not think it was. I thought my duty was to my aunt."

Miss Ravenscroft was silent for a minute.

"My dear," she said then gently, "you are new to the school. You have doubtless indulged in a very free-and-easy and unconventional life in your own country. I was once in Ireland, in the west, and I liked the people and the land, and the ways of the people and the looks of the land, and for the sake of that visit I am not going to be hard on a little Irish girl during her first sojourn in the school. In future, Kathleen O'Hara, I must insist on instant obedience. I will forgive you for your disregard of my message last night, but if ever I require you again I shall expect you to come to me at once. For the present we will forget last night."

"Thank you, madam. I am sure I should love you very much if I knew you well."

"That is not the question, my dear. I must insist on your treating me with respect. It is not very easy to know the head-mistress; the girls know her up to a certain point, but personal friendship as between one woman and another cannot quite exist between a little girl and her head-mistress. Yes, my dear, I hope you will love me, but in the sense of one who is set in authority over you. That is my position, and I hope as long as I live to do my duty. Now then, Kathleen, I will speak to you about the other matter which obliged me to send you a message last night."

"Thank you, ma'am," said Kathleen. She looked down, so that the fun in her eyes could not be seen.

"I am sure from your face that you will not tell me a lie."

"No," said Kathleen, "I won't tell you a lie."

"I must, however, ask you one or two direct questions. Is it true that you have encouraged certain girls in this school—"

"Oh, I encourage all the girls, I know. Poor things! I—"

"Don't interrupt me, Kathleen; I have more to say. Is it true that you encourage certain girls in this school"—here Miss Ravenscroft put up her hand to check Kathleen's words—"to rebellion and insubordination?"

"I don't know what insubordination is," said Kathleen, shaking her head.

"Is it true," continued the head-mistress, "that you have started a society which is called by some ridiculous name such as The Wild Irish Girls, and that you meet each week in a quarry a short distance from town; that you have got rules and badges; that you sing naughty songs, and altogether misbehave yourselves? Is it true?"

Kathleen closed her lips firmly together. Miss Ravenscroft looked full at her. Kathleen then spoke slowly:

"How did you hear that we do what you say we do?"

"I do not intend to name my informant. The girls who have joined your society and are putting themselves under your influence are the sort of girls who in a school like this get most injured by such proceedings. They have never been accustomed to self-restraint; they have not been guided to control themselves. Of all the girls in the school whom you, Miss O'Hara, have tried to injure, you have selected the foundationers, who have only been to Board schools before they came here. They look up to you as above them by birth; your very way, your words, can influence them. Wrong from your lips will appear right, and right will appear wrong. You yourself are an ignorant and unlearned child, and yet you attempt to guide others. This society must be broken up immediately. I will forgive you for the past if you promise me that you will never hold another meeting, that as long as you are at the school you will not encourage another girl to join this society. You will have to give me your word, and that before you leave this room. I do not require you to betray your companions; I do not even ask their names. I but demand your promise, which I insist on. The Irish Girls—or the Wild Irish Girls, whatever you like to call them—must cease to exist."

Miss Ravenscroft ceased speaking.

"Is that all?" said Kathleen.

"What do you mean? I want your promise."

"But I have nothing to say."

"You are not stupid, Kathleen O'Hara—I can see that—and I should hope you were too much of a lady to be impertinent. What do you mean to do?"

"Indeed," said Kathleen, "I don't mean to be impertinent, and I don't want to tell a lie. The best way on the present occasion is to be silent. I can't give myself or the other girls in the school away. You ask me to make you a promise. I cannot make that promise. I am sorry. Perhaps I had better leave the school."

"No, Kathleen, you cannot leave it in the ordinary way. You are connected with other girls now; your influence must be publicly withdrawn. I had hoped to spare you this, but if you defy me you know the consequences."

"May I go now?" said Kathleen.

"You may—for the present. I must consult with the other teachers. It may even be necessary to call a meeting of the Board of Governors. Your conduct requires stringent measures. But, my child"—and here Miss Ravenscroft changed her voice to one of gentleness and entreaty—"you will not be so silly, so wicked, so perverse. Kathleen, it is sometimes a hard thing to give up your own way, but I think an Irish girl can be noble. You will be very noble now if you cease to belong to the Irish Girls' Society."

"'Wild Irish Girls' is the name," said Kathleen.

"You must give it up. It was a mad and silly scheme. You must have nothing more to do with it."

Kathleen slightly shook her head. Miss Ravenscroft uttered a deep sigh.

"I am afraid I must go," said Kathleen. "I think you have spoken to me very kindly; I should like to have been able to oblige you."

"And you won't?"

Kathleen shook her head again. The next moment she had left the room.

The school was nearly over; but whether it had been or not, Kathleen had not the slightest idea of returning to her class-room. She stood for a moment in one of the corridors to collect her thoughts; then going to the room where the hats and jackets hung on pegs, she took down her own, put them on, and left the school. She walked fast and reached Mrs. Tennant's house at a quarter to one. Both Mrs. Tennant and Miss O'Flynn were out. There was a message for Kathleen to say that Miss O'Flynn expected her to be ready to go to town with her immediately after dinner. Kathleen smiled to herself.

"Dear Aunt Katie! She must get me out of this scrape. But as to thinking of giving up girls whom I meant to help, and will help, I wouldn't do it for twenty Miss Ravenscrofts." She stood at the door of the house; then a sudden idea struck her, and as she saw the girls; filing out of the school, she crossed the common and met Susy Hopkins, her satchel of books flung across her shoulder.

"Ah, Susy, here I am. I want to speak to you."

Susy ran up to her in excitement. It was already whispered in the school that their secret proceedings were becoming known. It had also been whispered from one to another that Kathleen had undergone a formidable interview with Miss Ravenscroft that very morning.

"What is it, Kathleen?" said Susy. "Was she very, very cross?"

"Who do you mean?" asked Kathleen, instantly on the defensive.

"Miss Ravenscroft. You went to see her; every one knows it. What did she say?"

"That is my affair. But, Susy, I want you to do something. We must not go to the quarry to-morrow evening. We want to have the meeting at your aunt's. I want to go to Mrs. Church's. You must run round this afternoon and make arrangements. There'll be about thirty or forty of us, and we must all be smuggled into the cottage."

"Oh, dear!" said Susy. "But how are we to get there? It's four miles away."

"Well, I suppose those who are really interested can walk four miles. I certainly can. Susy, you had better not miss it to-morrow night, for Aunt Katie O'Flynn is to be present, and there's no saying what she will do. She will help us if any one can. She is ever so kind, and so interested. It will be the greatest meeting the society has ever had; I wouldn't miss it myself for the world."

"Oh, hurrah!" said Susy. "You certainly are a splendid girl, Kathleen. And won't Aunt Church be pleased?"

"Tell her that if she wants to get one of the little almshouses she had better oblige us as far as she can," said.

Kathleen. "Now I must rush back to dinner. I am going to town afterwards."

Without waiting for Susy's reply, Kathleen turned on her heel and returned home. Susy watched her for a minute, then slowly and gravely went in the direction of her mother's shop. Mrs. Hopkins was getting in fresh stock that morning, and the little shop looked brighter and fresher than it had done for some time. It was a beautiful day in the beginning of winter, with that feeling of summer in the air which comes to cheer us now and then in November. Susy marched through the shop, still swinging her satchel.

"I wish you wouldn't do that, Susy," said her mother. "And I wish, too, that you wouldn't always be late home. Be quick now; there's pease-pudding and pork for dinner. Tom is in a hurry to be off to his football."

"Oh, bother!" said Susy.

Mrs. Hopkins frowned. Susy, in her mother's opinion, was not quite so nice and comforting as she once had been. But it was not Mrs. Hopkins's way to reproach her children; she bore her burden with regard to them as silently and patiently as she could.

Susy ran up to her room, tossed off her hat, washed her hands, and came down. Soon the three were seated at their frugal dinner.

"You seem to have got in a lot of fresh goods, mother," said Tom.

"I have," said Mrs. Hopkins, with a groan; "but I haven't paid for one of them. Parkins says he will trust me for quite a month; but however I am to pay your Aunt Church, and keep enough money for the new goods, beats me. Sometimes I think that my burden is greater than I can bear. I have often had a feeling that I ought to give up the shop and take service somewhere. I used to be noted as the best of good housekeepers when I was young."

"Oh, no, mother, you mustn't do that," said Susy. "What would Tom and I do?"

"If it wasn't for you and Tom I'd give notice to-morrow," said the widow. "But there! we must hope for the best, I suppose. God never forsakes those who trust Him."

"Mother," said Susy suddenly, "I hope you will be able to spare me this afternoon. I want to go and see Aunt Church."

"Why should you do that, child? There's no way for you to go except on your legs, and it's a weary walk, and the days are getting short."

"All the same, I must go," said Susy. "I suppose you couldn't shut up the shop and come with me, could you, mother?"

"Shut up the shop!" said Mrs. Hopkins. "What next will the child ask? Not a bit of it, Susan. But what do you want to see your aunt for?"

"It is a little private message in connection with Miss Kathleen O'Hara. It means money, mother; of that I am certain. It means that Aunt Church will forgive you last month's installment of the debt, and perhaps next month's, too. You had best let me go, mother. I am not talking without knowledge, and I can't tell you what I know."

"I know something," said Tom, and he gave utterance to a low whistle.

Susy turned and glanced at her brother in some uneasiness.

"There are a deal of funny things whispered about your school just now," he said. "I'm not going to peach, of course; only you'd best look out. They say if it got to the governors' ears every foundationer in the place would be expelled. It is something that ought not to be done."

"Don't mind him, mother. Do you think I'd do anything to endanger my continuing at the school, after all the trouble and care and anxiety you had in getting me placed there?"

"Really, child," said Mrs. Hopkins, "I don't know. The wilfullness of young folks in these days is past enduring. But you had better clearly understand, Susy, that if for any reason you are dismissed from the school there is nothing whatever for you but to take a place as a servant; and that you wouldn't like."

"I should think not, indeed. Well, mother, to avoid all these consequences I must go as fast as I can to see Aunt Church."

CHAPTER XVIII.
SUSY HOPKINS PERSUADES AUNT CHURCH.

Mrs. Hopkins said nothing more. Susy saw that she could have her own way, and as soon as dinner was over, without even waiting to help her mother to put the place in order, she started on her walk. She felt pleased and self-important. The day was a frosty one, and the sunset promised to be glorious. The road to Mrs. Church's house was flat and long and pleasant to walk on. Susy had no particular eye for pretty views, or she might have pleased herself with the wonderful tints of the sky, and the autumnal shades which had not altogether deserted the neighboring woods. Susy's thoughts, however, were occupied with very different matters.

"Mother is always grumbling," she said to herself; "and for that matter, so is Tom. As if I'd demean myself by taking a place! The idea of my being a servant. Why, I know I shall do very well in the future. I look high. I mean to be a lady, as good as the best. Would Miss Kathleen O'Hara take so much notice of me if I was not a very nice, lady-like sort of a girl? I am sure no one could look sweeter than I do in my pale-blue blouse. Even Tom says so. He said I looked very genteel, and that he'd like his great friend, Walter Amber, to see me. I don't want to have anything to do with Tom's friends. Poor Tom! if mother can apprentice him to somebody, that is the most that can be expected. But as for me, the very lowest position I intend to take in life in the future is that of a teacher. I shall probably be a teacher in this very school, and get my couple of hundred a year. A place indeed! Poor dear mother doesn't know what she is talking about."

Occupied with her own thoughts, the road did not turn out long to Susy. She reached Mrs. Church's very humble abode between three and four o'clock. It was still daylight. The little old lady was seated in her window; she looked very much surprised when she saw Susy, and limped to the door and opened it.

"Come in, Susy Hopkins," she said. "I suppose your mother has sent me my money. If so, it is very thoughtful of her. If you have brought the money, Susy, you shall have a cup of tea before you start on your homeward walk. It is a fine day, child, and your cheeks look very fresh. Come in, dear; come in."

Mrs. Church hobbled back again into her small sitting-room. She got back into her chair, and motioned to Susy to take one opposite to her.

"If that is the money you have in your hand," she said, noticing that the child held a small parcel, "you may give it to me, and then go over there and get me that black cash-box. I will put the gold and silver in immediately. It is never safe to leave money about."

"But I haven't got the money, Aunt Church. Mother couldn't have saved it in the time."

Mrs. Church's face became very bleak and decidedly wintry in appearance.

"Then what have you come for, Susan?" she said. "You needn't suppose I am going to waste my good tea on you if you haven't brought the money. If you think so, you are fine and mistaken."

"I don't think so, really, Aunt Church; but perhaps when you know all you will give me a cup of tea, and perhaps you won't be so cross the next time I wear my pale-blue blouse."

"Ah, my dear, I wasn't cross at the end of the time, although I did think it a bit suspicious: your mother losing nineteen-and-sixpence of my own money out of her till—you forget that fact, Susan Hopkins; it was my money—and then you decking yourself out in the most unsuitable garment I ever saw on a little girl of your age and station. It has pleased the Almighty, Susan, to put you in a low walk of life, and in that walk you ought to remain, and dress according—yes, dress according. But, as I said, I was not displeased at the end. That was a very bonny young lady who came into your mother's shop—miles and miles above you, Susan. And how she can demean herself to call you her friend passes my comprehension."

"You are very rude, Aunt Church," said Susy; "but I am not going to be angry with you, for I want you to help us. I have got news for you, and very good news, too. But I will only tell it to you on condition."

Mrs. Church looked first skeptical, then curious, then keenly desirous.

"Well, child?" she said. "Maybe you might as well put the kettle on the fire; it takes a good long time to boil. It's a very bobbish little kettle, and it has cranky whims just as though it were a human. There's a good child, Susan; take it out and fill it at the tap, and put it on the fire to boil up while you are telling me the rest of the story. I always liked you very well, Susan; not so much as Tom, but you are quite to my liking, all things considered."

"No, you never liked me, Aunt Church," said Susy; "but I will fill the kettle if you have a fancy—although perhaps I won't be able to stay to have that cup of tea that you seem all of a sudden willing to give me."

Mrs. Church said nothing. Susy left the room with the kettle.

"I could fly out at her," thought the old lady; "but where's the good? She's hand and glove with that beautiful Miss O'Hara, and for the sake of the young lady I mustn't get her back up too much."

So Susy put the kettle on to boil, and then resumed her place opposite Mrs. Church.

"Susan," said the old lady, "while the kettle is boiling you might as well lay the cloth and get out the tea-things."

"No, no," said Susy; "I haven't come here to act servant to you, Aunt Church."

"You have a very nasty manner, Susan; and whatever the Almighty may mean to do with you in the future, you had best change your tune or things will go ill with you."

Susy sat quite still, apparently indifferent to these remarks.

"Well, if you won't lay the cloth, and won't help your own poor old aunt, you may as well tell me what you came for."

"Not yet. I will presently."

Susy was now thoroughly enjoying herself. Mrs. Church edged her chair a little nearer; her beady black eyes seemed to read Susy through and through.

"Go on, child; speak. 'Tain't right to keep an old body on tenter-hooks."

"I will tell you if you will promise me something. I have brought you a little bag that I made my own self, and you shall have it if you promise me something. It is a bag for your knitting. You know you said that you were always losing the ball; it would keep running under your chair, and you could never get it without stooping and hurting yourself."

"To be sure I did, child, and it is thoughtful of you to think of me. Well, but we'll talk of the bag when you have said whatever else you have got at the back of that wise little head of yours."

"I have got news that may mean a great deal to you, but before I tell it I want you to give me a promise. I want you to let mother off this month's installment of her debt."

"What?" cried Mrs. Church, turning very pale. "The money that she owes me?"

"Yes, the money she owes you. A thief came into the shop and took some of her money, and she is very short of money and very worried. I will tell you the news if you will forgive mother."

"Well," said Mrs. Church, "of all the impertinent, bare-faced, wicked little girls, you beat them all. My answer to that, Susan Hopkins, is no; and you can leave the house, for that is the last word you will get."

"Thank you, Aunt Church," said Susy. "I will leave it. It doesn't matter whether you hear the message I have come to give you or not. It is from Miss Kathleen O'Hara, but that don't matter, either. What have you to do with a young lady like Miss Kathleen O'Hara. She's as unsuitable to be with you as she is to be with me. Good-bye, Aunt Church; good-bye."

Susy got as far as the door when Mrs. Church called her back.

"Come here, you bad little thing," she said. "Sit down on that chair. Now, what do you mean?"

"I say I will give you my message if you will forgive mother."

"Then I won't. I will never hear your message."

"All right, I will go," said Susy. "I'll tell Miss Kathleen; she will be disappointed, so to speak. It was about those almshouses, but—"

"Look here, child; you tell me first, and then I'll consider."

"No, no," said Susy. "I know something better than that. You make the promise first, faithfully and truly, and then I will tell you."

After this there was a considerable wrangle between the old woman and the young girl, but all in good time Susy won her desire, and Mrs. Church made the required promise.

"Now speak," she said. "There's that kettle singing like mad, and it will boil over in a minute. You shall have a cup of tea and a nice sweet bun with it, and what more can a poor old body like myself offer? What about Miss Kathleen O'Hara?"

"Aunt Church, you can help Miss Kathleen, and she is worthy of being helped. She wants you to do something for her."

"Me?" said Mrs. Church. "And what can a poor body like me do to help her? Things ought to be the other way round; it's she who ought to help me."

"And so she will, and she said as much. She said she'd do what she could to put you into one of those sweet little almshouses; and when Miss

Kathleen says a thing she means it. And there's an aunt of hers has come over from Ireland—and from all accounts she must be a perfect wonder—and she's coming, too. Oh, Aunt Church, you are in luck!"

"You are enough to distract any one, child. Susy, I told you the kettle would boil before we were ready for tea. Take it off and put it on the hob; and be careful, for goodness' sake, Susy Hopkins, or you'll scald yourself."

Susy removed the kettle from its position on the glowing bed of coals, and then resumed her narrative.

"They're all coming," she said, "and you will have to get them in by hook or crook."

"You're enough to deave a body. Who's coming, and where are they coming when they do come?"

"They're coming here, Aunt Church, a lot of them—girls like me—big girls and little girls, old girls and young girls, bad girls and good girls; girls who'll laugh at you, and girls who'll respect you; some dressed badly, and some dressed fine. They are all coming, up to forty of them in number, and Miss Kathleen O'Hara is the queen amongst them. Miss Katie O'Flynn is coming, too, and it's to your house they're to come; and it's to happen to-morrow night."

"Really, Susy, of all the impertinent children, I do think you beat all. Forty people coming into this tiny house, where we can scarcely turn round with more than two in the house! You are talking pure nonsense, Susan Hopkins, and I'll break my word if that's all you have to tell."

"It's true enough. Have you never heard of our society? Well, of course not, so I will tell you. It is this way, Aunt Church: When Miss Kathleen came to the school she took pity on us foundationers. She founded a society, and we used to meet in the old quarry just to the left of Johnson's Field; and right good times we had. She promised us all sorts of things. It was she who gave me that blouse that you seemed to think I had bought with the money which was taken from mother's till. And she gave me this. See, Aunt Church; if you look you will believe."

Here Susy pulled from the neck of her dress a little heart-shaped locket with the device and name of the society on it.

"Look for yourself," she said.

Mrs. Church did look. She put on her spectacles and read the words, "The Wild Irish Girls, October, 18—."

"Whatever does this mean?" she said. "The Wild Irish Girls! It doesn't sound at all a respectable sort of name."

"I am one," said Susy, beginning to skip up and down. "I am a Wild Irish Girl."

"That you ain't. You don't know the meaning of the thing. You are nothing but a little, under-bred Cockney."

"Thank you, Aunt Church. I do feel obliged for your kind opinion of me. But now, are you going to help Miss Kathleen, or are you not? She can't have the girls—the Wild Irish Girls, I mean—any longer at the quarry, for it's getting noised abroad in the school, and there are those who'd think very little of telling on us; and then we might all be expelled, for it's contrary to the rules of the governors that there should be anything underhand or anything of that sort in the place. So it is this way: we have got into trouble, we Wild Irish Girls, and dear Miss Kathleen is determined that, come what will, the society must not suffer; and she thinks you could help. And if you help in any sort of fashion, why, she'll take precious good care that you get into one of those little almshouses. She said I was to see you to-day, and I was to take her back the answer. And now, will you help or will you not?"

"Well, I never!" said Mrs. Church.

When she had uttered these words she sank back in her chair. Her knitting was forgotten; her old face looked pale with anxiety.

"Have a cup of tea; it will help you to think more than anything," said Susy, and in a brisk and businesslike fashion she dived into the cupboard, took out the cups and saucers, a little box of biscuits, a tiny jug of milk, a caddy of tea, and proceeded to fill the little teapot. By-and-by tea was ready, and Susy brought a cup to the old lady.

"There, now," she said. "You see what it means to have a nice little girl like me to wait on you. You'd have taken an hour hobbling round all by yourself. Now what will you do?"

"What shall I do?" said Mrs. Church. "Look round, Susan Hopkins, and ask me what I am to do! How many of those forty can be squeezed into this room?"

"Let me think," said Susy.

She looked round the room, which was really not more than twelve feet square.

"We couldn't get many in here," she said. "Four might stand against the wall there, and four there, and so on, but that wouldn't go far when there are forty. We must have the backyard."

"What! and upset the pig?" said Mrs. Church.

"Oh, Aunt Church, you really can't think of Brownie at a moment like this! They must all congregate in the yard, and you shall look on. Oh, you'll enjoy it fine! But you ought to have tea for Miss O'Hara and Miss Katie O'Flynn; you really ought. Think, Aunt Church; it is quite worth while when you have an almshouse in view; and you know that for all the rest of your life you are to have a house rent-free, coal and light, and six shillings a week."

"It's worth an effort," said Mrs. Church; "it is that. But I doubt me, now that the thing seems so near, whether I shall like the crossing. I can't abide finding myself on the salty sea. I have that to think over, and that is against the scheme, Susy Hopkins."

"And what do a few hours' misery signify," said Susy, "when you have all the rest of your life to live in clover?"

"That's true—that's true," said the old lady. "If you are positive that it won't upset Brownie—"

"You can lock Brownie up; I will take charge of the key."

"And have him grunting like anything."

"He won't be heard with forty of them."

"It does sound very insurrectionary and wrong," said Mrs. Church; "but if you are certain sure she will keep her word—"

"If I am sure of anybody, it is Miss Kathleen."

"She looks a good sort."

"And then, you know, Aunty Church, you can clinch matters by having a nice little tea for her; and afterwards, if you don't speak up, I will. I'll tell her you expect to get the almshouse after doing so much as to entertain forty of her guests."

"Well, look here, Susy, you have thrust yourself into this matter, and you must help me out. I suppose I must have a tea, but it must be a very plain one."

"No; it must be a very nice tea. Oh, I'll see to that. Mother shall send over some things from town—a little pink ham cut very thin, and new-laid eggs—"

"And water-cress," said Mrs. Church. "I have a real relish for water-cress, and it's a very long time since I had any."

"You have got your own fowls," said Susy, "so they will supply the eggs; and for the rest I will manage. You are very good indeed, aunty, and mother will be so pleased. Kiss me, Aunt Church. I must be off or I'll be getting into a terrible scrape."

CHAPTER XIX.
RUTH'S TROUBLES AND
SUSY'S PREPARATIONS.

The next day the suppressed excitement in the school grew worse. It is sad to relate, nevertheless it is a fact, that Kathleen O'Hara openly neglected her lessons. She kept glancing at Susy Hopkins, and Susy Hopkins once very boldly winked at her; and when she did this one of the under teachers saw her. Now, there were certain rules in the school which all the girls were expected to keep, and winking and making faces were always prohibited. But the teacher on this occasion did not complain of Susy; there were so many other things to be considered that she thought she would let the matter pass.

Ruth Craven was in her class, and more than one girl remarked on Ruth's appearance. Her face was ghastly pale, and she looked as though she had been crying very hard. Alice Tennant was also in her class, and she looked very bold and upright and defiant. Nothing ever induced Alice to neglect her studies, for did not the scholarship depend on her doing her very utmost? She worked just as assiduously as though nothing was happening. But each foundation girl—at least each who had joined the Wild Irish Girls—pressed her hand against the front of her dress, so as really to be certain that the little locket, the dear little talisman of her order, was safe in its place; and each girl felt naughty and good at the same time, anxious to please Kathleen and anxious to adhere to the rules of the school, and each girl resolved that, if she had to choose between the school and Kathleen, she would throw the school over and give allegiance to the queen of the society.

But Ruth's unhappy face certainly attracted attention. Cassandra Weldon noticed it first of all. In recess she went up to her and took her hand.

"Ruth," she said, "you must come home with, me to dinner. Afterwards we can have a good chat; and then you shall have a room to yourself in order to work up your lessons for Miss Renshaw. But what is the matter, Ruth? You don't look well."

"I am quite well," answered Ruth; "but I don't think I'll be able to come back with you to-day, Cassie."

"Oh, what a pity, dear! Is your grandmother ill?"

"No; she's quite well."

"And your grandfather?"

"They are both quite well. It is—no, it's not nothing, for it is something; but I can't tell you. Please don't ask me."

"You look very sad."

"I feel miserable."

"I wonder—" said Cassandra thoughtfully.

Ruth looked at her. There was absolute despair in the eyes generally so clear and steadfast and bright. At this moment Kathleen O'Hara was seen passing through the playground in a sort of triumphal progress. She was accompanied by quite a tail of girls: one hung on her right arm, another on her left; a third danced in front of her; and other girls followed in a thick procession.

"I feel like a queen-bee that has just swarmed," she remarked *en passant* to Cassandra Weldon.

Her rude words, the impertinent little toss of her head, and the defiant glance out of her very dark-blue eyes caused Cassandra to stamp her foot.

"Ruth," she said, "I don't like your friend Kathleen O'Hara."

"But I love her," said Ruth.

"That is just it. She makes you all love her and then she gets you into trouble."

"But getting into trouble for a friend doesn't make you hate that friend," said Ruth.

"Well, I fail to understand her. I agree with Alice Tennant about her. A girl of that sort—fascinating, handsome, dangerous—works havoc in a school."

"Listen, Cassie," said Ruth suddenly. "A good many people will be saying bad things about Kathleen before long, and perhaps you will be questioned. I know that Alice Tennant has been questioned already. Will you promise me something, Cassie?"

"You look so imploring that I'd like to promise you anything; but what is it?"

"Do take her part when the time comes. You are certain to be asked."

"But I don't know her. How can I take her part?"

"You can say—oh, the kindest things. You can explain that she has always been bright and gay and loving and kind."

"I don't know that she has."

"Cassie," said Ruth, "your goodness to me has been almost past understanding; but I could hate you if you spoke against her, for I love her."

Just then a teacher came out, touched Ruth Craven on her arm, and said:

"Will you go at once to see Miss Ravenscroft?"

"Why, have you got into a scrape, Ruth? Is that why you look so pale and excited and distressed?" said Cassandra.

She spoke in a whisper. Ruth's eyes looked full into hers.

"God help me," she said under her breath.—"Cassie, if you knew, if you could guess, you'd pity me."

Ruth turned away and followed the teacher into the school. A moment later she was standing before the head-mistress.

"Now, Ruth," said that lady, "I have given you as long a time as possible. Are you prepared to tell me what you know of the Wild Irish Girls?"

Ruth was silent.

"I can't give you any further time. There is to be a meeting of the governors at four o'clock this afternoon—a special meeting, convened in a hurry in order to look into this very matter. If you don't tell me in private what you can tell me, I shall be obliged to ask you to appear before the governors. In that case it would be a matter of insurrection on your part, and it is very doubtful if you would be allowed to remain in the school."

"It is very cruel to me," began Ruth.

"My dear, the path of right is sometimes cruel. We must put this matter down with a strong hand. Do you or do you not know where Kathleen O'Hara and her society are to meet this evening?"

"I've been thinking it out," said Ruth; "I have had no one to consult. If I were to tell I should be a traitor to Kathleen. I did not care for the society, although I love her. I joined it at first—I can't quite tell you how—but afterwards I left it. I left it entirely for my own benefit. There is a girl in this school whom you all love and respect. I don't suppose any other girl in the whole school bears such a high character. Her name is Cassandra Weldon."

"Of course I know Cassandra Weldon," said the head-mistress. "She is our head girl."

"She is; and she is not proud, and she is—oh, so kind! She offered me a very great help. She presented to me a tremendous temptation."

"What was that, Ruth?"

Miss Ravenscroft began by being cold and indifferent; she was now really interested.

"You can sit down if you like," she said.

But Ruth did not sit; she only put one pretty little hand on the back of a chair as though to steady herself.

"I will tell you everything that concerns myself," she said. "I don't mind how badly you think of me. I had joined the other foundationers as a member of Kathleen's society. Then Cassandra presented the temptation. She offered to give me the services of her coach, Miss Renshaw, to work up for the Ayldice Scholarship. That means sixty pounds a year. We are poor at home, Miss Ravenscroft. My grandfather and grandmother are very poor people; but my father was a gentleman, and my mother was a lady, and their great longing in life was to have me well educated. My grandparents can scarcely afford the expense of keeping me in this school. I know I am a foundationer and my education is free; but there are other small expenses that have to be met. Even for me to live at home is almost more than they can compass. You can therefore imagine the great and wonderful delight of being able to secure a scholarship of sixty pounds a year. I could scarcely have managed it without this help. It was noble of Cassandra to offer it, and I—I accepted it, Miss Ravenscroft. After that, of course, I couldn't remain in Kathleen's society, for Kathleen and Cassandra hate each other, and I couldn't be one moment with one girl and another with the other; so I gave up the society and joined Cassandra. But I can't now betray those who were my friends. I have made up my mind; I can't."

"You have really made up your mind?"

"Quite—quite; indeed I cannot."

"Do you know what this means?"

"I can guess."

"We shall be obliged to call a meeting of the governors. You will be had up before them. If you still persist in keeping your knowledge to yourself they will be obliged to strike your name off the school roll. You will not then be able to get the Ayldice Scholarship. You are a clever girl, Ruth. My dear child, the whole thing is a mistake. You do wrong to conceal insurrection. I can tell your special friend Kathleen, who will no longer be queen of the Wild Irish Girls, to-morrow morning, that I have forced this confession out of you. She will not hate you; she will forgive you. She will understand. My dear, why should you sacrifice everything for the sake of this naughty Irish girl?"

"Because I love her, and because it would be mean," answered Ruth, and now she burst into tears.

Miss Ravenscroft talked to her a little longer, but Ruth was firm. When she left the head-mistress's presence she felt a certain sense almost of elation.

"Now I don't feel so absolutely horrible," she said to herself. "Of course I will face the governors. I will just say that I know but that I can't tell. Yes, I believe I have done right. Anyhow, I don't feel quite so bad as before I went to see Miss Ravenscroft."

Meanwhile Susy Hopkins was having a busy time. She went to school in the morning, but as soon as ever lesson hours were over she flew back to her mother's shop. There Mrs. Hopkins awaited her with a tray full of good things.

"Now, Susy," she said, "Tom will help you, for I have got him to promise. He will borrow a wheelbarrow, and all the things can be stacked away tidily into it, and he will take them straight off to Aunt Church's house with you immediately after dinner. You had best spend the afternoon with the old lady and encourage her all you can. It is a blessed relief to have two months of that debt wiped out, and I am very much obliged to you, child, and I will help you all I can."

"You can't think how exciting it is, mother," said Susy. "And you know the best of the fun is, they are making no end of a fuss in the school. They're trying to find out all about poor Kathleen's society, in order to put a stop to it and to call the foundationers to order; but the only effect of the fuss is to make more and more of the girls want to join. I saw Kathleen for a few minutes this morning, and she said that she had twelve applications for badges already to-day, but she told the new girls that they had best not come to the meeting to-night, as there wouldn't be room for them. Kathleen is in the highest spirits; she is just laughing and dancing about and looking like a sunbeam."

"Dear, dear!" said Mrs. Hopkins. "I do hope it's nothing wicked. You girls of the present day are so queer, there's no being up to half your pranks. It would be a sorry day for me if you were banished from the school, Susy."

"Oh, I won't be. It will be all right. Anyhow, this is delicious fun, and I mean to go on with it. What have you got for the old lady's tea, mother?"

"Well, now, look here. Of course, she's only going to give tea to Miss O'Hara and Miss O'Flynn—I haven't seen that lady—and yourself and Tom. That's about all."

"And Tom will have a pretty keen appetite," said Susy. "I'll tell Miss Kathleen that she is to be at Aunt Church's house quite half-an-hour before the rest of the girls, so that aunty can have her talk with her and arrange about the almshouse, and also that Kathleen and Miss O'Hara may have their meal in comfort. What's the grub, mother? Tell me at once."

"Bread-and-butter," said Mrs. Hopkins, beginning to count on her fingers, "a pot of strawberry-jam—"

"Oh, golloptious!" burst from Susy.

"A plumcake—"

"Better and better!" cried Susy.

"A little tin of sardines—some ladies are fond of a savory—"

"Yes, mother; quite right. And so is aunty, for that matter. You haven't forgotten the water-cress, have you?"

"Here's a great bunch of it. You must turn the tap over it and wash it as clean as clean. And what with new-laid eggs, and tea with cream in it, and loaf-sugar, why, I think that's about enough."

"So it is, mother; and it's beautiful. But, mother, I do think Aunt Church would relish a pound of sausages. It isn't often she has anything of that kind to eat; she lives very penuriously, you know, mother."

"Well, I suppose I can fling in the sausages. I'll just run round to the shop and buy them. Now then, eat your own dinner, Susy, and be quick. Tom has eaten his, and has gone to fetch the wheelbarrow from Dan Smith, the cartwright."

Mrs. Hopkins's programme was carried out. Tom arrived at the door with the wheelbarrow about two o'clock. The provisions were stowed safely away in the bottom and covered over with a piece of old matting, and then Tom and Susy started off. Both boy and girl were in high spirits. The day was as fine as it had been on the previous day, and Susy chattered to her heart's content.

"My word," said Tom, "I must be in it!"

"But you can't, Tom. You are a boy. That would be the final straw. If the ladies of the school and those awful governors were to come along and to see a boy in the midst of forty girls, I do believe we'd all be put in prison. You must clear out, Thomas; make up your mind to that as soon as ever you have handed over the things to Aunt Church."

"You wait and see," said Tom. "You may suppose you are a favorite with Aunt Church, but you are nothing at all to me; I can just twist her round my fingers. It's a fine time I mean to have. I won't worry you at all when you are having your commotion in the yard. For the matter of that, I'll creep into the pig-sty with Brownie, and we can look over the doorway."

"Oh, Tom, you are certain to be discovered. And you'll just pinch that pig and make him squeal like anything."

Tom laughed.

"I mean to have my fun," he said; "and don't you suppose for a moment I'm going to funk a lot of stupid, silly girls. How much do you think I'm going to eat, miss?"

"I'm sure you are going to be horribly greedy. But perhaps when you see Miss O'Hara and Miss O'Flynn you'll take a fit of shyness. It's to be hoped you will."

"Shyness!" cried Tom. "What's that?"

"It's what you ought to have, Tom, and it's to be hoped you will have it when the time comes."

"Looks like it!" cried Tom, rubbing his hands in a meaning way. "Never frightened of anybody in the whole course of my life. Mean to have a lark with your pretty Miss Kathleen; mean to get a sov. or two out of that charming Miss O'Flynn; mean to coax Aunty Church to give me that microscope when she moves across the sea to Ireland. Tell you, Susy, I'm up to a lark, and the best of the supper goes down my throat. Now you know, and there's no use worriting, for what can't be cured must be endured. Tom Hopkins is part and parcel of this 'ere feast, and the sooner you make up your mind to endure me the better."

Susy felt slightly alarmed, but she knew from experience that Tom's bark was worse than his bite; and she trusted to Aunt Church desiring him in a peremptory manner to go when the time approached, and to Tom's being forced to obey her.

They arrived in good time at their destination, and Mrs. Church received them figuratively with open arms. And now began the real fuss and the real preparation. Tom took a brush and kicked up, as Aunt Church expressed it, no end of a shindy. The little sitting-room was a cloud of dust. The table, the chairs, and the little sideboard were pushed about; everything seemed to be at a loss until Susy peremptorily took the duster out of Tom's hand and reduced chaos to order. Then the tea was unpacked. A very white cloth from Mrs. Hopkins's most precious store was produced; real silver spoons—from the same source—made their appearance; a few cups and saucers of good old china were added. The table looked, as Tom expressed it, "very genteel." Then the provisions were placed upon the board.

"Now we are ready," said Mrs. Church; "and I must say," she added, "that I am pleased. I have known good genteel living in my lifetime, and I expect that Providence means me to know it again before I die. Susy and Tom, you are both good children. You have your spice of wickedness in you, but when all is said and done you mean well, and I may as well promise you both now that when I get to Ireland I will have you over in the holidays. You will enjoy that—won't you, Thomas?"

"See if I don't, Aunt Church. And I always was your own boy, wasn't I? And you won't mind, old lady—say you won't mind—leaving me the microscope when you cross the briny? I'm fairly taken with that microscope. I dream of it at night, and think of it every minute of the day."

"Come here and look me in the eyes, Tom," said Mrs. Church.

Tom went over. Out of his freckled face there beamed two honest light-blue eyes. His forehead was broad and slightly bulgy; his carroty hair was cut short to his head. Mrs. Church raised her wrinkled old hand and laid it for a minute on Tom's forehead.

"You resemble your great-uncle, my husband," she said. "He was the cleverest man I ever came across. He had a real turn for the microscope."

"Then, of course, you will leave it behind you; of course you will give it to me," said Tom, quite triumphant with eagerness.

"No, my boy, that I won't. If you are a good boy, and do me credit, and get on with your books, and do well in that calling which Providence means you to work in, why, I may leave it to you when I am called hence, Tom."

"There, Tom!" said Susy, coming forward. "Don't worry Aunt Church any more. She's got plenty to think about.—Won't you turn him out now, Aunt Church? It is time for you to be dressing, you know."

"So it is," said Mrs. Church, looking round her in some alarm. "Whatever is the hour, child?"

"It is going on for six o'clock; and they will be here at half-past seven at the latest."

"Very well," said Tom; "if I must go I will have a talk with Brownie."

He looked at Susy as if he meant to defy her, but Susy was too wise to anger him at that moment. As soon as ever he was out of the house she fetched hot water, soap and a clean towel. Having helped old Mrs. Church with her ablutions, she produced a clean cap and a little black shawl. The old lady said that she felt very smart and refreshed, and altogether in a state to do honor to that dear little almshouse.

"I am quite taking to you, Susy," she said. "But I do hope you will marshal those dreadful girls into the backyard without frightening my hens or Brownie."

"Pigs aren't remarkable for sensitiveness," said Susy. "But I tell you what, Aunt Church; Tom's after mischief; he means to witness all the proceedings of dear Miss Kathleen's great society, and we oughtn't to let him. It would do a lot of mischief if the school heard of it, and we would most likely be expelled. He don't mind a word I say, so will you talk to him, aunty?"

"But he can't be in the yard without being seen; you say that they are bringing lamps and will make the place as bright as day."

"Yes, but he will be in the sty with Brownie; and he as good as said he'd give her a pinch to make her squeal."

"Oh, indeed! I'm afraid that must be put a stop to," said the old lady. "Send him to me this minute."

Susy went out and called her brother. There was no answer for a minute; then Tom appeared, looking somewhat rakish and disheveled.

"Brownie and I were chumming up like anything," he said; then he pushed Susy aside and walked into the old lady's presence.

What she said to him even Susy did not hear, but when the little girl returned to Mrs. Church, Tom was nowhere to be seen.

"Has he gone home, Aunt Church," she asked.

"You leave the boy alone," was Mrs. Church's answer. "He's a good boy, and the moral of his grand-uncle; and I'll leave him that microscope. See if I don't."

CHAPTER XX.
THE GOVERNORS OF THE
SCHOOL EXAMINE RUTH.

At four o'clock that afternoon the governors of the Great Shirley School met in the room set aside for the purpose. There were six governors, and they were all ladies. Their names were Miss Mackenzie, Mrs. Naylor, Mrs. Ross, the two Misses Scott, and Miss Jane Smyth. The founders of the Great Shirley School had ordained that it should always be governed by women — that women should conduct its concerns, should see to the best possible education of its pupils, and should manage these things to the best of their ability. Even the trustees of the trust fund were women.

Amongst these ladies Miss Mackenzie was reckoned as head. She was a tall, strong-minded woman, with iron-gray hair, false teeth, a prominent nose, and small steel-gray eyes. Miss Mackenzie was between sixty and seventy years of age; she always dressed in the severest and most old-fashioned manner, and wore her iron-gray hair in ringlets on each side of her head. She was an excellent woman of business, and was dreaded not only by the schoolgirls, but also by one or two of the ladies of the committee; those who most feared her were the two Misses Scott and Miss Jane Smyth. Mrs. Ross was a fashionable woman who went a good deal into London society, talked about the Great Shirley School to her different friends, and was considered an expert on the subject of girls' education. Mrs. Ross had a husband and a beautiful home; she dressed remarkably well, and was looked down on in consequence by Miss Mackenzie. Mrs. Naylor was the oldest of the governors. She was a little, wizened lady with a face like a russet apple, a kindly smile, and a sweet voice.

It was the custom of the governors to meet four times a year as a matter of course, and as a matter of expediency they met about as many times again. But a sudden meeting to be convened within forty-eight hours' notice was almost unheard of in their experience.

When they were all seated round the table Miss Mackenzie, who was chairwoman, took out the agenda and read its contents aloud. These were brief enough:

"To inquire into the insurrection amongst the foundationers, and in particular to cause full investigation to be made with regard to the Irish girl, Kathleen O'Hara."

"This is really very astonishing," said Miss Mackenzie, turning to the other governors. "An insurrection amongst the foundationers! Had we not better summon Miss Ravenscroft, who will tell us what she means?"

A clerk who attended the meetings (also a woman) went away now to summon Miss Ravenscroft. She appeared in a few minutes, was asked to seat herself, and was requested to give a full explanation. This she did very briefly.

"At the beginning of the term," she said, "a girl of the name of Kathleen O'Hara joined our number. She was eccentric and untrained. She came from the south-west of Ireland. I had her examined, and found that she knew extremely little. We were forced to put her into much too low a class for her years and general appearance."

"Well," said Miss Smyth, "that, after all, isn't a crime. I don't quite understand."

"If you will kindly resume your story we shall be obliged, Miss Ravenscroft," said Miss Mackenzie.

Miss Ravenscroft did resume it. She traced Kathleen's conduct from the first day of her arrival to the present hour. Short as the time was—not more than six weeks—she had worked havoc in the school. Her influence was altogether felt amongst the foundationers. They crowded round her at all hours; a glance from her eyes was sufficient to compel them to do exactly what she wished. They ceased to be attentive to their lessons; they were often discovered in school in a state of semi-drowsiness; they were rebellious and impertinent to their teachers—in short, they were in a state of insurrection.

"And you trace this disgraceful state of things to the advent of the Irish girl?" said Miss Mackenzie.

"I am sorry to say, Miss Mackenzie, that I do. When I noticed that Kathleen O'Hara had a disturbing influence over the girls I caused further inquiries to be made, and I then made a discovery which distressed me very much. My eyes were first opened by the fact that one of our teachers picked up off the floor, just where a certain Clara Sawyer, one of the best and most promising of the foundationers, was sitting, a small locket, evidently a badge. She brought it to me, and I now hand it to you ladies for inspection."

The little silver heart-shaped badge was passed from one lady to another. The Misses Scott thought it pretty and quaint. Miss Jane Smyth murmured the words "Wild Irish Girls" under her breath. Mrs. Ross pushed it away from her as though it was beneath notice. Mrs. Naylor said:

"Very pretty; quite touching, isn't it? Heart-shaped. I always think that such a sweet emblem, don't you, Miss Mackenzie?"

But Miss Mackenzie, with a sniff, took up the little talisman and turned it from right to left.

"'Wild Irish Girls,'" she said aloud. "What can this mean?"

"I can throw some light on the subject, but not much," said Miss Ravenscroft. "It is quite evident that a society calling itself by this name exists, and that it has been instituted and formed altogether by Kathleen O'Hara, who has induced a great number—I should say fully half—of the foundationers to join her. They meet, I have discovered, at night; their rendezvous being, up to the present, a certain quarry a short distance out of town. What they do at their meetings I cannot tell, but I believe they are very riotous, with singing and dancing and sports of all sorts. Of course, as you know, Miss Mackenzie, such proceedings are altogether prohibited in our school."

"But this takes place out of school," said Mrs. Naylor.

"Mrs. Naylor, I should be much obliged if you would allow Miss Ravenscroft to continue," said Miss Mackenzie.

Miss Ravenscroft did continue.

"Putting aside that question," she said, "the effect on the girls is most disastrous. They are completely out of my control, and I know for a fact that they do not care to please any one except Kathleen O'Hara."

"Of course our duty is plain," said Miss Mackenzie. "We must get the ringleader into custody, so to speak, and either bind her over to break up the society, and so keep the peace, or expel her from the school."

"She is a difficult girl to deal with," said Miss Ravenscroft. "She has a great deal that is good in her; she is handsome and rich, very affectionate, and full of spirit."

"But what has a girl who is handsome and rich to do in a school like the Great Shirley?" asked Mrs. Ross.

"That is the curious part of it. Kathleen's mother was educated in this school, and she made up her mind that her daughter should never go to any other. Kathleen lives with the Tennants. I should be sorry if she were expelled; there is so much that is good in her. It would be a pity to harden her or hold her up to public disgrace. I hope some other way may be discovered of bringing her to order."

"You are quite right. Miss Ravenscroft," said Miss Smyth. "I never did hold with the severe hardening process."

"Certainly in the case of Kathleen it would do no good," said Miss Ravenscroft.

"But what do you propose to do, then?" said Miss Mackenzie. "You have not, I presume, asked us to come here without having some plan in your head."

"The first thing to do is to get hold of all possible facts," said Miss Ravenscroft. "Now, there is one girl in the school who could tell us—a charming girl, a new girl—for she also only joined this term—but in all respects the opposite of Kathleen O'Hara. She for a short time belonged to the rebels, as I must call the Wild Irish Girls, but she saw the folly of her conduct and left them. She could tell us all about them if she liked, and help us to bring the insurrection to an end."

"Then that is capital," said Miss Mackenzie in a tone of enjoyment. "Have the girl summoned, please, Miss Ravenscroft."

Miss Ravenscroft turned to the clerk, who went away at once in search of Ruth. Ruth came in looking very white, her face dogged, her usual beauty and charm of manner having quite deserted her. She wore her little school-apron and she kept folding it between her fingers as she stood in the presence of her judges.

"Your name?" said Miss Mackenzie.

"Ruth Craven."

"Your age?"

"I am fourteen."

"Where do you live?"

"In No. 2 Willow Cottages."

"Oh, I know," said Miss Mackenzie, looking with more approval at the child. "I have often met your grandfather. You live with him and his wife, don't you?"

"Yes, madam."

"And you have been admitted here as a foundationer?"

"Yes, madam."

"In what class is Ruth Craven, Miss Ravenscroft?"

"Ruth is a very diligent pupil. She is in the third remove," replied Miss Ravenscroft, looking with kindly eyes at the child.

Ruth just glanced at her teacher, and then lowered her eyes. Her beautiful little face was beginning to have its usual effect upon most of the ladies present. Some of the stony despair had left it; the color came and went in her cheeks. She ceased to fiddle with her apron, and clasped her two little white hands tightly together.

"My child," said Mrs. Naylor, "your object in coming to school is doubtless the best object of all."

Ruth raised inquiring eyes.

"I mean," said the little old lady, "that you want to learn all you can—to gain knowledge and wisdom, to learn goodness and forbearance and long-suffering and charity."

"Oh, yes," said Ruth, her eyes dilating.

"If," continued Miss Mackenzie, interrupting Mrs. Naylor, and speaking in a very firm tone—"if, instead of these pleasant things happening, a little girl learns to join insurrectionists, to forget those to whom she is indebted for such tremendous advantages, then how do matters stand—eh, Ruth Craven?"

"I don't understand," said Ruth.

Her trembling and fear had come back to her.

"The dear child is frightened, Miss Mackenzie," said Mrs. Naylor.

"I hope not," said Miss Mackenzie; "but I as chairwoman am obliged to question her.—Ruth Craven, is it true that you became a member of a silly schoolgirl society called the Wild Irish Girls, and that you wore a badge like this?"

Ruth nodded.

"Don't nod to me. Speak."

"It is true," said Ruth.

"Are you now a member of that society?"

"No."

"Why did you join it?"

"Because I loved Kathleen O'Hara."

"She is the promoter, then?"

Ruth was silent.

"You have heard me?"

"Yes, madam."

"Kathleen O'Hara is the promoter?"

Again Ruth was silent. Miss Mackenzie glanced at the other ladies. After a pause she continued:

"We will leave that matter for the present. Please write down, Miss Judson"—here she turned to the clerk—"that Ruth Craven has refused to answer my question with regard to Kathleen O'Hara. We will return to that point later on.—Why did you leave the society?"

"I did so because I wanted to join a scheme proposed by a girl who was not a foundationer and not a member of the society. Her name is Cassandra Weldon."

"One of our best and most promising pupils," interrupted Miss Ravenscroft.

"I know her," said Miss Mackenzie. "We have every reason to be proud of Cassandra Weldon.—And so she, this charming and excellent Cassandra Weldon, is your friend, little Ruth Craven?"

"She has been extremely good to me, madam. She offered me the services of her own coach in order that I might work up for the Ayldice Scholarship."

"And do you think you have a chance of getting it?"

"I don't know. I mean to try."

Her dark-blue eyes flashed with intelligence and longing as she uttered these words.

"I think we are now in possession of the facts," said Miss Mackenzie. "Is that not so, Mrs. Ross? Ruth Craven was a member of the objectionable society; she very wisely left it, knowing that she would better herself by doing so.—Now then, Ruth, we expect you to tell us all about the society— where it meets, and as much as you know about its rules. And you must also acquaint us with the names of the girls who are members."

Ruth again was silent, but now she held herself erect and looked full at Miss Mackenzie.

"You hear me, child. Speak. You can make your narrative brief. Where does the society meet? What does it do? What are its rules? Go on; you are not stupid, are you?"

"No, Miss Mackenzie," said Ruth, "I am not stupid; and I am very, sorry indeed to seem rude, but I cannot answer your questions. You know that Kathleen's society exists; that fact I cannot hide from you, but you will not hear anything more from me. It would be a very terrible thing for me to be expelled from this school; it would mean great sorrow to my grandfather and grandmother; but I cannot betray my friend Kathleen, nor any of the other girls of the society."

Miss Mackenzie was silent for quite a minute. The other ladies fidgeted as they sat. Ruth, having delivered her soul, looked down. After a long pause Miss Mackenzie said quite gently:

"Ruth Craven, you scarcely realize your own position. We cannot possibly let a little girl who is rebellious, who keeps secrets to herself which she ought to tell for the benefit of the school, continue in our midst. We will give you three days to think over this matter. If at the end of three days you are still obstinately silent, there is nothing whatever for it but that you should be expelled from the school. Do you understand what that means?"

"It means that I must go, that I shall lose all the advantages," said Ruth.

"It means that and more. It means that in the presence of the whole school you are pronounced unworthy, that you leave the school publicly, being desired to do so by your teacher. It is an unpleasant ceremony, and one which you will never be able to forget; it will haunt you for life, Ruth Craven. I trust, however, my dear child, that such extreme measures will not be necessary. You think now that you are honorable in making yourself a martyr, but it is not so. We who are old must know more than you can possibly know, Ruth, with regard to the benefits of a great establishment like this. Insurrection must be put down with a firm hand. You will see for yourself how right we are, and how wrong and silly and childish you are.—Miss Ravenscroft, a special meeting of the governors will take place in this room on Saturday morning. This is Wednesday. Until then we hope that Ruth Craven will carefully consider her conduct, and be prepared to answer the very vital questions which will be put to her.—You can go, Ruth."

Ruth left the room.

"An extraordinary child," said Miss Mackenzie.

"A sweet child, I call her," said Mrs. Naylor. "What a beautiful face!"

"My dear Mrs. Naylor, does the beauty of Ruth Craven's face affect this question? She is, in my opinion, extremely silly, and a very naughty child.—Miss Ravenscroft, we leave it to you to bring the little girl to reason. I have known her grandfather ever since he kept a grocer's shop in the High Street. I have respected him more than any man I ever knew. This child in appearance is one of Nature's ladies, but we must get her to see things in the right light, and if necessary she must be made an example of. It will be very painful, but it must be done."

"I will do what I can," said Miss Ravenscroft; "but from the little I have seen of Ruth, I imagine she would go to the stake before she would betray those who are kind to her. I will, however, confide in Cassandra; she is extremely fond of Ruth, and she may influence her where others fail. I can't help saying, Miss Mackenzie, that it would be a very terrible thing, and would, I believe much injure the school, if a girl like Ruth were expelled. The other foundationers would feel it; there would be a sense of martyrdom. Sides would be taken for and against her. I trust that this extreme step will not be necessary."

"If she does not tell us what she knows, it will be not only necessary, but it will be carried into effect, and in my presence," said Miss Mackenzie. "But now to return to the more immediate business. You say these girls meet in a quarry?"

"I have heard rumors to that effect."

"Do you think they meet there every night? Are their scandalous proceedings a nightly occurrence?"

"Oh, no; I do not think they meet oftener than once a week."

"Have you any idea what night they choose?"

"I am rather under the impression that this is the night."

"Then send some one to see, Miss Ravenscroft. One or two of the teachers would be the best. They could go to the quarry to-night and wait there in order to see if the girls arrive. If they do, my orders are that they take no apparent notice of them, but write down the names of all present. If that can be done, and you are successful in finding the girls, we shall have the matter, as it were, in a nutshell, and we shall soon crush this disgraceful rebellion."

"And what about Kathleen?" asked Miss Ravenscroft.

"There is very little doubt that she will have to be expelled. Such a girl as that is a firebrand in a school, and however rich she may be, and however well-born, the sooner she leaves us the better."

CHAPTER XXI.
THE SOCIETY MEETS AT MRS. CHURCH'S COTTAGE.

That evening at about a quarter to eight a band of perfectly silent girls might have been seen walking along the road that led to Mrs. Church's cottage. They walked as much as possible on the grass, and glided in single file. Each one, as they expressed it, had her heart in her mouth. Occasionally they looked behind them; sometimes they started at an ordinary shadow, thinking that a policeman at least would be waiting for them. The foundationers who called themselves the Wild Irish Girls had very little doubt what it would mean if their scheme was discovered. They knew, of course, that Miss Ravenscroft would be furiously angry, that the governors would have something to say to them, and that they might be dismissed from the school unless they promised to cease to belong to the society. Perhaps there were worse things than that. There was a timid little girl called Janey Ford, who whispered to her friend that the Wild Irish Girls belonged to the rebels in Ireland, and that it might be considered necessary by the government of the country to have them taken up and put into prison. Nobody for a single moment believed Janey Ford's silly remarks, but nevertheless they gave a sort of thrill to the occasion. It was all delightful, this stealing away in the dark, this pressing one against another as they walked down the little road. And then Kathleen was so fascinating; her eyes were so bright; she was such a valiant sort of leader. If they were men and she was a man, Janey Ford had whispered to her great friend Edith Hart, they would follow her to the death.

"We'd form a crusade for her," Edith had whispered, back. "She is magnificent."

And then both girls felt the little heart-shaped lockets round their necks and thought of themselves as heroines.

The entire party, numbering about forty-three in all, arrived at the cottage. Susy suddenly put in her appearance.

"Girls," she said, "it isn't at all certain that we are safe. I saw a man going by not ten minutes ago, and he looked suspiciously at the house. Miss

Ravenscroft would do anything to catch us; but Aunt Church says that if you go into the yard she doesn't think you will be seen or heard.—May I take the girls into the yard, Kathleen? And may I take you and Miss O'Flynn into the house to see Aunt Church?"

Kathleen nodded in reply. She also felt excited and pleased and completely carried out of herself.

Susy ushered her visitors with great pride and pomp into Mrs. Church's little sitting-room. Really she felt herself quite rising in the social scale as she saw her old relative dressed in her best, with the manners she used to wear when she was housekeeper at Lord Henshel's, and with that most appetizing, most *recherché* tea on the table.

"I will be back in a minute," said Susy.—"Aunt Church, here they are, and I know you will give them welcome."

"I am proud to do that," said Mrs. Church. "I presume I am talking to Miss O'Flynn? Will you take a chair here by the fire, miss? I'm afraid the night is a little bit chilly.—Miss Kathleen, I wish I could get up and offer you a seat, but as it is—"

"Oh, nonsense!" said Kathleen. "What are young legs for if not to wait on old legs? Oh, what a heavenly, delicious tea! What is that I see? Honey! Oh, don't I just adore honey? Don't you, Aunt Katie?"

"That I do," said Miss O'Flynn; "and I eat it comb and all. It never yet disagreed with me; but then I've got the digestion of an ostrich."

"Indeed, then, madam, I think you are rather silly to eat the comb," said Mrs. Church; "and you ought always to put butter on your bread when you eat honey. My poor mother told me so, and I have always followed in her steps. If you butter your bread and don't eat the comb, honey agrees with you as well as anything else."

"Mrs. Church," said Kathleen, "you are perfectly sweet, and I can't tell you how grateful we are; but we are in something of a hurry, so perhaps you wouldn't mind telling the rest of that story about butter and honey to Aunt Katie when you are in Ireland. Have you made the tea, Mrs. Church? Shall I make it?"

"The tea is in that little brown caddy," said Mrs. Church, "and there's a measuring spoon close to it. I allow—"

"Oh, I know," said Kathleen.

She began to ladle out spoonful after spoonful and put it into the little brown teapot, which she then filled up with hot water. Mrs. Church looked on with a mingled feeling of approval and disapproval. She was being carried completely off her feet. She to give up her dear little neat house in this reckless way; she to give up her most precious tea to be absolutely wasted and practically lost—for Kathleen put in quite three times too much tea into the little teapot; she to forgive Susy's mother two months of that debt which she owed her. Oh, what did it mean? She was going to be ruined in her old age!

"I'd just like to say, miss," she said, looking at Miss O'Flynn and then at Kathleen—"I'd like to say that I am willing to help the young ladies, and the old ladies too for that matter, but I want to know if it is settled that I am to have the almshouse and six shillings a week. I am a plain-spoken body and I'd like to know it; for if so it can be done, I ought to give notice to the landlord of this little house, where I have lived in peace and comfort for over twelve years. I'd like to know, and as soon as possible."

"We have written about it, Mrs. Church," said Miss O'Flynn. "I wrote to my brother-in-law this very day, and I expect an answer soon. Of course, we can't tell you to a certainty whether the house is still to be had, but I didn't hear that it was let. We must hope for the best."

"And if it is let," said Kathleen suddenly, running up to the old lady and whispering in her ear, "I'll get Dad to send me a cheque, and you shall have it, so you won't lose one way or the other."

This whisper of Kathleen's was very soothing to Mrs. Church. She nodded her head twice and said:

"Thank you, dear," and just then Susy returned, and tea began in real earnest.

While the ladies were enjoying their meal they did not observe that a round boyish face occasionally appeared at the little glass partition which divided Mrs. Church's sitting-room from her bedroom. The glass reached down about two feet from the ceiling, and was the only light the bedroom had. The boyish face bobbed up now and again, made appealing faces in Mrs. Church's direction, and then disappeared. Mrs. Church shook her head at the apparition, but for a time no one noticed the circumstance. Then Susy began to observe it.

"What can it mean?" she thought, and she turned and looked.

The face appeared, the tongue now stuck into the cheek, one eye winking furiously.

"Well, I never!" said Susy.

"What are you saying, 'Well, I never!' for?" asked Kathleen. "And why do you and Mrs. Church keep gazing up at that ugly glass across the room? What is the glass for?"

"It is the window that lights my bedroom, miss," said Mrs. Church. "And I don't see," she added, "why I may not look at any part of my own house that I take a fancy to."

"Of course," said Kathleen. But Tom was now making pantomimic signs for refreshments. He was touching his mouth, which he opened into a round O, pointing at the cake and honey, and going on altogether in a way that distracted poor Susy. And just as Susy looked up Kathleen looked up, and the latter burst into a loud laugh, and said:

"I do declare there's a boy in there."

The next instant she had burst into the bedroom and dragged Tom out.

"Oh, you are Tom Hopkins," she said; "you are Susy's brother. Now sit down here and have a right good meal. It was silly of you to hide in there; as if we minded."

"But Kathleen, you ought to mind," said Susy; "for it would be the very last straw if we were discovered and there is a boy found amongst us. I declare I never felt so nervous in my life.—Do go back to the bedroom, Tom.—Aunt Church, oughtn't he to go?"

"Come and sit by me," said Mrs. Church. "And here's a fresh egg for you. Take your place, Tom; and when the others go into the yard for their foolish mummeries—for I can't make out that there's a bit of sense in this scheme from first to last—why, you and I will finish up what is left of the good things."

"You are a brick, Aunt Church," said Tom.

He took a seat at the table, and gazed with wonder, delight, and admiration at Kathleen. He told his school-fellows that at that moment he lost his heart to Kathleen. He said that she bowled him over completely.

"I haven't a scrap of heart in my body to-day," he remarked to his chosen friends. "I took it out and put it at her feet; and if you'll believe me, she spurned it. That's the way of girls. Don't you have anything to do with them, boys."

But the boys only begged more earnestly than ever to have a look at Kathleen. Tom finally promised to secure her photograph by hook or by crook, and to show it to them.

When the meal, which was but a short one after all, came to an end, Miss O'Flynn and Kathleen got up and were preparing to go to the yard at the back of the house, when there came the sound of horse's hoofs on the stones outside. They stopped at the cottage, and a loud knock at the door was next heard.

"They have come," said Susy, her face white as a sheet. "I knew they would. I wonder what will happen, Kathleen. Aren't you awfully frightened?"

"Not I," said Kathleen. "Why should I be afraid? Whoever is there has nothing to do with us."

Susy's state of panic amused both Miss O'Flynn and Kathleen, and Tom was the only one found brave enough to go to the door in answer to the knock. He came back the next instant with a telegram, which was addressed to Miss O'Flynn. She tore it open, and gave a loud scream.

"It's my poor cousin Peggy Doharty. She has fallen from her horse and has concussion of the brain. I must go to her at once. Oh, alannah, alannah! What is to be done?"

Here Miss O'Flynn turned a face of anguish in Kathleen's direction.

"It is I that must leave you, my darling," she said. "I will go back to town with the messenger, get off to London to-night, and cross in the morning. Ah, the creature! And she's my dearest friend. Let us hope that Providence will spare her precious life. Oh dear, dear, dear! This is awful!"

"I don't see why you should go, Aunt Katie," said Kathleen. "I want you very badly indeed just now."

"Then, my sweet child, come straight away with me to Dublin; for as to leaving Peggy in her hour of extremity, I wouldn't do it even for you, Kathleen, and that's saying a good deal."

"But how can I come? I have my society and—and the school."

"Well, then, stay, love; only don't keep me now. Good-bye to you, pet; I haven't a minute to lose—Tom—is that your name?—go out and tell the messenger that I will go back with him to Merrifield."

"And what about my almshouse?" screamed out Mrs. Church. "This is a nice state of things, I must say. Who minds what a slip of a young lady says?—meaning no offence to you, miss; but I have been spending my money right and left, getting tea that beats all for gentility, and now one of the ladies is off as it were in a flash of an eye. What about my almshouse?"

Miss O'Flynn looked rather indignant.

"You shall have your almshouse if it can be got. How unfeeling you are to think only of yourself when my dearest friend may be at death's door. Here's a sovereign, which will more than cover the expenses of the tea.— Good-bye, Kathleen, core of my heart.—Good-bye, all of you."

Miss O'Flynn flung a sovereign on the table. Mrs. Church made a grab at it, and held it tightly in her hand, which was covered by a black mitten. The next moment the good lady had departed, and Kathleen, looking thoroughly bewildered, was left alone.

"Dear, dear!" she said. "Yet I am an Irish girl, and I'm not going to show funk. There are all those poor girls waiting in the yard so long. I will go to them at once. Come with me, Susy."

There were about forty girls in the yard, and they sat close together. The night was sufficiently cold to make them somewhat chill, and the fears which little Janey Ford had put into their hearts began to grow greater and more fixed each moment. When Kathleen appeared all was immediately changed. Susy preceded her, carrying the little paraffin lamp. This was placed on the table which was arranged in the yard for the purpose, and its light fell now on the vivid coloring and beautiful face of the Irish girl. She took off her favorite blue velvet cap and pushed her hand through her masses of radiant hair, and then flung herself into what she was pleased to call an attitude, but which was really a very graceful and natural pose. Then she said, speaking aloud:

"Girls of the society, Wild Irish Girls, I am sorry to tell you that my aunt, Miss O'Flynn—Miss Katie O'Flynn—who I hoped would have joined our numbers to-night, and would have been a perfect rock of strength for us all, has been obliged to suddenly go back to Ireland, owing to an accident that has happened to her dearest friend."

"Dear, dear, how sad!" said one or two.

"So we are without her, girls," continued Kathleen. "And now I want to know if you are prepared to stand by me through thick and thin?"

"That we are!" was shouted in one vivid, clear girlish note.

"I am glad to hear it. And if you will stand by me, you may be quite sure that I will stand by you. It is whispered in the school that we are found out, and the school, bless it! is angry. It doesn't want us, you foundationers and me, to have our fun—our little bit of innocent fun."

"Very mean of it!" said one or two, while the others groaned.

"It wants to crush us," continued Kathleen. "We mean the school no harm, and why shouldn't it let us alone? All we want is our fun, a little bit of liberty, and to show those companions who look down upon us that we are as good as they, and that we will fight for each other, and have our own way, and meet when we please, and do as we like out of school hours. It is a sort of Manifesto of Independence, that is what it is, girls, and I want to know if you will stick to it."

All the hands were raised up at this juncture, and all the voices said:

"Yes, yes, yes."

"That's splendid," said Kathleen. "I didn't know I had such an enthusiastic following. Well girls, we'll have to run a certain risk. We will have to conceal all we can about this society; we'll have to be true to each other, whatever happens; and we'll meet wherever we like, girls. Let the head-mistress and the governors say what they please."

"Hurrah for Kathleen O'Hara! Hurrah for the Wild Irish Girls for ever!" they shouted.

"That's about it," said Kathleen. "I called you all to-night to tell you that we are suspected, and we are called insurrectionists; but let them call us what they like."

"Please," here put in the timid voice of Janey Ford, "are we likely to be put in prison? For that would break mother's heart, and do none of us any good."

"Oh, you little goose!" cried Kathleen, with her ringing laugh. "Not a bit of it. The worst that could happen to us is to be expelled from the school."

Now this worst, which was really a matter of little importance in the eyes of Kathleen, was somewhat serious to the other girls. To be expelled meant to deprive them of their chance of being well educated and of earning a decent living by-and-by. They all felt very grave, and Kathleen, who had a great power of reading what went on in the hearts of those in whom she was interested, felt somehow that their enthusiasm had abated.

"But nothing will happen," she cried, "if we are faithful to each other, stand shoulder to shoulder, and do not whatever happens, betray each other. Why girls, Miss Ravenscroft and the governors can do nothing to us unless they have proof, and they will have no proof if we are all true to each other. Now that's the whole of it for to-night. We'll meet in the quarry on Saturday night, and then we'll make a plan for a great expedition all by ourselves to London in the course of next week."

"Oh dear," said Susy, "doesn't it make your heart throb?"

"And I want to add," continued Kathleen, "that I will frank you. I can't do it always, but I will on this occasion. Aunt Katie O'Flynn has given me some money for that purpose. So you will stick to me, won't you girls?"

"That we will!" came from the mouths of all.

"And I am your captain, am I not girls?"

"Indeed you are. We could die for you," said one or two. "And we'll never betray you or one another."

CHAPTER XXII.
RUTH'S HARD CHOICE: SHE CONSULTS HER GRANDFATHER.

The next morning Cassandra Weldon was much surprised, on arriving at the school, to receive a message asking her to step into Miss Ravenscroft's special sanctum. She went there at once, wondering if the head-mistress wanted to give her particular instructions with regard to the great scholarship examination which would take place at the end of the term. Cassandra was remarkable for her calm and somewhat stately bearing; she was the sort of girl who never gave herself away. She was admired rather than passionately loved by her companions. No one could help giving her a most sincere respect. But one or two adored her, and amongst these was Florence Archer, a handsome, bright-faced, original sort of girl who was in the same form as Cassandra.

"Be sure you come and tell me afterwards what it all means, Cassie," said Florence, touching her friend affectionately on the shoulder.

Cassandra nodded. She did not suppose the matter was of special import. The rest of the girls proceeded to their different classes, and Cassandra found herself in Miss Ravenscroft's presence. Now to Kathleen the fact of being interviewed by Miss Ravenscroft only caused a sense of annoyance, and unwonted irritation; Ruth was surprised, partly delighted and partly afraid; but Cassandra, whose father had been a teacher, and who lived all her life in the scholastic world, considered it an honor almost too great for words that she should be specially interviewed by so great a person as Miss Ravenscroft. She made, therefore, a most respectful curtsy, and stood modestly before the head-mistress.

"Sit down, dear," said Miss Ravenscroft kindly. "I have sent for you, Cassandra, neither to reprove nor to give you ordinary counsel. I have sent for you to consult you, my dear child."

"You are very good," said Cassandra, flushing all over her delicate face; "and I am sure," she added, "if it is possible for me to help one like you, I should be only too proud."

"That is what I feel; and I think you can help me. We are at present in a very unpleasant position in the school. The unanimity and harmony of this entire large place is in danger, and the foundationers are in extreme peril. You perhaps know to what I allude."

"I could not be in the school without having heard rumors of a sort of insurrection which seems to be spreading a good deal," said Cassandra.

"Of course," said Miss Ravenscroft. "It has been brought to our ears that a society has been formed by an Irish girl of the name of Kathleen O'Hara. She has called it the Wild Irish Girls. There are several members, and she herself is the leader. Now, Cassandra, without going into particulars, it is the firm intention, not only of myself as head-mistress, but also of the governors, to crush this matter in the bud. It is true that the bud is rapidly blossoming into most dangerous flower and fruit, but if we are in time we shall stop all further mischief. Now to do this we must get all particulars. There is one girl who can furnish us will all we want to know, but she dreads, doubtless from conscientious motives, to betray her late companions. I allude to Ruth Craven."

"Poor little Ruth!" said Cassandra. "I thought as much. The child is very unhappy. I take a great—- very great—interest in Ruth, Miss Ravenscroft. She is a most sweet girl; she is a lady placed in a position which a lady should scarcely occupy, but through it all she will never betray the true instincts of her nature."

"I am sure of that. I quite like the child myself," said Miss Ravenscroft; "and your opinion of her, Cassie, confirms my own. She told me, too, that you have been extremely kind to her. I quite expect that is the case. But, my dear, the time has come when Ruth will either have to tell us what she knows or to resign her place in the school."

Cassandra's face looked troubled.

"There are no two opinions on the matter," continued Miss Ravenscroft. "Yesterday a meeting of the governors was convened. They assembled in the committee-room, and I was present. Ruth was sent for and questioned by Miss Mackenzie, our chairwoman. She was asked certain questions, which she absolutely refused to answer. The only thing we could get out of her was that she had been a member of the society but was one no longer."

"She left them because of me," said Cassandra. "She felt she could not be with me and with those who do not approve of the paying girls."

"There you are!" said Miss Ravenscroft. "Think of the monstrous mischief that is going on in our midst. Children like the foundationers, who are received at the school without being expected to pay anything, who get the most admirable education free of all cost, daring to set up their opinion against girls who, without being in any sense their superiors—one doesn't want to imply that for an instant—are yet vastly superior in numbers. The thing must be put a stop to, and with a high hand; and to show you, my dear, what we mean to do, we have presented an ultimatum to Ruth Craven. She will either tell publicly what she knows of the Wild Irish Girls or be publicly expelled."

"Oh, poor Ruth!" said Cassandra.

"We are naturally most anxious that such a painful scene should not take place," said Miss Ravenscroft. "I beg of you, therefore, Cassie, to see her and use your influence to induce her, not from quixotic motives, to ruin herself and injure the other girls of the school."

"I will do what I can. But Ruth is peculiar. She is, with all her sweetness, very obstinate. Still, I faithfully promise to do what I can."

Cassandra left the presence of Miss Ravenscroft and returned to her place in class. Nothing would induce her not to work with her usual diligence, but when on certain occasions she raised her head she saw that Florence Archer was watching her with curiosity and affection, and that Ruth darted quick glances at her and then bent her head, with its curly hair falling over her face, to resume her lessons.

This was a half-holiday, and the classes broke up at twelve o'clock. Cassandra hoped to have a talk with Ruth before she went home, but when she looked round for her little favorite she could not find her anywhere. The foundationers were standing in knots talking eagerly to each other. There was a sort of buzz or whisper going on in their midst. Kathleen O'Hara darted from one group to another, smiled at one set of girls, patted the shoulder of a favorite girl in another group, laughed one time, said an emphatic word to another, and presently disappeared, accompanied by Susy Hopkins.

Alice Tennant was standing by herself; she looked dull and depressed. Cassandra went up to her.

"It there anything the matter, Alice?" she asked.

"Matter!" replied Alice. "Surely you must know that for yourself. Have you not heard what a condition the school is in?"

"I have, of course, heard about the Wild Irish Girls," said Cassandra, lowering her voice. "But surely the fact that there are a few naughty girls in our midst need not upset the whole school?"

"It upsets me, anyhow," said Alice, "for I feel that I have brought it on the school. I could cry. I only wish that mother had never been induced to take Kathleen as a boarder. She is worse than troublesome; she is a girl without principle."

"Oh, I don't think quite so bad as that, dear," said a gay voice at that moment; and turning, Alice saw the piquant and beautiful face of the girl she loathed. "I guessed, of course, that you must be alluding to me," said Kathleen. "I am bad, but I have my own principles—and a good old-fashioned set, worth a great deal."

She nodded impertinently to both the girls, and then reentered the school.

"I left my satchel and came back for it," she said as she vanished from their view.

"Yes," said Alice, "that is just like her—just the sort of thing she would do. She is always daring every one. I do wish some strong influence could be brought to bear on her. There is no doubt she is very clever, and when she likes she can be extremely agreeable."

"She is extremely pretty, you know, and that goes a long way."

"Not with me, thank goodness!" said Alice. "In fact, I almost hate her face. I detest people who are always grinning and smiling and showing themselves off. My opinion is that schoolgirls ought to be modest, and attentive to their books, and not thinking of giving themselves airs. But there! no one agrees with me. Mother and the boys are fairly mad on Kathleen; and as to the servants, there's nothing they wouldn't do for her. Every one combines to spoil her; I don't see that she has the least chance."

Cassandra talked a little longer to Alice, and then prepared to go home. She was disappointed that she had not seen Ruth; but Ruth had promised to be with her quite early in the afternoon. They were both to work for two hours, and afterwards their coach was to arrive. Ruth would spend the entire afternoon at Cassandra's home. On her way back Florence Archer suddenly joined her.

"Now, Cassie," she said, "what is it?"

"Oh, can't you guess for yourself, Flo? It is this. The school has got into trouble, and the governors and Miss Ravenscroft mean to sift the matter to the very bottom. It is pretty bad when all things are considered, for if the girls won't tell they will be expelled—expelled without any hope of returning. And I rather fancy Kathleen is the sort of girl whom no one will betray. It is extremely awkward, and I feel very miserable about it."

"You look it; and yet it isn't your affair. Your place in the school is secure enough."

"What does that matter, Flo, when those you love are in danger?"

"Those you love in danger, Cassie! What do you mean now?"

"I mean just what I say. I am decidedly fond of little Ruth Craven. She is placed in a hard position, but she is so clever and so pretty that she could do anything. Well, I am certain that Ruth won't betray her companions."

"I forgot," said Florence, "that she did belong to that silly society. What a little goose she was!"

"She was led into it by Kathleen. They all were for that matter. Kathleen seems to have a singular power over them."

"But Ruth doesn't belong to it now."

"No. I can't in justice to her explain any further, Florence. I will tell you all I can, of course; but may I say good-bye now, for I have a good deal to do before dinner?"

"You are not half as friendly as you used to be," said Florence, pouting. "You hardly ever ask me to your house, and when I ask you to mine you always have an excuse ready. It is somewhat hard on me that Ruth Craven should have come between us."

"But she hasn't. I wish that you would believe that she hasn't. I have to give her a sort of protecting love; but you and I, Flo, are equal in our love. Surely we can afford to be kind to a little girl who has not our advantages."

"Oh, if you put it in that way, I don't mind a bit," said Florence cheerfully. "Well, good-bye for the present. We'll meet to-morrow morning."

The girls parted, and Florence went on her way home.

Meanwhile Ruth had also gone on her way. She walked slowly. Once or twice she stopped. Once when in a somewhat narrow and lonely path she paused and looked up at the sky, and then down at the ground beneath her feet. Once she uttered a short, expressive sort of sigh; and once she said half-aloud:

"I do hope God will help me. I do want to do just what is right."

Thus, lagging as she walked, she by slow degrees reached her home. Mrs. Craven happened to be out, but old Mr. Craven was seated by the fire. He was feeling rather poorly to-day. He had a large account-book open in front of him, and when Ruth entered he laid down the pen with which he had been summing up his figures.

"I can't make them quite right," he said slowly.

"Why, grandfather, what is the matter?" said Ruth in some surprise.

The old man's large clear blue eyes were fixed on the child.

"I had a curious feeling this morning," he said; "but I know now it was only a dream. I thought I was back in the shop again. I was up, my dear; I had taken a bit of a walk, and I came in and sat down by the fire. It came over me all of a sudden how lazy I was, and how wrong to neglect the shop and not give your grandmother a bit of help with the customers; and so strong was the notion over me that I unlocked the old bureau and took out the account-books. I said to myself I can at least square everything up for her, and that will help her as much as anything. She was always a rare one to see a good balance at the end of the week. If she had a good balance and all things nicely squared up, we'd have a nice little joint for Sunday; and she'd put on her little bonnet and best mantle, and we'd go for a walk in the country arm-in-arm, just like the Darby and Joan we were, Ruthie, and which we are. But if the balance didn't come out on the right side she'd stay at home. She'd never cry or despair; that wasn't her way, bless you! She'd say, 'We must think of some way of saving, John, or we must do a bit more selling of the stock.' She was a rare one to contrive."

Ruth had heard this story of her grandmother many and many a time before, but her grandfather's look frightened her. She went up to him and closed the big account-book.

"You have balanced things a long time ago," she said. "Don't fret now. May I put the account-book aside?"

"You may, darling; you may. But the accounts ain't balanced, Ruthie; we are on the wrong side of the ledger, my love—on the wrong side of the ledger."

Ruth said nothing more. She put the book back into the drawer and locked it. Then she sat down by her grandfather's side.

"Would you rather I got you your dinner," she said, "or would you rather I talked to you for a little?"

"I'd a sight rather my little Ruth sat near me and let me place my hand on her hair. Your hair is jet-black, Ruthie—almost blue-black. So was your father's hair, my child. He was a very handsome boy. I never looked for it that he would die in the foreign parts and leave you to your grandmother and me. But you have been a rare blessing to us—a rare blessing."

"Sometimes I think," said Ruth slowly, "that I have been a great care. It must have cost you a great deal to feed and clothe me."

"No, no, child; far from that. You were always the bit of good luck—on the right side of the balance—always, always."

Ruth took the old man's hand and pressed it between both her own. Presently she rubbed her cheeks softly against it.

"Grandfather," she said, "are you all right now—quite wide awake, I mean? Has the dream about the shop and the wrong accounts passed out of your head?"

"Why, yes, darling; of course it was only a dream."

"Then I'd like to ask you something."

"Ask away, my little Ruth. You are such a busy little maid now, what with your school, and what with your lessons, and what with that big scholarship—sixty pounds a year. Ah! we shall have a fine right side of the ledger when little Ruth has brought home sixty pounds a year."

Ruth stifled a groan.

"I am rather puzzled," she said, "and I want to put a question to you."

"Yes, my darling; I am prepared to listen."

"I know a girl," said Ruth after a pause—she thought that she would tell her story that way—"I know a girl at school, and she has been kindly treated. She is one of the foundation girls, but some of the girls who are not foundationers have singled her out and been specially good to her."

"Eh, eh! Well, that's good of them," said old Mr. Craven.

"They have been very good to her; but that Irish girl whom I told you about, she started a society—no special harm in itself—at least it didn't seem harm to the girl I have been telling you about, and she joined it. She joined it for a bit, and she liked it—that is, on the whole—but afterwards a girl who had not joined the society and did not belong to the foundationers, one whom I am sorry to say the foundationers did not care for at all, offered a great kindness to this girl—a very special and tremendous kindness—and the girl in her own mind decided that she would be doing wrong not to accept it. So she did accept it, and—Are you listening, grandfather?"

"Indeed I am, little maid. Go on, my child; I'm attending to every word."

"The girl decided to accept the kindness from the paying girl, and to do that she had to give up the society. She was sorry to give it up, but it seemed to her that it was the only right and honorable thing to do. She could not belong to both—to one side of the school and to the other; she must take her stand with one or the other; so she decided for her own special benefit to take her stand with the paying girls."

"On the whole, perhaps, she was right," said the old man. "Can't say unless I know everything; but on the whole, perhaps, she was right."

"I think she was, grandfather," said Ruth slowly. "But now please listen. The head-mistress at the school and the governors have found out about the secret society. They have found out that it exists, but they don't know much more. They know, however, that its influence is bad in the school, and they are determined to crush it out. In order to do this they must get full particulars. They must get the name of the leader. I am afraid that they know the name of the leader, but they must also get the names of her companions—all the names—and as much as possible of the rules of the society. Now the only girl not a member of the society who can give those particulars is the girl I have been talking about; for, of course, she knows, as she belonged to it at one time although she has now left it. And the governors and the head-mistress sent for this girl and asked her to betray her companions—those girls to whom she had sworn fealty—and the girl refused."

"Quite right," said old Mr. Craven.

The color rushed into Ruth's cheeks. She clasped her grandfather's hand firmly.

"She thought it right, but something dreadful is going to happen. It will be terribly hard for the girl if she sticks to her resolve, for the governors of the school have presented what they call an ultimatum to her; they have given her from now till Saturday to make up her mind, and if she refuses on Saturday grandfather, she is to be expelled publicly. Her sentence will be proclaimed in the presence of all the school, and she will be watched walking out of the schoolroom and out of the big gates, which will close behind her for ever, and all her chance goes—all her golden prospects. Nevertheless, grandfather, speaking to me from your own heart, ought the girl to betray her companions?"

"Upon my word!" said the old man, who was intensely moved by Ruth's story. It did not occur to him for one moment that the little girl was talking about herself. "I tell you what, Ruth," he said; "I must think over it. I pity that poor girl. I don't think the governors ought to put any girl in such a position."

"They are sorry, but they say they must. They must get at the truth; they must crush out the insurrection."

"But it is turning king's evidence," said the old man. "I don't see how a girl is to be expected to betray her companions."

"That is the position, grandfather. And now I think I will get you your dinner."

Ruth went out of the room into the little kitchen. For a minute she pressed her hands against her face.

"Grandfather agrees with me," she said to herself. "I am glad I consulted him. No one ever had a clearer head for business or for right and wrong than grandfather when he is at his best. He was at his best just now. I feel stronger. I won't betray Kathleen O'Hara."

CHAPTER XXIII.
RUTH WILL NOT BETRAY KATHLEEN.

Soon after dinner Ruth walked over to Cassandra's house. Cassandra was so anxious to see her, so determined to use her influence on what she considered the scale of right, that she was waiting for Ruth at the little gate.

"Ah! here you are," she said. "I am so glad to see you. Mother has gone out for the day; we will have a whole delightful afternoon to ourselves. We can do some good work."

"Let us," said Ruth.

She felt feverish and excited. As a rule she was very calm, but now her heart beat too fast. She was thinking of her grandfather, and of what it would mean to him and the old grandmother when she came back on Saturday a disgraced girl, expelled from her high estate, her golden chance snatched from her. Nevertheless she had always been pretty firm, and pretty well resolved to do what she thought right. She was firmer now, and quite resolved.

"Shall we go in at once and set to work?" she said. "I want to read that bit of Tasso over again before Miss Renshaw comes."

"No, no," said Cassandra. "You are always in such a fidget to learn, Ruth. Come into the garden; I want to talk to you."

Ruth looked full round at her companion. She saw something in Cassandra's eye which made her slightly shiver. Then she said:

"Very well."

Cassandra opened the little gate which led into the tiny fruit and vegetable garden. There was a narrow path, bordered on each side with a box-hedge, down which the girls walked. Presently Cassandra slipped her arm round Ruth's waist.

"You knew, of course," she said, "how much I love you."

"You are awfully good to me, Cassie."

"As a rule I am not fond of what schoolgirls call falling in love," continued Cassandra; "but I love you. There is nothing I wouldn't do for you."

"Thank you," said Ruth again.

She wondered what Cassandra would say on Saturday. Surely after Saturday no girl who belonged to the Great Shirley School would like to speak to her.

"Now I want to tell you something," continued Cassandra. "I saw Miss Ravenscroft this morning. She told me about you and your position with the governors."

"Oh, need we talk of that?" said Ruth coloring, stopping in her walk, and turning to face Cassandra.

"Why shouldn't we? I wish you would tell me everything. Why are you going to be so obstinate? But of course you won't be. You will—you must—change your mind. She told me—Miss Ravenscroft did—because she likes you, Ruth, and she would be so terribly sorry if you got into trouble over this matter. She said you are certain to get into most serious, terrible trouble, for the governors will on no account depart from their firm resolve to expel you from the school. You will have defied their authority, and that is what they cannot permit. It is on that ground they will expel you, but it is strong enough; no one can suppose for a moment that they are acting with injustice."

"I am glad it is on that ground," said Ruth softly.

"Then of course you will be wise, Ruth. It is silly and quixotic, for the sake of a girl like Kathleen O'Hara, to ruin all your own prospects."

"It is scarcely that—and yet it is that," said Ruth slowly. "It is because I will not be a traitor," she added, lowering her voice, then flinging up her head and gazing proudly before her.

"I knew you were quixotic. I knew that was at the bottom of it," said Cassandra. "But you will think it over, Ruth. It would be too terrible to see you denounced in the presence of the whole school, and sent out of the school for ever. Think of losing your scholarship. Think of the help you want to give your grandparents. Think of your own future."

"I think of them all," said Ruth; "but I also think of what father would have said if he were alive. You see Cassandra, before all things he was a gentleman."

Cassandra started. She looked full at Ruth.

"Is that a slap at me?" she asked.

"No; I did not mean it as a slap at you or anybody. I only see how the matter looks to me, and how it would have looked to father, and how it looks to grandfather. There are some people born that way; I think, after a fashion, I am one of them. There are others who would look at the thing from a different point of view, but I don't think I envy those others. Shall we go in now and set to work?"

"You are an extraordinary girl," said Cassandra. "I really don't know whether I love you or hate you most for being such a little goose. Well, Ruth, if that is your mind, I don't know why you care to go in to work, for it will be all over in a day or two—all over—and your fate sealed."

"Nevertheless I should like to read that piece of Tasso, and do my work with Miss Renshaw. Shall we go in?" said Ruth.

Cassandra somehow did not dare to say any more. Afterwards, when Ruth had returned to her own home, Cassandra sat with her head in her hands for the best part of an hour. Her mother asked her what ailed her.

"I have a headache," she replied. "I was with a girl to-day who is fifty times too good for me."

"What nonsense you are talking, Cassandra! There are few people good enough for you."

"To think of her gives me a headache," continued Cassandra. "If you don't mind, mother, I will go to bed now."

Meanwhile things were moving rather rapidly in another direction. Kathleen O'Hara, walking home that day in the company of Susy Hopkins, eagerly questioned that young lady.

"How prim and proper every one looked in the school to-day!" she said. "What is wrong?"

"There is plenty wrong," said Susy. "I tell you what it is, Kathleen, I feel rather frightened. I suppose it will come to our all being expelled."

"Oh, not a bit of it," said Kathleen.

"Well, it looks rather like it," said Susy. "Do you know what they are doing?"

"What?"

"They are bringing pressure to bear upon Ruth Craven. The governors convened a special meeting yesterday; they had Ruth before them, and then tried by every means in their power to get her to tell. You see, she is in the position of the person who knows everything. She belonged to us for a time, and now she doesn't belong to us."

"Well?" said Kathleen, feeling interested and a little startled.

"She wouldn't tell."

"Of course she wouldn't. She is a brick. The Ruth Cravens of the world are not traitors," said Kathleen. "And so that is what the governors are doing—horrid, sneaky, disagreeable things! But they are not going to subdue me, so they needn't think it. I tell you what it is, Susy. Why should we put off till next week our picnic to town? Can't we have it this week?"

"I wish we could," said Susy. "It would be glorious," she continued. "I do think somehow, Kathleen, that they will catch us in the long run. It might be dangerous to put off our glorious time till next week."

"It might? It certainly would," said Kathleen. "We will go to-morrow evening. School is always over at four. We can meet at the railway station between five and six, and go off all by ourselves to—But where shall we go when we get to town?"

"Couldn't we go to a theatre—to the pit at one of the theatres?"

"If only Aunt Katie O'Flynn was with us it would be as right as right," said Kathleen; "but dare we go alone?"

"I am sure we dare. I shouldn't be frightened. I think some of the girls know exactly how to manage."

"Well, I tell you what. You know most of the names of the members. Go round to-day and see as many as you can. Tell them that I am game for a real bit of fun, and that I will stand treat. We will go to town by the quarter-to-six train to-morrow evening. We will have some refreshments at a restaurant, and then we will go to the pit of one of the theatres. It will be a lark. There will be about forty of us altogether."

"We are sure to be found out. It is too risky; and yet I think we'll do it," said Susy. "Oh, there never was such a lark!"

"Nothing could happen to forty of us," said Kathleen. "I am going to do it just to defy them. How dare they try to make dear little Ruth betray us? But she won't. I am certain she won't."

Susy talked a little longer to Kathleen, and finally agreed to take her message to as many of the Wild Irish Girls as she could possibly reach.

"They will all hear of it safe enough," said Susy. "The whole forty of us will meet you at the station to-morrow night. Oh dear! of course it is wrong."

"It is magnificently wrong; that is the glorious part of it," said Kathleen. "Oh dear! I feel almost as jolly as though I were in old Ireland again."

She laughed merrily, parted from Susy, and ran all the rest of the way home.

CHAPTER XXIV.
KATHLEEN AND GRANDFATHER CRAVEN.

Friday was emphatically a summer's day in winter. The sky was cloudless; the few leaves that still remained on the trees looked brilliant in their autumn coloring. The ground was crisp under foot; the air was soft, gentle, and pleasant. Girls, like all other creatures, are susceptible to weather; they do their best work and have their best feelings aroused when the sun shines and the day looks cheerful. The sunshiny weather puts heart into them. But it is sad to relate that when a girl is bent on mischief she is even more mischievous, more daring, more defiant when the sun shines and the earth looks gay.

Kathleen awoke on the special morning after a night of wild dreams. She raised herself on her elbow and looked across at Alice.

"What a lovely day! Why, I see sunshine quite plainly from where I am lying. Wake up, won't you, Alice?" she said.

"How tiresome of you to rouse me!" said Alice, opening her eyes and looking crossly at Kathleen.

Kathleen smiled back at her. Her face was rosy. Her hair was tossed in wild confusion about her head and shoulders; it tumbled also over her forehead, and made her eyes look more dancing and mischievous than ever beneath its heavy shadow.

"I wonder—" said Kathleen softly.

If she had spoken in a loud voice Alice would have taken no notice, but there was something pathetic and beautiful in her tone, and Alice raised herself and looked at her.

"I wonder," she said "why you hate me so much?'

"Fudge!" said Alice.

"But Alice, it isn't fudge. Why should I have made myself so terribly obnoxious to you? The others are fond of me; they don't think me perfect— and indeed I don't want them to—but they love me for those qualities in me which are worthy of love."

"How you chatter!" said Alice. "I have hitherto failed to perceive the qualities in you that are worthy of love. It wants another quarter of an hour before our hot water is brought in. Do you greatly object to my sleeping during that time?"

"No, cross patch," said Kathleen, turning angrily on her pillow. "You may sleep till doomsday as far as I am concerned."

"Polite," muttered Alice.

She shut her eyes, folded her arms, and prepared for further slumber; but somehow Kathleen had effectually aroused her. She could not get the radiant face out of her head, nor the words, a little sad in their meaning, out of her ears. She looked up as though moved to say something.

"As you have asked me a question, I will give you an answer. I know a way in which you can secure my good opinion."

"Really!" said Kathleen, who was too angry now to be properly polite. "And what may that way be?"

"Why, this: if you will tell the truth about your horrible society, and spare dear little Ruth Craven, and make Cassandra Weldon happy."

"I don't care twopence about your tiresome Cassandra; but little Ruth — what ails her?"

"The governors are going to insist upon her telling what she knows."

"But she won't," said Kathleen, laughing merrily. "She is too much of a brick."

"Then she'll be expelled."

"What nonsense!"

"You wait and see. You don't know the Great Shirley School as well as I do. However, I have spoken; I have nothing more to say. It is time to get up, after all."

The girls dressed in silence. Alice had long ceased to torment Kathleen about her own side of the room. Provided Alice's side was left in peace, she determined to shut her eyes to untidy wardrobes, to the chest of drawers full to bursting, to a boot kicked off here and a shoe disporting itself there, to ribbons and laces and handkerchiefs and scarves and blouses scattered on the bed, and even on the floor. Alice had learnt to put up with these things; she turned her back on them, so to speak.

The two girls ran downstairs together. Just for a moment Kathleen had felt frightened at Alice's words, but then she cast them from her mind. It was quite, quite impossible to suppose that anything so monstrously unfair as that a little girl should be expelled from the school could happen. Ruth, too, of all the girls—Ruth who was absolutely goodness itself. So Kathleen ate her breakfast with appetite, remarked on the brightness of the day to Mrs. Tennant and the boys, and then with Alice started off to school with her satchel of books slung over her shoulder, her gay, pretty dress making her look a most remarkable figure amongst all the girls who were going towards the great school, and her saucy bright face attracting attention on all sides. There was nothing about Kathleen to indicate that that evening she meant to steal from home and, in company with forty companions, go to London. She was able to keep her own counsel, and this last daring scheme was locked tightly up in her heart. On her way to school she met Ruth.

"There is Ruth," she said, turning to Alice. "Oh! and there's Susy in the distance. I want to speak to them both. You can go on, of course, Alice; I will follow presently."

"We are rather late as it is," said Alice. "In addition to your misdemeanors, I should advise you not to be late for prayers just at present."

"Thanks so much!" said Kathleen in a sarcastic tone.

She left Alice and ran towards Ruth.

"Why, Ruth," she said, "you do look pale."

"Oh, I am all right," said Ruth, brightening at the sight of Kathleen.

"Then you don't look it. Ruth, is it true that they want you to tell?"

"They want me to, Kathleen," said Ruth; "but I am not going to. You can rest quite satisfied on that point."

"You are a splendid, darling brick," said Kathleen, "and I love you to distraction. Dear Ruth, what can I do for you?"

"Give up the society as fast as you can," said Ruth.

"What? And yet you won't tell!"

"It's because it's dishonorable to tell," said Ruth. "Don't keep me now, Kathleen; I want to get into school in good time. Grandfather is not well, and I must hurry back to him."

"Your nice white-haired grandfather that you have talked to me about?"

"He was ill all night. He talked about you a little. Do you know, Kathleen, I think he'd like to see you. Would you greatly mind coming back with me after school, just to see him for a minute? I have told him so much about you, and I have told granny too, and they both picture you somewhat as you are. Do you think you could come, just to give them both pleasure?"

"Come?" said Kathleen gaily. "Why, of course I'll come, heart of my life. I'd do anything on earth to please you. I'll join you after school, and well go straight away. It doesn't matter a bit about my being late for dinner at the Tennants'. Ah! there's Susy. I want to have a word with her."

Kathleen pushed past Ruth and ran up to Susy. Susy was looking intensely agitated: there were vivid spots of color on her cheeks, and her eyes were as bright as stars.

"I have managed everything," she said in a whisper. "It's all right; it's splendidly right. We are all coming; not one of us will stay behind. We know what it means, of course."

"You look very mysterious," said Kathleen. "I wonder why you talk like that. What does it mean, in your opinion?"

"Oh, Kathleen, can't you understand? And one does it sometimes in life. I have read about it in story-books, and there are cases of it in history; you have one great tremendous fling; you do what is wrong; you have a good—a very good—time, and you know it won't last; you know that afterwards will come—the deluge."

"You are a silly!" said Kathleen. "Why, what could happen? Nobody need know; we will be far too careful for that. I can't tell you how splendidly I have planned things. I have got up my headache already, in order to go to my room and thus avoid all suspicion."

"Oh dear!" said Susy. "It doesn't sound right, does it?"

"Right or wrong, it is fun," said Kathleen. "I am going to have it so. I have got the money, and I mean to have a magnificent time. Now don't keep me; I must run into school. It is horrid of them to grudge us our little bit of amusement."

Susy agreed with her friend; indeed, during those days she was nearly lifted off her feet, so excited was she, so charmed, so altogether amazed at Kathleen O'Hara's condescension to her. Before Kathleen arrived at the school Susy was a good little girl, who helped her mother in the shop, and had dreams of going into another shop herself by-and-by. In those days she did not consider herself a lady, nor expect ladies to take any special notice of her. But those dull and stupid days were no more. Gold and sunshine and rich color and marvellous dreams had all come into her life since the arrival of Kathleen at Merrifield. For Kathleen had discrimination; it mattered nothing to her whether a girl paid or did not pay for her lessons, whether she belonged to the despised foundationers or was respected and looked up to by paying girls. Indeed, if anything, Kathleen had a decided leaning towards the foundationers; and she, Kathleen, was a lady—she belonged to what her mother and Aunt Church called the "real quality." "None of your upstarts," Aunt Church had said, "but one who for generations has belonged to the aristocrats; and they are of the kind who are too great in themselves to be proud. They are proud in the right way, but they never look down on folks." Yes, Susy was a happy girl now.

But, after all, was she quite happy? Was she not at this very minute more or less oppressed by a secret fear? Suppose any single individual in Merrifield heard of the midnight picnic—the great, daring, midnight excursion into the heart of London. Susy knew far better than Kathleen what a mad action the girls were about to perpetrate. She knew because she lived with the class who discussed such things very openly. If their frolic was not discovered, all would be well; if it was, it would be ruin—ruin complete and absolute. The ladies of the town would fight shy of her mother's shop. Aunt Church would be very unlikely to get her little almshouse in Ireland, for surely even Kathleen's friends would be very angry with her if they knew. Susy herself would be expelled from the school, and she in her fall would bring down her mother and brother. Yes, terrible would be the consequences *if* they were discovered. But then, they needn't be. Plucky people were not as a rule brought into trouble of that sort. It only needed a brave heart and a firm foot, and courage which nothing could daunt; and the other girls, the thirty-eight who were to join Kathleen and Susy, would keep them company. Nevertheless Susy was as unhappy as she was happy that day. She was so absorbed in her feelings, and in wondering what would happen during the next twenty-four hours, that she was not attentive at her lessons, and did not notice how the teachers watched her and made remarks. It was very evident to an onlooker that the teachers were particularly alert that morning, and that their gaze was principally fixed upon the foundationers.

No remarks, however, were made. The school came to an end quite in the usual manner. Immediately afterwards Kathleen dashed off to find Ruth. Ruth was waiting for her just outside the gates.

"Here I am," said Kathleen. "Take my arm, won't you, Ruthie? I shall be very glad indeed to be introduced to your grandfather."

Ruth made no answer. Her face was white, but this fact only increased the rare delicacy, the sort of fragrance, which her appearance always presented. Kathleen and Ruth, did they but know it, made a most charming contrast as they walked arm-in-arm across the common; for Ruth belonged more or less to the twilight and the evening star, and Kathleen—her face, her eyes, her voice, her actions—spoke to those who had eyes to see of the morning. Kathleen was all enthusiasm, gay life, valor, daring; Ruth's gentle face and quiet voice gave little indication of the real depth of character which lay beneath.

"This is such a lovely day," said Kathleen, "and somehow I feel so downright happy. Perhaps I am wrong, perhaps I am right, but I feel happy. I think it is on account of the day."

They had now reached the little path which led up to the cottage. Ruth went first, and Kathleen followed. What a tiny place for her darling favorite to live in! But Kathleen felt she loved her all the better for it.

Ruth softly unlatched the door and peeped in. The front-door opened right into the kitchen, and Mrs. Craven was seated by the fire.

"Hush!" she said, putting her finger to her lips; "he is asleep."

"I have brought Kathleen O'Hara, granny. I thought you'd like to see her, and I thought granddad would like to see her."

"To be sure, child," said Mrs. Craven, bustling up and removing her cooking-apron. "Bring Miss O'Hara in at once. Is she waiting outside? Where are your manners, Ruth?—Ah, Miss O'Hara, I'm right pleased to see you! I am sorry my dear husband is not as well as could be wished; but perhaps if you'd be good enough to sit down for a minute or two, he would wake up before you go."

Kathleen entered, held out her hand, greeted Mrs. Craven with a frank smile, showing a row of pearly teeth, and then sat down near the fire.

"This is cosy," she said. "Aren't you going to give me a little bit of dinner, Mrs. Craven?"

"Oh, my dear young lady, but we live so plain!"

"And so do I when I am at home," said Kathleen. "I do hate messy dishes. I like potatoes better than anything in the world. Often at home I go off with my boy cousins, and we have such a good feed. I think potatoes are better than anything in the world."

"Well, miss, if you'd like a potato it's at your service."

"I should if it is in its jacket."

"What did you say, miss?"

"If the potato is boiled in its jacket. Ah! I see they are. Please let me have one."

Kathleen did not wait for Mrs. Craven's reply. She herself fetched a plate and the salt-cellar from the dresser, and putting these on the table, helped herself to a potato from the pot.

"Now," she said, "this is good. I can fancy I am back in old Ireland."

Mrs. Craven began to laugh.

"Ruth, do have a potato with me," said Kathleen; "they are first-rate when you don't put a knife or fork near them."

But Ruth had no inclination for potatoes eaten in the Irish way.

"I will go in and see how grandfather is, granny," she said, and she disappeared into the little parlor.

"You know," said Kathleen, helping herself to a second potato, and fixing her eyes on Mrs. Craven's face—"you know how fond I am of Ruth."

"Indeed, my dear young lady, she has been telling me about you; and I am glad you notice her, dear little girl!"

"But it is not only I," said Kathleen; "every one in the school likes her. She could be the primest favorite with every one if she only chose. She is so sweetly pretty, too, and such a lady."

"Well, dear, her mother was a real lady; and her father was educated by my dear husband, and was in the army."

"It doesn't matter if her father was a duke and her mother a dairymaid," said Kathleen with emphasis. "She is just a lady because she is."

Before she could add another word Ruth came in.

"Do come, Kathleen," she said. "He is much better after his sleep. I told him you were here, and he would like to see you."

"He has been bothered like anything about those accounts," said Mrs. Craven. "I can't make out what has put it into his head. Years ago it was an old story with him that something had gone wrong with the books; but, dear hearts! he had forgotten all about it for a weary long while. Now within the last week he has been at it again, just as if 'twas yesterday."

"He has an old account-book on the table now, granny," said Ruth.

"Well," said Mrs. Craven, "we must humor him.—Don't you take any notice, Miss O'Hara; don't contradict him, I mean."

Kathleen nodded. There was a look on Ruth's face which made her feel no longer interested in the Irish potatoes. She slipped her hand inside her friend's, and they went into the parlor. Mr. Craven was seated by the fire. His white locks fell about his shoulders; there was a faint touch of pink on each of his sallow cheeks, and his blue eyes were bright.

"Ah!" he said, raising his face when he saw Kathleen. "And is this the little lady—the dear little lady—- from over the seas, from the heart of

Ireland itself? I was once in Ireland. I spent a month in Dublin, and I bought the very best paper for packing my sugars and teas in that I ever came across. Ah! I had a good time. We used to sit in Phoenix Park. I liked Ireland, and I could welcome any Irish maiden.—Give me your hand, missy; I am proud to see you."

Kathleen gave her hand. She came up close to the old man and said:

"Do you know, you have a look of my own old grandfather. He is dead and in his grave; but he had white, white hair like yours. Do you mind if I put my hand on your hair and stroke it just because of grandfather?"

"Ah, my dear, you may do what you like," said the old man. "And you have been good to my little lass—my little woman here. She has told me you have been good to her."

"She has been very good to me. I am glad to see you, Mr. Craven. I hope when you get strong again you will come over and stay with father and mother and me at Carrigrohane Castle."

"No, no, my love. There was a time when I'd have liked it well, but not now. You see, dear—" his voice faltered and his eyes grew anxious—"I must mind the shop. When a man doesn't attend to his own business, accounts go wrong. Now there was quite a deficiency last week—the wrong side of the ledger. It was really terrible. I think of it at night, and when I wake first thing in the morning I remember it. I must get to my accounts, little miss, but I am right glad to see you."

Kathleen felt a lump in her throat. Ruth, with her bright eyes fixed on her grandfather, stood close by.

"But there!" said the old man hastily. "It's splendid for Ruth. She's got into that school, and she's trying for a scholarship. I know what Ruth tries for she will get, for her brain is of that fine quality that could not brook defeat, and her mind is of that high order that it must adjust itself to true learning. I was a bit of a scholar when I was young, although I made my money in grocery. Well, well! Ruth is all right. Even if the old man can't square up the ledger, Ruth is as right as right can be. Thank you, Miss—I can't remember your name—- but thank you, little Irish miss, for coming to see me; and good-bye."

Kathleen found herself outside the room. Mrs. Craven was not in the kitchen. Ruth and Kathleen went into the garden.

"How can you stand it?" said Kathleen. "Doesn't it break your heart to see him?"

"Oh no," said Ruth. "You see, I am accustomed to him. He talks like that. I am sorry he is so bothered about the accounts, but perhaps that phase will pass."

"He is so pleased about you and the scholarship."

"Yes," said Ruth. She turned pale. "Whatever happens," she added, "he must never know."

"What do you mean about whatever happens?"

"He must never know if I do not get it. Good-bye now, Kathleen. I am glad you have seen grandfather and granny. I must go back to granny now. She is very tired; she gets so little rest at night."

Kathleen went slowly home. The meal was over at the Tennants', but somehow her couple of potatoes had satisfied her. She felt much more sober than she had done in the morning; she was inclined to think, to consider her ways. She felt an uncomfortable sensation of being haunted by the faces of Ruth and the old man.

"But of course Ruth will get her scholarship," she said to herself. "Of course—of course her grandfather is right. Her brain is of the right order, and her mind is attuned to learning. How nicely he spoke, and how beautiful he looked—how like my dear old grandfather who has been with God for so many years now."

There came a loud rat-tat at the front-door. David went out and brought in a telegram. It was addressed to Kathleen. She opened it in some surprise, and read the contents slowly. There was amazement on her face; a feeling of consternation stole into her heart. The telegram, not a long one, was from her father:

"Have just seen Aunt Katie O'Flynn. Do not approve of your society. Squash the whole thing at once, or expect my serious displeasure.—O'Hara."

"Is there an answer?" asked David.

"No," said Kathleen. "I mean yes. Yes, I suppose so. Can I have a form? Mrs. Tennant, can I have a telegraph form?"

Mrs. Tennant began to hunt about for one. Telegrams were by no means common things at the Tennants' house. David suggested that the messenger boy might have one. This turned out to be the case. Kathleen began to write, but she suddenly changed her mind.

"No, no; there is no answer," she said. "I can write by post."

She crushed the telegram up and thrust it into her pocket. After this she went out for a little; she was too restless to stay still. The fascination of the coming sport grew greater as obstacles appeared in the way of its realization. Whatever her father might say, she could not desert the girls who belonged to her society now.

"What can have ailed Aunt Katie to betray me in such a fashion?" she thought.

She came home in time for tea; but, to her amazement she found another telegram waiting for her. This was from Dublin, from Aunt Katie herself:

> "Have told your father. He received letter from schoolmistress this morning. Very angry about Wild Irish Girls. You must give the whole thing up or you will incur his serious displeasure. Don't be a goose; nip the thing in the bud immediately.—Aunt Katie."

"But indeed I won't," thought Kathleen. "Whatever happens, we will have our fun to-night. Whatever happens, neither father nor Aunt Katie, nor Ruth Craven can keep me back."

CHAPTER XXV.
KATHLEEN HAS A GOOD TIME IN LONDON.

So the head-mistress had written; she had dared to write to Kathleen's father. What she said to him was a matter of no moment; she had written, and to complain of her!

"She thinks, I suppose," said Kathleen, "that she'll subdue me by these means. She wants to bring, not the long arm of the law, but father's arm right across the sea to stop me. No, no, daddy, your Kathleen will be your Kathleen to the end—always loving, always daring, always true, but always rebellious; the best and the worst. I am going to-night, and I am going all the more surely because you wired to me not to go, and because they are daring to bully dear little Ruth Craven. And after I have had my fling I will come back in good time. No fear; nothing will go wrong. Your Kathleen wouldn't hurt a fly, much less your heart. But I mean to have my fun to-night."

Kathleen quite sobered down as these thoughts came to her. It was now getting dusk. The girls were to meet at the station at half-past five. They were to go in quite quietly by twos and twos; each couple of girls was to go to the booking-office and take their tickets, and walk away just as though nothing special had happened. They were on no account to collect in a mass. They were not even to take any notice of each other until they were off. Once the train was in motion all would be safe; they might meet then and talk and be merry to their hearts' content. Oh, it was a good, good time they were about to have!

This arrangement about meeting one another had been suggested by Kate Rourke, who knew a good deal about theatres, and who also knew how dangerous it would be for so many girls to be seen at the station together; but dressed quietly, and just dropping in by couples, nobody would remark them.

"And then we must go straight to the theatre," she said, "and stand outside the pit, and take our chance; but we will have time enough for that if we leave Merrifield by the quarter-to-six train."

Kathleen noticed that evening that Alice watched her as she moved about the room; that Alice occasionally lifted her eyes and glanced at her when she sat down to read; and when she approached the tea-table and helped herself to tea and bread-and-butter and jam, Alice also kept up that gentle sort of espionage. It annoyed Kathleen; she found herself watching for it. She found herself getting red and annoyed when the calm, steadfast gaze of Alice's brown eyes was fixed on her face. Finally she said:

"What are you doing? Why do you stare at me?"

"Sorry," replied Alice. She bent over her book, and did not glance again at Kathleen.

By-and-by Kathleen went upstairs. She went to their mutual room, and turned the key in the lock.

"I must get out of the window," she said to herself. "I can easily do it; it is but to swing on to that thick cord of ivy and I shall reach the ground without the slightest trouble. The back-gate that leads into the garden is never locked, and the window I mean to emerge from looks into the garden. I shall go off without anybody's noticing me."

Kathleen had to take a great deal of money with her. If there were forty girls, their tickets would cost a good deal. It is true they were to buy their own in the first instance, but Kathleen was to return them the money in the train. Then the omnibuses they were to go on, the seats at the theatre, their supper of some sort must be paid for by the head of the society.

"I promised to frank them, and I must frank them," thought the girl.

She slipped some sovereigns into her purse, tucked it for safety into the bosom of her dress, and then put on her hat and jacket. Some instinct told the wild, ignorant child to dress quietly. She put on her plainest hat and a little reefer coat which looked neat and substantial. She was just drawing a pair of gloves on her hands when Alice was heard turning the handle of the door.

"Let me in at once, Kathleen," she cried.

Kathleen did not reply at all for a moment; then she said in a sleepy, smothered sort of voice which seemed to proceed from the bed:

"I have a splitting headache; don't disturb me."

"Very sorry," answered Alice, "but I really must come in."

Kathleen made no answer. After a long pause, during which Alice once or twice felt the handle of the door again, the sound of her retreating footsteps was heard.

"Now is my time," thought Kathleen.

To tell the truth, Alice was not at all taken in by Kathleen's headache.

"She is very clever," thought that young lady, "but she has tried that dodge on so often before that I am not going to be deceived by it now."

Accordingly she went into her mother's room and stood by the window. Now the window of Mrs. Tennant's bedroom looked also into the garden, and was really parallel with the window by which Kathleen meant to escape. There was an interval of silence, and then Alice had her reward! for the window of their mutual bedroom was flung wide open, and Kathleen, neatly dressed, appeared on the window-sill. She looked around her for a minute. Alice caught a glimpse of her bright face by the light of the moon, which was already getting up in the sky. The next minute Kathleen caught firm hold of the arm of old ivy and let herself down deftly and quickly to the ground. The action was done so neatly, and in fact so beautifully, that Alice in spite of herself felt inclined to cry "Bravo!" She knew that if she were to trust herself to that ivy she would probably fall to the bottom and get, if not really killed, at least half so. But Kathleen stood serenely on the ground, and glanced up at the window from which she had let herself down. Just at that moment Alice rushed into their bedroom. Kathleen had shut the window behind her before she trusted herself to the ivy; she had also unlocked the door. In a moment Alice had put on her hat and jacket, had rushed downstairs, opened the hall door, and was following Kathleen across the common. Now, quite the nearest way to the railway station was across the common. Kathleen walked fast.

"Kathleen, Kathleen!" cried Alice.

Kathleen looked behind her. She saw Alice, and took to her heels.

"No, no, Kathleen; I will follow you until I drop. You must let me come up with you."

But Kathleen made no answer. If she could do anything well, she could run in a race. Her swift feet scarcely touched the ground. She ran and ran. How soon would Alice get tired? She did not dare to go to the railway station as long as she was following. And the time to catch the train was very short. At the other side of the common was a long, narrow, winding passage which, after a quarter of a mile of tortuous turning, led right up a back-way to the great terminus. Kathleen had given herself exactly the right length of time. Had nothing happened to hinder her, she would have been on the platform three minutes before the train came in. For reasons of her own she did not wish to be long there. She had crossed the common when she looked behind her; Alice was still running, but she was also in the distance.

"If I could only double, hide for a minute, and make her give up the chase, all would be well," thought the mischievous Irish girl.

There was a great tree, which cast a huge shadow, just before the winding passage was reached. Kathleen darted towards it. In an instant she had climbed up and was seated securely in one of its lower branches.

"Now, if only she will be quick, she will run past me into the passage. She will never get to the end in time. I shall slip down and go the long way. I know it is a good bit farther, but she is not in it with me as far as running is concerned," was Kathleen's thought.

Alice came up as far as the tree; she paused a minute and looked around her. Kathleen in the gray darkness looked down at her. Kathleen's face was completely in the shadow, but the light fell full on Alice's, and her face, white and anxious, almost made the other girl laugh.

"If the situation wasn't quite so tremendous I could enjoy this," she thought.

Presently Alice ran down the passage. Kathleen waited until her footsteps had died away, and then she descended from the oak-tree. She flew as fast as she could the long way to the railway station.

"Alice can't think that I want to go by train," thought Kathleen.

Now she was truly a very swift runner, but as she was running to-night, whom should she meet but Mrs. Hopkins. Mrs. Hopkins was on her way home after doing a little shopping on her own account. She saw Kathleen, observed her panting for breath, and stood directly in her path.

"Miss O'Hara," she said, "can I speak to you for a moment? It is something very particular indeed. I am very thankful I happened to meet you."

"I will see you to-morrow—to-morrow," panted Kathleen. "I am in a great hurry. To-morrow, Mrs. Hopkins."

"No, Miss O'Hara; it ought to be to-night. You are going to the railway station, aren't you, miss?"

Kathleen felt inclined to knock that interfering woman down. She darted to one side of the road.

"Oh, let me pass!" she said. She was shaking with her quick run. She knew the moments were flying; already she heard the bell at the station ring. The train for London was signaled; she had not an instant to lose.

"Don't—don't keep me," she said.

"But you mustn't go, miss; it would be madness—wicked. You musn't; you daren't."

Kathleen pushed past her. This time Mrs. Hopkins had no power to stop her. She rushed on, reached the station, flew up the steps, and found herself on the platform just as the train was coming in.

Instead of the forty girls she expected to meet, she saw not more than about half-a-dozen. They all crowded up to her at once.

"I have got your ticket for you," said Susy. "I was just able to screw out the money to get one for you and myself. Here's the train; let us hop in at once."

"But where are all the others—the forty?" gasped Kathleen.

"They funked it, almost all of them. Oh! come along; here's the train."

The great train thundered into the station. The girls ran wildly looking for a third-class carriage. At last they found one and tumbled into it; the door was slammed, and they were off. Kathleen wondered—she was not sure, but she wondered—if she really did see, or if it was only a dream, a pair of brown eyes looking at her from the station, and the severe young figure and shocked face of Alice Tennant.

"It must have been a dream; she could not have guessed that I was going to the station. What a good thing she didn't meet Mrs. Hopkins!" thought Kathleen. Then she turned to her companions—to the six girls who had decided to brave all the terrors of their expedition. They were Susy Hopkins, Kate Rourke, Clara Sawyer, Rosy Myers, Janey Ford, and Mary Wilkins.

Kathleen sat quite still for a minute until she had recovered her breath. She looked around her. To her relief, she saw that they were alone. There was no one else in the compartment.

"Now then," she said, "how is it that all the others have funked it?"

"There has been so much muttering and whispering and suspecting going on during the whole livelong day that they were positively afraid," said Susy. "Indeed, if it hadn't been for you, Kathleen, I doubt if any of us would have come."

"Well, girls, we can't help it," said Kathleen. "If the rest are so timid, there's more fun for us; isn't that so?"

She looked round at her companions.

"I mean to enjoy myself," said Kate Rourke. "I have been to a theater twice before. Once I went with my grandfather, and another time with an uncle from Australia. I didn't go to the pit when I went with uncle. He took me to a grand stall, and we rubbed up against the nobility, I can tell you."

It suddenly occurred to Kathleen that Kate Rourke was rather a vulgar girl. She drew a little nearer to her, however, and fixed her very bright eyes on the girl's face."

"But we needn't go to the pit, need we?" she said. "I meant to pay for forty. If there are only six, why shouldn't we have jolly seats somewhere, and not waste our time outside the theater?"

"That would be nice," said Kate Rourke. "I always enjoy myself so much more if I am in good company. I have been looking up the plays at the theaters, and there is a very fine piece on at the Princess'. That is in Oxford Street. It is a sort of melodrama; there's a deal of killing in it, and the heroine has to do some desperate deeds."

"Oh, dear!" said Susy, with a sigh; "I don't feel, somehow, as if I much cared where we went. It will be awful afterwards when the fun is over."

"But we will enjoy ourselves, Susy, while the fun lasts," said Kathleen. She tried to believe that she was enjoying herself and was having a right good time. She tried to forget the fact that Alice Tennant might really have seen her off, and that Mrs. Hopkins had justice in her remarks when she begged and implored of Kathleen not to go to the train.

"What can she have found out?" she thought.

She now turned to Susy.

"Has your mother learned anything, Susy?" she said.

"What do you mean?" said Susy, turning very pink.

"Well, you know, as I was running here—Oh, girls, I had such a lark! What do you think happened? That horrid Alice—Alice Tennant—ran after me as I was leaving the house. I raced her across the common, and then to get rid of her I climbed up into an oak-tree. She never saw me, and ran on down the passage. Of course, my only chance of getting to the station was to go by the long way.—Half-way there I came across your mother, Susy, and she tried to stop me, and said she must speak to me. Dear, she did seem in a state! Evidently there's a great deal of excitement and watching going on in that school."

"There will be a great deal of excitement to-morrow," said Susy. "It strikes me it will be all up with us to-morrow—that is, if Ruth tells."

"If Ruth tells! What do you mean?"

"They are going to do their utmost to get her to tell; and if she does tell they will call out our names and expel us, that's all. Oh! I can't bear to think of it—I can't bear to think of it."

Susy's voice broke. Tears trembled in her bright black eyes, and she turned her head to one side. Kathleen gave her a quick glance.

"It will be all right," she said. "Ruth won't tell. Ruth is the kind who never tells. She told me to-day she wouldn't."

"She'll be a brick if she doesn't," said Kate Rourke. "But then, of course, you know—"

"I know what?"

"Oh, nothing. What's the good of making ourselves melancholy on a night like this?"

"If I were expelled," said Clara Sawyer, "I should leave Merrifield. I could never lift up my head again. You can't think what impudent sort of boys my brothers are, and they have always twitted me for my good fortune in getting into the Great Shirley School. They say that if we are to be expelled it will be done in public. The governors are determined to read us a lesson. That's what they say."

"Who cares what they say?" said Kathleen. "Let them say."

"Well, that's what I think; and I dare say half of it is untrue," said little Janey Ford.

"I am sure, Janey, wonders will never cease when we see you in this thing," said Susy. "It was disgusting of the others to funk it. But I suppose they were on the right side; only I do sometimes hate being on the right side.—Don't you, Kathleen?"

"Yes," said Kathleen in a whisper, and she squeezed Susy's hand. It seemed to her that her soul and Susy's had met at that moment, and had saluted each other like comrades true.

"But how was it you came, Janey? Didn't your little heart funk it altogether?" continued Kate.

"I was so mad to come," said Janey. "I am shaking and trembling now like anything. But I had never been to a theater, and it was such a tremendous temptation. I said about ten times to myself that I wouldn't come, but eleven times I said that I would; and the eleventh time conquered, and here I am. I do hope we'll have a right good time."

With this sort of chatter the girls got to London. Here Kate Rourke took the lead. She marshaled the little party in two and two, and so conveyed them out of the station. Outside the yard at Charing Cross they all climbed on the top of an omnibus, and soon were wending their way in the direction of the Princess' Theater, which Kate most strongly advocated. There was no crowd at the theater this special evening. The piece which was presented on the boards happened to be a fairly good one. The girls got excellent seats, and found themselves in the front row of the family circle. From there they could look down on dazzling scenes, and Kathleen, who had never been to a theater in the whole course of her life, was delighted. She at least had forgotten what might follow this expedition. Oh, yes, they were having a glorious time; and it was quite right to do what you liked sometimes, and quite right to defy your elders. Oh, how many she was defying: Ruth Craven, who would almost have given her life to keep her back from this; Miss Ravenscroft, the head-mistress, to whom Kathleen's heart did not go out; her own father; her own aunt; Alice Tennant—oh, bother Alice Tennant! And last, Mrs. Hopkins.

"Quite an army of them," thought Kathleen. "I have dared to do what none of them approved of, and I am not a bit the worse for it. Darling dad, your own Kathleen will tell you everything, and you may give me what punishment you think best when the fun is over. But now I am having a jolly time."

So Kathleen did enjoy herself, and made so many saucy remarks between the acts, and looked so radiant notwithstanding her very plain dress, that several people looked at the beautiful girl and commented about her and her companions.

"A school party, my dear," said a lady to her husband.

"But I don't see the chaperone," he remarked.

And then the lady, who looked again more carefully, could not help observing that these seven girls were certainly not chaperoned by any one. A little wonder and a little uneasiness came into her heart. She was a very kind woman herself; she was a motherly woman, too, and she thought of her own girls tucked up safely in bed at home, and wondered what she would feel if they were alone at a London theater at this hour. Presently something impelled her to bend forward and touch Kathleen on her arm. Kathleen gave a little start and faced her.

"Forgive me," she said; "I see that you and your companions are schoolgirls, are you not?"

To some people Kathleen might have answered, "That is our own affair, not yours;" but to this lady with the courteous face and the gentle voice she replied in quite a humble tone:

"Yes, madam, we are schoolgirls."

"And if you will forgive me, dear, have you no lady looking after you?"

"No," said Kate Rourke, bending forward at that moment; "we are out for a spree all by our lone selves."

Kate gave a loud laugh as she spoke. The lady started back, and could not help contrasting Kathleen's face with those of the other girls. She bent towards her husband and whispered in his ear. The result of this communication was that, the curtain having fallen for the last time, the actors having left the stage, the play being completely over, and the seven girls being about to get back to Charing Cross as best they could, the lady touched Kathleen on her arm.

"You will forgive me, dear," she said; "I am a mother and have daughters of my own. I should not like to see girls in the position you are in without offering to help them."

"But what do you mean?" said Kathleen.

"I mean this, my dear, that my husband and I will see you seven back to your home, wherever it is."

Kathleen burst out laughing; then she looked very grave, and her eyes filled with tears as she said:

"But wouldn't mother approve of it?"

"If your mother is the least like me she would not approve of it; she would be horrified."

"I don't think the lady can see us home," here remarked Clara Sawyer, "for we live at Merrifield, a good long way from London."

Again the lady and her husband had a talk together, and then she suggested that they should take the girls back with them to Charing Cross and put them into their train.

"But we thought we'd have a bit of supper," said Kate Rourke.

"I can get you some things at the railway station; you ought not to wait for supper in town," said the gentleman in a stern voice.

Then somehow all the girls felt ashamed of themselves, Kathleen slightly more ashamed than the others. They left the theater very slowly, with all the lightsomeness and gladness of heart gone.

Two cabs were secured for the little party, and with their kind protectors they were taken back to Charing Cross. Eventually they got seats in a comfortable carriage, and found themselves going back again to Merrifield.

"Well, it has been a dull sort of thing altogether," said Clara Sawyer. "What meddlesome people!"

"Don't!" said Kathleen.

"Don't what, Kathleen O'Hara? Why should you speak to me in that reproving voice?"

"It isn't that; only they were like two angels. I know it; I am sure of it. We did an awful thing coming to town; I know we did, and I feel—oh, detestable!"

Kathleen bent her head forward, covered it with her hands, and sat still. No tears shook her little frame, but there was a storm within. To her dying day Kathleen never forgot that return journey. Truly the fun was all over; the dregs of the cup of pleasure were in their mouths, and there was a fear, great, certain, and very terrible, in their hearts. But with all her fears—and they were many—Kathleen thought again and again of the lady who had girls of her own, and of the gentleman who was both stern and chivalrous, who had the manners of a prince and the look of a gentleman. As long as she lived she remembered those two faces, and the words of the lady, and the smile with which she said good-bye. She never learned their names; perhaps she did not want to.

CHAPTER XXVI.
THE RIGHT SIDE OF THE LEDGER.

Ruth got up rather earlier than usual on that Saturday morning. She had a dull, stunned kind of feeling round her heart. She was glad of that; she was glad that she was not acutely sorry, or acutely glad, or acutely anxious about anything.

"If I could always be like this, nothing would matter," she said to herself.

She dressed with her usual scrupulous neatness, and after hesitating for a moment, put on her best Sunday serge dress. It was a dark-blue serge, very neatly made. She combed back her luxurious hair and tied it with a ribbon to match the dress. She then ran downstairs.

"Why, Ruth?" said her grandmother, who was pouring some porridge into bowls, "what are you wearing that frock for?"

"I thought I would like to, granny."

"Well, to be sure. I trust to goodness you are not getting extravagant. It will be doomsday before we can get you another like it. You must remember that I saved up for it sixpence by sixpence, and it took me all my time and my best endeavors to get it."

"I know it, granny; and when I wear it I feel that you were very kind to give it me. A girl who wears a dress like this ought to be very, very good, oughtn't she, granny?"

"Well, to be sure, little woman; and so you are. There never was a better child. Sit down now and sup your porridge. It is extra good this morning, and there's a drop of cream in that jug which will give it a flavor."

Ruth sat down to the table and drew her bowl of porridge towards her. The warm, nourishing food seemed to choke her; but, all the same, she ate it with resolution."

"That's right, dear," said her grandmother. "'It's putting a bit of color into your cheeks. You are too white altogether, Ruth. I hope, my dear, you are not working too hard."

"Oh, that's all right," said Ruth, keeping back a groan.

"It's a fine thing your getting into that school," continued Mrs. Craven; "it gives you a chance. Do you know, now, when I look at you and see the pretty little girl you are turning into, and observe your lady-like ways, which every one remarks on, I think of the time when your father was your age."

"Yes, granny," said Ruth, brightening up and looking earnestly at the old lady; "you never care to talk about father, but I should greatly like to hear about him this morning."

"Well, child, I don't talk of him because it hurts me too much. He was the only child I ever had, and if I live to be a hundred I sha'n't get over his death. But he was like you—very neat in his person, and very particular, and always keen over his books. And do you know what he said to his father? It was when he was fifteen years old, just for all the world about the age you are now. I mind the time as well as if it was yesterday. Her father and I were sitting by the hearth, and the boy came and stood near us. Your grandfather looked up at him, and his blue eyes seemed to melt with love and pride, and he said:

"'What will you be, my boy? Will you let me teach you the business, and save up all the money I can for you to sell groceries on a bigger scale? There's many a small business like mine which, when built up, means a great big business and much wealth. If you have a turn that way I could set you on your legs; I am certain of it. I'd like to do it. Would you like that best, or would you rather have a profession and be made a gentleman?'

"'The gentleman part doesn't matter,' said our boy in reply to that; 'but I think, father, if you can give me my choice, I'd like best to be that which, if necessary, would oblige me to give my life,'

"'What do you mean?' asked his father, and the lad explained with his eyes shining.

"'I have only got one life,' he said, 'and I'd like to give it if necessary.'"

"To tell the truth, Ruth, I could not understand him."

"But I can," said Ruth. She hastily put down her porridge spoon and jumped to her feet. "I can understand," she continued; "and I am proud of him."

"So he went into the army. I wish you could have seen him in his uniform; and his father paid for every scrap of the whole thing, and educated him and all. Oh, dear! it was a proud moment. But we weren't proud afterwards when we heard that he was killed. His father reminded me of his words: 'I'd like to be that for which I could give my life if necessary,'"

There was quite a pink color in each of Ruth's cheeks now, and her eyes were very bright.

"I will go and see grandfather," she said, "and then I must be off to school."

She left the kitchen and went into the tiny parlor where the old man was seated. It was his fashion to get up early and go straight to the parlor and read or talk softly to himself. For a couple of months now he had never sat in the kitchen; he said it caused a buzzing in his head. Mrs. Craven brought him his meals into the little parlor. He had finished his breakfast when Ruth, in her neat Sunday dress, entered the room. There was an exalted feeling in her heart, caused by the narrative which her grandmother had told her of her father.

"Well, little woman," said the old man, "and you are off to school? Or is it school? Perhaps it is Sunday morning and you are off to church."

"No, grandfather; it is Saturday morning—quite a different thing."

"Well, my love, I am as pleased as Punch about that school. I can't tell you how I think about it, and love to feel that my own little lass is doing so well there. And if you get the scholarship, why, we will be made; we won't have another care nor anxiety; we won't have another wrinkle of trouble as long as we remain in the world."

Ruth went straight over to the old man, knelt down by his side, and looked into his face.

"Stroke my hair, granddad," she said.

He raised his trembling hand and placed it on her head.

"That is nice," she said, and caught his hand as it went backwards and forwards over her silky black hair, and kissed it.

"Granddad," she said after a pause, "is it the best thing—quite the best thing—always to come out on the right side of the ledger?"

"Eh? Listen to the little woman," said the old man, much pleased and interested by her words. "Why, of course, Ruth; it is the only thing."

"But does it mean sometimes, grandfather—dishonor?"

"No, it never means that," said Mr. Craven gravely and thoughtfully. "But I will tell you what, Ruthie. It does mean sometimes all you have got."

"Yes," said Ruth, "I understand." She rose to her feet. Do you think my father would have come out on the right side of the ledger?"

"Ah, child! when he lay dead on the field of battle he came very much out on the right side, to my thinking. But why that melancholy note in your voice, Ruth? And why are your cheeks so flushed? Is anything the matter?"

"Kiss me," said Ruth. "I am glad you have said what you did about father. I am more glad than sorry, on the whole, this morning. Good-bye, grandfather."

She kissed him; then she raised her flower-like head and walked out of the room with a gentle dignity all her own.

"What has come to the little woman?" thought the old man.

But in a minute or two he forgot her, and called to his wife to bring him the account-books.

"Why do you bother yourself about them?" she asked.

"It has come over me," he replied, "that I have counted things wrong, and that I'll come out on the right side if I am a bit more careful. Put the books on this little table, and leave me for an hour or two. That's right, old woman."

"Very well, old man," she replied, and she pushed the table towards him, put the account-books thereon, and left the room.

Meanwhile Ruth went slowly to school. She was in good time. There was no need to hurry. The morning was fresh and beautiful; there was a gentle breeze which fanned her face. It seemed to her that if she let her soul go it would mount on that breeze and get up high above the clouds and the temptations of earth.

"I am glad," she said to herself, "the right side of the ledger means giving up all, and the best of life is to be able to lose it if necessary. I will cling to these two thoughts, and I don't believe if the worst comes that anything can really hurt me."

When she got near the school she was met by Mrs. Hopkins. She was amazed to see that good woman, as at that hour she was usually busily engaged in her shop. But Mrs. Hopkins took the bull by the horns and said quietly:

"I came out on purpose to see you, Ruth Craven."

"Well, and what do you want?" asked Ruth.

"My dear, you are not looking too well."

"Please do not mind my looks."

"It is just this, dear. There will be no end of a fuss in the school to-day."

Ruth did not reply.

"And they will press you hard."

Still Ruth made no answer.

"You know what it will mean if you tell?"

Ruth's grave eyes were fixed on Mrs. Hopkins's face.

"Child, I don't want to doubt you—nobody who knows you could do that—but it will mean ruin to poor Susy and to many and many a girl at the Great Shirley School. It isn't so much Miss O'Hara we mean. Miss O'Hara has gone into this with her eyes open; and she is rich, and what is disgrace to her in this little part of England, when she herself lives in a great big castle in Ireland, and is a queen, lady, and all the rest? But it means—oh, such a frightful lot to so many! Now, Susy, for instance. I meant to apprentice her to a good trade when she had gone through her course of work at the Great Shirley; but she will have to be a servant—a little maid-of-all-work—and I think that it would break my heart if she was expelled."

"And what do you want me to do, Mrs. Hopkins?"

"Oh, my dear, not to think of yourself, but of the many who will be ruined—not to tell, Ruth Craven."

Ruth gave a gentle smile; then she put out her small slim hand and touched Mrs. Hopkins, and then turned and continued her walk to the school.

There were a group of foundationers standing round the entrance. Ruth longed to avoid them, but they saw her and clustered round her, and each and all began to whisper in her ears:

"You will be faithful, Ruth; nothing will induce you to tell. It will be hard on you, but you won't ruin so many of us. It is better for one to suffer than for all to suffer. You won't tell, will you, Ruth?"

Ruth made no reply in words. The great bell rang, the doors of the school were flung wide, and the girls, Ruth amongst them, entered.

CHAPTER XXVII.
AFTER THE FUN COMES THE DELUGE

Kathleen O'Hara's nature was of the kind that rises to the top of the mountains and sinks again to the lowest vales. She had been on the tip-top of the hills of her own fantasy all that evening. When she ran quickly home under the stars she began to realize what she had done She had done something of which her mother would have been ashamed. Not for a moment had Kathleen thought of this way of looking at her escapade until she read the truth in the eyes of the unknown but most kind lady. She despised herself for her own action, but she did not dread discovery. It did not occur to her as possible that what she and her companions had done could be known. If no one knew, no one need be at all more sorry or at all more unhappy on account of her action.

"Poor Wild Irish Girls! they are getting into hot water," she said to herself. "But this little bit of fun need never be told to any one."

Kathleen had let herself out of the house by the strong rope of ivy; she meant to return to her bedroom the same way. Alice was a very sound sleeper; it did not occur to her that Alice on that particular night might be awake. She reached the foot of the window in perfect safety, saw that the ivy looked precisely as it had looked when she climbed down it, and began her upward ascent. This was decidedly more difficult than her downward one; but she was light of foot and agile. Had she not climbed dangerous crags after young eaglets at home? By-and-by she reached the window-sill. How nice! the window was partly open. She pushed it wider and got in. The room was in darkness. So much the better. She stepped softly, reached her own bed, undressed, and lay down. How nice of Alice to be sound asleep! Then of course it was not Alice she saw standing on the platform looking at her with reproachful, horrified eyes.

"I must have dreamt it," thought Kathleen. "Now all is well, and I shall sleep like a top until the morning."

This, however, was no easy feat. Alice's quiet breathing sounded not many feet away, and after a time it seemed to get on Kathleen's nerves. She moved restlessly in her bed. Alice awoke, and complained of the cold.

"The window is a little open," said Kathleen. "Shall I shut it?"

Alice made no answer. Kathleen jumped up, shut the window, and fastened it. She then got back into bed. In the morning Alice called out to her:

"Is your headache better?"

"Had I one?" began Kathleen. Then she blushed; then she laughed; then she said, "Oh, it's quite well."

Alice gazed steadily at her. It seemed to Kathleen that Alice's eyes were full of something very terrible.

"Are you coming to school to-day?" asked Alice the next moment.

"Of course. Why do you ask such a strange question?"

"I shouldn't think you would wish to; but there is no accounting for what some people can live through."

"Alice, what do you mean?"

"What I say."

"Explain yourself."

"No."

"Is there anything very awful going to happen at school?"

"You will find out for yourself when you get there."

"Dear me!" said Kathleen; "you look as if the deluge was coming."

"And so it is," said Alice.

She had finished dressing by now, and she went out of the room. The two girls went down to breakfast. Alice's face was still full of an awful suppressed knowledge, which she would not let out to any one; but Mrs. Tennant was smiling and looking just as usual, and the boys were as fond of Kathleen as was their wont. She had completely won their immature masculine hearts, and they invariably sat one on each side of her at meals, helped her to the best the table contained, and fussed over her in a way that pleased her young majesty. Kathleen was very glad that morning to get the boys' attention. She determined to sit with her back slightly turned to Alice, in order not to look into her face. They were about half-way through breakfast when there came a ring at the front-door, and Cassandra Weldon's voice was heard.

Alice went out to her. The two girls kept whispering together in the passage. Presently Alice returned to the breakfast-room, and Kathleen now noticed that her eyes were red, as though she had just been indulging in a bout of crying.

"What can be the matter?" she thought.

"Why, my dear Alice," said her mother, looking up at this moment, "what did Cassandra want? And what is the matter with you? Have you had bad news?"

"Yes, mother," answered Alice.

"But what is it, dear?"

"You will know soon enough, mother."

"That is exactly what you said to me upstairs," said Kathleen, driven desperate by Alice's manner. "I do wish you would speak out.—Do get her to speak out, Mrs. Tennant. She hints at something awful going to happen at school to-day. I declare I won't go if it is as bad as that."

"It would be like you not to come," said Alice. "But I think you will come. I don't think you will be allowed to be absent."

"Allowed!" said Kathleen. "Who is going to prevent me staying away from school if I wish to?"

"The vote of the majority," said Alice very firmly. "Now, look here, Kathleen; don't make a fuss. It is wrong for the girls of the Great Shirley School to absent themselves without due reason."

"Well, I have a headache. I had one last night."

"No, you had not."

"Alice, dear, why do you speak to Kathleen like that?" said her mother. "What is the matter with you?—Kathleen, do keep your temper.—Alice, I am sorry something has annoyed you so much."

"It is past speaking about, mother. You will understand all too soon.—Kathleen, it is time for us to be going."

"I am not going," said Kathleen, "so there!"

"Kathleen, you are."

"No."

"Come, Kathleen; come."

"You needn't fuss about me; I am not coming."

"Kathleen, dear, I think you ought to go. Go for my sake," said Mrs. Tennant.

Kathleen looked up then, saw the anxiety in Mrs. Tennant's face, and her heart relented. She was in reality not at all afraid of what might be going to happen at school. If there was to be a fray, she desired nothing better than to be in the midst of it.

"All right," she said, "I will go; but I won't go yet. I am going to be late this morning. I can see by your manner, Alice, that I have got into disgrace. Now, I can't think what disgrace I have got into, unless some horrid girls have been prying and telling tales out of school. That sort of thing I should think even the Great Shirley girls would not attempt. Unless some one has been mean enough to act in that way, there is nothing in the world to prevent my going to school, and taking my accustomed place, and disporting myself in my usual manner. I shall get a bad mark for being late; that is the worst that can happen to me. I am going to be very late, so you can go on by yourself, Alice."

Alice very nearly stamped her foot. She went so far as to beg and implore of Kathleen, but Kathleen was imperturbable.

"You are very naughty, Kathleen," said Mrs. Tennant, but Kathleen ran up to her and kissed her.

"You and I·will have some fun, perhaps, this afternoon," she said. "I have got a lot of new plans in my head; they are all about you, and to make you happy and not so tired. Don't be cross with me. I'll promise that I will never be naughty again after to-day."

Mrs. Tennant said nothing more. A minute or two later Alice left the house.

It was quite an hour after Alice had departed that Kathleen took it into her head that she might as well stroll towards the school. On Saturdays school was over a little earlier than other days. There was a special class which she was anxious not to miss, for in spite of herself she was becoming interested in certain portions of her lessons. Her depression had now left her, and she felt excited, but at the same time irritated. A spirit of defiance came over her. She went upstairs and selected from her heterogeneous wardrobe one of her very prettiest and most fashionable and most unsuitable dresses.

She put on a hat trimmed with flowers and feathers, and a sash of many colors round her waist. Over all she slipped her dark-blue velvet jacket, and with rich sables round her neck and wrists, she ran downstairs.

"Why, Kathleen, any one would suppose you were going to a concert," said Mrs. Tennant.

"Ah, my dear good friend, I like to look jolly once in a way. I am certain to get a bad mark for unpunctuality, so I may as well get it looking my best as my worst. You don't blame me for that, do you?"

"No. Go off now, dear, and don't let me find you so troublesome again."

Kathleen started off. She ran across the common, and reached the doors of the great school exactly one hour after she ought to have arrived. To her amazement, she saw quite a crowd of people waiting outside, and amongst them was Mrs. Hopkins. There were several other mothers as well, and when they saw Kathleen they turned their backs on her, and one or two were heard to say aloud:

"It's she who has done it."

But Mrs. Hopkins did not turn her back on Kathleen; she came close to her, and even took her hand.

"Why are you late, miss?" she said. "But perhaps it is best. Miss O'Hara, you won't forget my poor aunt; you will be sure to get her the little almshouse in Ireland?"

"Yes, of course I will," said Kathleen. "Aunt Katie has written about it already, and I will write to-night. You may tell Mrs. Church that it is absolutely quite certain that she will get it. What is the matter, Mrs. Hopkins? How strange you look! And all those other women—they seem quite cross with me. What have I done?"

"Ah, miss! I keep saying to them that it is because you are Irish and don't know frolic from serious mischief. Bless your heart, miss! it is you that are kind. You mean kindly—no one more so—and so I have said to them."

"But it will be a nice thing if my girl gets expelled owing to her," said a sour-faced woman, coming forward now and placing her arms akimbo just in front of Kathleen.

"Is it that that every one is thinking about?" said Kathleen. She stood still for a minute. The color left her face. She felt a wave of tempestuous blood pressing against her heart; then it all rushed back in a fiery color into her cheeks and in brightness to her eyes.

"And Alice knew of this," she said to herself; "and when I didn't come to school this morning she thought that I was afraid. Afraid!—Don't keep me, good people," said Kathleen. "Make way, please. I am sorry I am a little late."

She walked past them all. When she got as far as the school door she turned to Mrs. Hopkins.

"You can tell your aunt that the almshouse is safe," she said, and then she blew a kiss to her and disappeared into the school.

CHAPTER XXVIII.
WHO WAS THE RINGLEADER?

In the passage a monitress was standing, and when she saw Kathleen she came up to her and said in an agitated tone:

"They are all assembled in the great hall. Go in quickly; you may be in time, after all."

The voice of the monitress quite shook, and there was a troubled, very nearly tearful expression in her eyes.

"But why is the whole school in the central hall?" asked Kathleen. "Why are they not in their different classrooms?"

"Go in—go in," said the monitress. "You will know when you find yourself there; and there is not a moment to lose."

So Kathleen, impelled by a curious power which seemed to drive her whether she will it or not, opened the door of the great central hall and entered. She found it quite full. The four hundred girls who composed the Great Shirley School were all present; so were the teachers, and so were the professors who came to give them music and drawing and literature lessons. So was the head-mistress, Miss Ravenscroft; and also, seated on the same little raised platform, were the six ladies who formed the governors. The governors sat in a little circle, Miss Mackenzie in the middle. Miss Mackenzie looked hard and very firm. Her iron-gray hair, her false teeth, her prominent nose, and her rather cruel steel-gray eyes made themselves felt all down the long room. The other ladies also looked as they usually did, except that Mrs. Naylor had traces of tears in her eyes, and bent forward several times to whisper something to Miss Mackenzie, who invariably shook her head and looked more stern than ever. There was evidently a moment's pause, and the whole school was in a waiting attitude when Kathleen made her appearance. All eyes were then turned in her direction; all eyes fixed themselves on the showily dressed and very handsome child who suddenly entered the room.

"It is Kathleen O'Hara;" "It is Kathleen O'Hara herself;" "Well, she has come at last;" "Yes, it is Kathleen O'Hara," passed from lip to lip, until

Kathleen felt that her name had got round her and above her and to right and left of her. She had an instant's sensation of absolute fear. She had a flashing desire to turn tail and run out of the room; but the same power which had pushed her into the room now sent her right up the long central hall past all the watching, expectant, eager-looking girls. Outside some one had said that she would be afraid. No, whatever the danger, she knew she could keep her own. She was not Kathleen O'Hara of Carrigrohane Castle for nothing.

"Come here, Miss O'Hara," said the voice of Miss Ravenscroft at that moment.

Kathleen obeyed at once. She found a seat on the front bench, dropped into it, and at the same moment encountered the almost malicious glance of Alice Tennant. She turned away from Alice. That look seemed suddenly to steady her nerves. She was afraid just for a moment that she might give way to something, she knew not what, but Alice's look hardened her heart. Time had been given Kathleen to take her place, to recover any emotion she might have felt by her sudden entrance, and then Miss Ravenscroft rose to her feet.

"It is my painful duty," she said, "to have to say something which distresses me far more than I can give you any idea of. My dear girls, you have all been summoned to attend in this hall to-day in order to meet the governors of the school, Miss Mackenzie, Mrs. Naylor, Mrs. Ross, the Misses Scott, and Miss Jane Smyth. These ladies have come to meet you, because they wish thoroughly to investigate a most disgraceful matter which has lately been going on in the school."

Miss Ravenscroft paused and looked round her.

"I allude," she said, "to the insurrection in our midst—a sort of civil war in our camp. There are, I am given to understand, in the midst of this hitherto well conducted and admirable school, a number of girls who have banded themselves together in disregard of its laws, and who have made for themselves laws contrary to the peace-abiding principles of this great school and noble institution: who meet at unseemly hours, who preach rebellion each to the other, who dare to publicly break the laws of the school, and who defy the express wishes of myself as head-mistress and the governors of the school by insisting on continuing their wicked meetings. And last night a certain number of these girls actually took it upon themselves to go to London—to do what, I can't say—and to return at midnight, alone and unchaperoned. Such conduct is so unworthy, so undignified, and so absolutely sinful that there is only one course to pursue. The girls who are rebellious in the school must be exposed; their conduct must be investigated, and a very heavy punishment awarded to them."

Here Miss Ravenscroft looked round her. She caught the eye of Miss Mackenzie, who beckoned to her and whispered something in her ear.

"Miss Mackenzie bids me say that if the girls who belong to this society will at this moment give up the name of their ringleader they themselves will be forgiven. What punishment they receive will only be connected with their work in the school, and may possibly exclude them from competing for certain scholarships during this present term, but for the rest nothing further will be said. But it is essential that the name of the ringleader, as well as her rules and her motives, should be declared."

Miss Ravenscroft paused again and looked down the whole length of the long hall. She looked to right and left.

"Don't let any girl think," she said after a pause, "that she is acting nobly by suppressing information which is for the benefit of the school. I do not ask the girls who are spoken of as the paying girls to expose their companions, nor do I ask those foundationers who have not joined the band of insurgents to betray their fellows; but what I do ask is this: that the girls themselves—the rebels—should rise in a body and point to their leader. With that leader the governors will deal. The girls themselves will have forgiveness."

Miss Ravenscroft again paused. The silence which followed might be felt. Susy Hopkins bent her head and sobbed. Janey Ford trembled all over, and clutched tightly the hand of her companion. But no one spoke. It was at that moment that Kathleen calmly and slowly raised her face and looked around her. She looked back, and caught the eyes of at least a dozen of those foundationers whom she had pitied and helped and been jolly with. She looked to the right then, and met as many more faces of girls whom she knew, and who were members of the Wild Irish Girls' Society. Then very calmly she resumed her nonchalant attitude in the front row of the schoolgirls. Miss Ravenscroft meanwhile stood waiting. Still no one spoke.

"Will no one speak?" she said. "Will no girl present be brave enough to save the school?"

Still there was silence.

"This is a very good and a great school," said Miss Ravenscroft. "It gives for a very trifling sum an education worthy of the very best and most expensive schools in England. It was founded some hundred years ago, by those who thought much and in advance of their time. In an age when girls were almost uneducated, when nothing further was required from them than a smattering of reading and writing, these wise and far-seeing people said that they would give the girls of the future a chance. So they left money for the purpose, and that money, wisely invested, has borne fruit. The great school was built, and has for generations helped many girls who otherwise might not have been able to earn their own bread. Even for the paying girls the expense for all they receive is but a trifle. But the school does more than that. It was the wish of the founders that there should always be one hundred foundationers on the school lists, and these girls are admitted free; they pay nothing in hard cash for what they receive. They are taught liberally; they have the best rooms, the best laboratories; the best music, the best art, are supplied to them. If they have talent they have every chance of bringing it to the fore, for the education is thorough and generous. But the school does even more than this. It opens up scholarships—many scholarships—of great value for those special girls who call themselves foundationers. Now my dear girls of the Great Shirley School, you must clearly understand that no establishment of this kind can be worked except on certain lines, and these lines mean order, method, and obedience. Rules must be made, and these rules at any cost must be obeyed. These rules are made not only to enable the girls to get the best possible education out of the school, but also that the greater education of mind and heart, which alone can build up a fine and useful character, may not be neglected. That sort of education can only be given by conforming to principles. Now, there are certain principles which every girl who comes into this school is bound to adhere to. She is bound on all occasions to behave with sobriety, with a sense of modesty and true womanly feeling; she is never, if she is a true member of the school, to join herself to rebels who do not believe in its rules. Now, there is not the slightest doubt that the society which you girls—a certain number of you— have joined is rebellious, has bad effects, and has rules of its own which are absolutely contrary to the rules of the Great Shirley School. It is impossible for you to be members of this society and to be members of the Great Shirley School. If, therefore, you do not immediately forsake that society, and immediately promise here and now that you will give it up forever, we shall have the painful duty of expelling you from the school. You have a few minutes in which to decide. Nobody wants to be hard on you; nobody wants to be hard on your founder, although she must no longer take her place as a member of this school; but if you don't confess, very stringent and terrible methods will have to be resorted to."

Miss Ravenscroft here resumed her seat. There was a faint applause which came from different parts of the room, but was not unanimous, and soon died away. After that there was silence. Miss Mackenzie bent forward and made some notes in a little black book which she held upon her lap. Mrs. Naylor took her handkerchief and wiped the tears from her eyes; the other governors looked depressed and uneasy. Meanwhile Miss Ravenscroft sat with her eyes fixed on the different girls in their different forms. There was no movement. Kathleen drew herself up proudly.

"They're not quite such cads," she said under her breath.

But just as the thought came to her, Miss Mackenzie, the woman most respected and most dreaded in the whole of Merrifield, rose slowly to her feet.

"Girls of the Great Shirley School," she said, "your head-mistress, Miss Ravenscroft, has conveyed to you a message from me and from the other governors. The message is to the effect that if those silly girls who have allied themselves to that most ridiculous society, the Wild Irish Girls, will give the name of their leader, they shall be forgiven. Do you accept, foundationers, or do you decline?"

Dead silence ensued.

"I presume," said Miss Mackenzie after a pause of a full minute, "that your silence means refusal I have therefore to turn to a certain young girl in this school who was a member of the Wild Irish Girls' Society, and who has now left it.—Ruth Craven, have the goodness to step forward."

Ruth had been seated in the fourth bench. She rose slowly. Kathleen felt a curious tremor run through her, but she did not move a muscle; only when Ruth appeared at the edge of the platform, it was with the greatest effort she could keep herself from jumping up, taking her hand, and mounting the platform by her side.

"Step up here, Miss Craven," said Miss Mackenzie.

Ruth did so.

"Will you have the goodness to stand just here, Miss Craven?"

Ruth went to the place indicated.

"You can now face me, and your schoolfellows can also see you.— Girls, I have requested Ruth Craven to take the prominent position she now occupies in order that you may all see her. You all know her, do you not? Those who know Ruth Craven, hold up their hands."

Immediately there was a great show of uplifted hands.

"I presume that you all like her?"

Again the hands went up, and Kathleen's was raised the highest of all. Ruth's little face, however, remained perfectly white and still; only her eyes were dark with emotion. She kept thinking of her father.

"I should like that which would make me give *my life* if necessary," he had said; and her grandfather had said, "Sometimes when you come out on the right side of the ledger it means giving *all* that you possess.»

Ruth could scarcely see the faces which rose up like a great ocean beneath her, but she remembered her father's words very distinctly.

"You all see Ruth Craven," continued Miss Mackenzie. "As far as I know, she is a good girl; and I judge by your method of answering my question that she is a popular girl. I know, alas! that she is poor. I have heard a great deal about her intellectual endowments, and believe that this school could be of immense advantage to her. I believe, in short, that she is the typical sort of girl of whom the founders thought when they instituted this great and noble house of learning. Nevertheless, Ruth Craven must fall if necessary for the good of the many.—Ruth, I wish to ask you a certain question. You were a member of that rebellious society, the Wild Irish Girls?"

"Yes, Miss Mackenzie."

Ruth's "Yes" was very clear; her face looked modest but firm. There was not the slightest hesitation in the words she uttered. Her speech was not loud, but it could be heard to the end of the great hall.

"You are no longer a member?"

"No."

"Three days ago I and the other governors sent for you to ask you certain questions. You refused to answer those questions then. We gave you three days to consider, telling you that if at the end of that time you still kept to your resolution there was only one thing for us to do, and that was to make an example of you in the presence of the entire school—in short, to take from you your right of membership, and to expel you from the school, taking from you all privileges, all chances of acquiring learning and the different valuable scholarships which this school was opening to you. We came to this most painful resolve knowing well that it would cast a blight upon your life, that wherever you went the knowledge that you had been publicly expelled from the Great Shirley School would follow you— that you would, in short, step down, Ruth Craven. I quite understand from the expression of your face that you are the sort of child who imagines that she is doing right when she keeps back the knowledge which she thinks she ought not to betray; but we governors do not agree with you. There are six of us here, and we wish to tell you that if you now refuse the information which we wish to obtain from you, you will do *wrong*. You are young, and cannot know as much as we do. We earnestly beg of you, therefore; not to make a martyr of yourself in a silly and ridiculous cause.—Mrs. Naylor, will you now say what you think to Ruth Craven?"

"I think, dear child," said Mrs. Naylor, speaking in a tremulous voice, which could scarcely be heard half-way down the room, "that it would be best for you not to conceal the truth."

"And I agree," said Mrs. Ross.

"We all agree," said the Misses Scott and Miss Jane Smyth.

"We all think, dear," continued Mrs. Naylor, "that for the sake of any chivalrous ideas, quite worthy in themselves, it is a considerable pity for you to spoil your life. You are not the sort of child who could stand disgrace."

"And you don't look the sort of child who would under ordinary circumstances act the idiot," said Miss Mackenzie sharply. "As to the chivalrous nature of your silence, I fail to see it. I hope you have carefully considered the position and are prepared to act openly and honorably. By go doing you will save the school and yourself. Now then, Ruth Craven, will you come a little more forward? Stand just there.—Girls, you can all see Ruth Craven, can you not?"

The girls held up their hands in token that they could.

"I will therefore at once proceed to question her," continued Miss Mackenzie.

There was just a moment's pause, and during that complete silence a dreadful rushing noise came into Kathleen O'Hara's head. The floor for an instant seemed to rise up as though it would strike her; then she felt composed, but very cold and white. She fixed her eyes full on Ruth.

"I will hear her out. I must hear the thing out," she kept saying to herself. "Afterwards—afterwards—But I must hear the whole thing out."

Miss Mackenzie turned, and in a very emphatic voice began to question.

"You are prepared to reply to the following questions?" she said.

Ruth's very steady eyes were raised; she fixed them on Miss Mackenzie. Her lips were firmly shut. Nothing could be quieter than her attitude; she did not show a trace of emotion. Always pale, she looked a little paler now than her wont. Her darks eyes seemed to darken and grow full of intense emotion; otherwise no one could have told that she was suffering or feeling anything in particular.

"But I know what she is going through," thought Kathleen. She clenched her hands so tightly that the nails went into the delicate flesh. She was glad of the pain; it kept her from screaming aloud.

"The first question I have to ask," said Miss Mackenzie, "is this: How many of the foundation girls have joined the rebels?"

Ruth came a step nearer.

"How many? I can't quite hear you."

"I am sorry," said Ruth then, "but I can't tell you."

Miss Mackenzie, without any show of emotion, immediately entered Ruth's answer in a little book which she held in her hand.

"Oh, don't, Miss Mackenzie! Don't be harsh," gasped little Mrs. Naylor.

Miss Mackenzie, as though she had not heard the voice of her sister governor, proceeded:

"What is the name of the founder of the society?"

"I am not prepared to say," replied Ruth.

Again this answer was recorded.

"Can you give me an exact account of the rules of the society, its motives, its bearing generally?"

The same negative reply was the result of this question.

"Do you know anything whatever of the disgraceful escapade which took place last night, when a certain number of the members of this society went to London and returned by themselves at midnight?"

Ruth's face cleared a little at this question.

"I cannot answer because I know nothing," she said.

A slight look of relief was visible on the faces of the unfortunate girls who had gone to town with Kathleen on the preceding night. A few more questions were asked, Ruth replying on every occasion in the negative. "I can't say," or "I will not say," were the only words that were wrung from her lips.

"In short," said Miss Mackenzie very quietly, "you have decided, Ruth Craven—you, an ignorant, silly little girl—to defy the governors of this school. All justice has been dealt out to you, and all patience. The consequence of your mad action has been explained to you with the utmost fullness. You have been given time—abundant time—to consider. You have chosen, from what false motives it is impossible to say—"

"My dear," interrupted Mrs. Naylor, "the child means well, I am assured."

"From what false motives it is impossible to say," continued Miss Mackenzie, not taking the slightest notice of the little governor's futile appeal, "you have decided to wreck your own life and to ruin the school. It was to have been your noble privilege to save the school in a time of extremity. You have chosen the unworthy course. It is therefore my painful duty to call upon Miss Ravenscroft as head-mistress to expel you, Ruth Craven, from this school. You are no longer a member of the Great Shirley School; you are—"

"Hold!" cried Kathleen.

Her voice rang out sharp and clear. It was heard all over the school, and was so imperative, so startling, so unexpected, that even Miss Mackenzie lost her self-control and fell back in silence.

"Hold!" cried Kathleen again. "You have said enough. I don't think you ought to go on. You are torturing the noblest girl in the world. But Kathleen O'Hara, bad as she is, cannot endure this last insult. Girls—Wild Irish Girls, you who belong to my society—I as your queen desire you to come forward. Come forward in a body at once."

What was there in the young voice that impelled? What was there in the young face that stimulated, that caused fear to slink out of sight and courage to come to the fore, that caused hearts to beat high with generous emotion? Not a single girl failed Kathleen in this moment of her appeal. They clambered over their seats; they bent under the forms; they got out in any fashion, until she was surrounded by the sixty girls who formed her society. She glanced round her; her dark-blue eyes grew full of sweetness, and there was a look on her face which made the girls for the moment feel that they would die for her.

"Come, girls," said their queen—"come; there is room on the platform."

She sprang up the couple of steps without another word, and the girls followed her.

"Do what you like with Ruth Craven, Miss Mackenzie," she cried; "but put your questions over again to me, and I will answer them one after the other. Then expel me and my companions; turn us out of the school, but keep the girl who would be a credit to you."

CHAPTER XXIX.
END OF THE GREAT REBELLION.

No one quite knew what happened next. Some of the girls went off into violent hysterics; others rushed out of the great hall, half-fainting; while others controlled themselves and listened as best they could. The scene was vivid and picturesque. Mrs. Naylor sobbed quite audibly, and took hold of Ruth's hand, and even kissed it. But as she did so Kathleen herself came near and flung her arm round Ruth's neck.

"If you mean to expel Ruth you will expel me," she said. "But won't you forgive her? If her ideas were wrong, they were at least generous; and you know that I won't trouble you any more. I am very sorry, but I don't think that I was made to suit a great school like this, and I give up the society — yes, absolutely — so you won't have any rebels present in your midst again. Expel me, but keep her, for she will be the flower of your school, the greatest ornament, one you will talk of in the dim years of the future. Don't let me feel that I have spoilt her life."

"But why did you act so, Kathleen O'Hara?" said Miss Mackenzie. "Why did you, a silly young girl, come over here, a stranger, to ruin the school and make us all unhappy?"

"I can't answer you that," said Kathleen, flinging out her hands. "I did what I was made to do. I am a rebel by nature. I believe I shall always be a rebel. I shall go home to father and mother and tell them I am not suited for a school like this. But don't expel Ruth, and don't expel the others."

"But we will all go if you are not kept," suddenly cried one of the sixty, Kathleen never quite knew which; and suddenly one girl after another began to speak up for her, and all promised that if Kathleen were allowed to remain, and if the whole story of the great rebellion was allowed to blow over, they would work as they had never done before. They wanted their queen to stay with them. Would the governors forgive their queen, just because she was an Irish girl and like no one else?

How it came to pass it was impossible to tell. There was something about Kathleen — the bold, bright, and yet generous look on her face, the love which darted out of her eyes when she grasped Ruth's hand — that even impressed Miss Mackenzie. She said after a pause that she was willing to reconsider matters, and that she and all the other governors would meet in a day or two to give their opinion.

Thus the school broke up. It had lived through its greatest and most exciting hour. But when Kathleen was seen going through the gates, her arm flung round Ruth's waist, and all the sixty girls following at her heels, such a cheer went up from the anxious mothers and fathers and brothers — for many fresh people had come to swell the crowd since Kathleen entered the school — as was never heard before in Merrifield.

Thus ended the great rebellion. It is spoken of to this day as the greatest and most conspicuous event in the school's history. For, after all, the governors were lenient, and no girl was expelled. Kathleen, as years went on, became far and away the most popular girl in the school. Her talents were of the most brilliant order; her very faults seemed in one way to add to her charms. In one sense she was always a more or less troublesome girl; but where she loved she loved deeply, and from that hour she gave up all thought of rebellion either against the governors or against Miss Ravenscroft. Ruth was Kathleen's greatest friend. Her grandfather got better; his heart was never broken by the knowledge of that terrible disgrace which the child so feared that she would bring him. Mrs. Church became one of the Irish alms-women, and grumbled a good deal at the change in her position. Mrs. Hopkins's debt was cleared off; and all the characters in this story did well, and were proud to admit that they owed most of their future prosperity to the Wild Irish Girl, Kathleen O'Hara.